The Art and Science of Reading

Custom Edition Mercer County Community College

Adams | Patterson

CENGAGE
Learning·

Australia • Brazil • Japan • Korea • Mexico • Singapore • Spain • United Kingdom • United States

CENGAGE
Learning·

**The Art and Science of Reading:
Custom Edition Mercer County
Community College**

Senior Project Development Manager:
 Linda deStefano

Market Development Manager:
 Heather Kramer

Senior Production/Manufacturing Manager:
 Donna M. Brown

Production Editorial Manager:
 Kim Fry

Sr. Rights Acquisition Account Manager:
 Todd Osborne

For product information and technology assistance, contact us at
Cengage Learning Customer & Sales Support, 1-800-354-9706

For permission to use material from this text or product,
submit all requests online at **cengage.com/permissions**
Further permissions questions can be emailed to
permissionrequest@cengage.com

This book contains select works from existing Cengage Learning resources and
was produced by Cengage Learning Custom Solutions for collegiate use. As such,
those adopting and/or contributing to this work are responsible for editorial
content accuracy, continuity and completeness.

Compilation © 2013 Cengage Learning
ISBN-13: 978-1-285-87597-2

ISBN-10: 1-285-87597-4

Cengage Learning
5191 Natorp Boulevard
Mason, Ohio 45040
USA
Cengage Learning is a leading provider of customized learning solutions with
office locations around the globe, including Singapore, the United Kingdom,
Australia, Mexico, Brazil, and Japan. Locate your local office at:
international.cengage.com/region.

Cengage Learning products are represented in Canada by Nelson Education, Ltd.
For your lifelong learning solutions, visit **www.cengage.com/custom.**
Visit our corporate website at **www.cengage.com.**

Printed in the United States of America

Table of Contents

Chapter Two - Recognizing Tone, Figurative Language, and Point of View   **78**

Chapter Four- Developing Computer Reading Skills   191

UNIT 1

Use Questions to Zero In on Valuable Information

You must not only aim right, but draw the bow with all your might.

Henry David Thoreau
(1817–1862), American author, philosopher, and naturalist

You don't have all day. You've got textbooks to plow through, articles to read, research to do, and lectures to attend. In addition, you might take time to watch the news, read the headlines, check your e-mail, or text a friend. How in the world are you going to retain all this information?

You're not.

The simple fact is that you can't possibly hold on to all the information you're bombarded with on a given day. You have to make some choices. That's why it's essential to be able use questions to zero in on the most valuable information. This chapter explains how to use questions to:

- **Figure Out Whether Information Is Relevant**
- **Decide Whether Information Is Important**
- **Determine Whether Information Is Reliable**

Critical Thinking Excerpted from *How to Study in College* 10th edition by Walter Pauk and Ross J. Q. Owens

Why is so much information so readily available?

There has never been a time when more information has been more readily available than right now. Thanks primarily to the Internet but also to a wealth of electronic documents and databases, many of us have at our fingertips what students in the past had to walk or drive miles to gain access to. But this mountain of available information has its drawbacks. Author David Shenk calls it "data smog." As Shenk explains, "We thrive on the information, and yet we can also choke on it."

So, how can we benefit from all this information without being asphyxiated by it? Questions are the key. Questions turn you from a passive learner into an active one. They provide the engine that drives the whole understanding process. Humans have realized the power of questions for more than twenty-four hundred years when the Greek philosopher Socrates (469–399 BC), found that instead of simply lecturing, he could pose a series of carefully directed questions that enabled the students who answered them to arrive at their understandings or conclusions themselves.

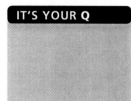

IT'S YOUR Q

How do questions aid learning?

Students have been using questions ever since to activate their learning and make sense out of their studies. Time and time again, questions have provided a needed breakthrough for those who had been struggling with a subject. Instead of expecting meaning to simply pop up magically like a jack-in-the-box, active learners take the initiative, using their own questions to extract meaning from readings and lectures.

How do you pinpoint the most valuable information?

By employing this questioning method, you should be able to pierce the thick haze of data to pinpoint what's truly valuable in the things you read and hear. With questions as your laser beam, you can focus your attention on the information that is relevant, important, and reliable—in other words, on the stuff that's worth retaining.

Figure Out Whether Information Is Relevant

How can you tell if information is relevant?

Relevant information has a connection to your focus. If you're living in Los Angeles, today's weather in New York probably isn't relevant. That's because it has no obvious connection to your life in Los Angeles. On the other hand, the temperature in Los Angeles and the traffic conditions there will probably be relevant, particularly if you're venturing outside.

What's wrong with irrelevant information?

Irrelevant information is a little like the distractions described in Chapter 3. It can gum up the works of understanding, making it difficult to concentrate properly, to think clearly, or to make decisions quickly and effectively. Math instructors frequently assign word problems that deliberately contain some irrelevant information. For example, a problem designed to see if you can calculate the distance that a person will be able to travel at a particular rate of speed in a set amount of time may describe the color of the person's shoes or running shorts. Neither of these details is relevant, because they have nothing to do with the focus of the problem, namely, how far someone can travel at a given speed in a given amount of time.

4

How can you reduce irrelevant information?

The sharper your focus, the more readily you'll be able to discard irrelevant information. If you want to learn everything you can about the Empire State Building, then the height of the building (1,472 feet) is relevant. But if your purpose is to find what you need to know to visit the Empire State Building, your focus is sharper and the height is no longer relevant. What *is* relevant is the location of the building and how to get there, its hours, and how much it will cost to visit. That's because all of this information has a connection to your purpose: visiting the Empire State Building.

How do you find relevant information?

You can't tell whether information is connected unless you know what it's connecting to. That normally requires a clearly articulated focus. This is where questions come in. The more specific your question, the sharper your focus is likely to be. Asking a question is like pointing a camera at a field of facts. All those facts you can see in the viewfinder are relevant. All those that you can't see are not.

How do you find relevant information using a search engine?

There are lots of books and websites devoted to search engine tips. Most of them devote a fair amount of time to the individual idiosyncrasies of particular search engines, the symbols and keywords that certain engines recognize that will help you focus your search. These details are helpful, although most of them are typically explained in the particular search engine's "advanced search" area. What's more important and more fundamental is to know what you're searching for before you begin searching. Back before the Web was commonplace, it was often possible to do computer-based searches of online databases with the help of a librarian or other trained researcher. These searches took time and in some cases they cost money. Both factors tended to discourage the casual, hit-or-miss approach that has gradually become more common.

What are the differences between a bull's-eye search and a ballpark search?

In general, there are two types of searches: bull's-eye and ballpark. With a bull's-eye search, you are looking for a specific document or fact. With a ballpark search, you are seeking information on a particular topic, but you don't have a specific fact or document in mind.

Do a Bull's-Eye Search

`FOCUSING` `QUESTIONING`

What approach should you use for a bull's-eye search?

With a bull's-eye search, your best approach is to be as specific as possible. After all, if you know exactly what you're looking for, there's no real value in being vague about it.

How do you do a bull's-eye search in a book?

Searching in a book. If you're doing a bull's-eye search in a book, begin with the index. If the index is detailed and your search is sufficiently specific, you should be able to find an entry that takes you straight to the page or pages you're looking for. If the index is sparse or doesn't list what you're searching for, try the table of contents. Based on the chapter titles, find the chapter most likely to contain the information you're looking for, turn to that chapter, and then use the 35,000-foot scanning technique (see Chapter 5) to locate it.

How do you do a bull's-eye search in a magazine or journal?

Searching in a magazine or journal.   Individual magazine or journal articles are rarely indexed. To do a bull's-eye search in these articles, your only real option is the 35,000-foot scanning technique (see Chapter 5). If the article uses subheadings, they can help to narrow your search. Skim the subheadings first and find the one that seems most likely to contain the information you're searching for. Then focus your attention on that section with your bull's-eye search.

Searching online or other electronic text.   Doing a bull's-eye search in a specific online or other electronic text is comparatively easy. Most applications that read electronic documents (web browsers, word processors, portable document readers) have a Find command that should enable you to type in the name, word, or phrase you're seeking and then go straight to it. By the way, these tools don't care if you've typed in the entire word or phrase; they just take the characters you've typed and find a match within the document. So, for example, if you're not sure how to spell the name of German composer Ludwig van Beethoven, you'd be safer searching for a part of his name—such as "hoven"—rather than run the risk of spelling it wrong. (A search for "Ludvig von Baythoven," for example, would turn up nothing.) On the other hand, if you've spelled your search words correctly and there are several occurrences of them within the text, most tools will normally take you to the first instance of their occurrence and enable you to search again for others.

Do a Ballpark Search

OVERVIEWING — QUESTIONING

What approach should you use for a ballpark search?

A ballpark search differs from a bull's-eye search in that you don't know exactly what you're looking for. You just have a general idea. Perhaps you're searching for information on Beethoven, but for some reason you don't remember his name. However, you know the person you are thinking of was German and a composer. The more clues you can assemble for a ballpark search, the more focused your search will be. But you have to be careful. If you include a clue that turns out to be incorrect, you may leave the ballpark entirely.

How do you do a ballpark search in a book?

Searching in a book.   If your ballpark search is in a book in hard-copy format, you'll eventually be doing the treetop skimming described in Chapter 5. Once again, you can start with the index to see if you can find any clues, although it's less likely this time that you'll be able to find something this way. Then move on to the table of contents to see if there's a chapter title that will put you in the ballpark. For example, if you were skimming a book called either "Famous Germans" or "Famous Musicians," you might find a chapter that would help to refine your search further (perhaps "Germans in Music" in the former and "German Composers" in the latter). If you're lucky enough to be searching a particular chapter, you may be able to zero in even further by reading the chapter subheadings for additional clues. Beyond that point, the treetop skimming begins in earnest as you try to grasp the context that might be likely to surround the information you're seeking.

6

How do you do a ballpark search in a magazine or journal?

Searching in a magazine or journal. Because a magazine or journal probably won't have an index, your only real hope of further narrowing a ballpark search in a magazine or journal article would be in its subheadings. Beyond that, you'll have to do your search using treetop skimming.

How can you do a ballpark search for an online document or in an electronic text?

Searching a single online or other electronic text. It's unlikely that a ballpark search of a specific online or other electronic text document will take you exactly where you want to go. But it may get you in the vicinity. The Find tool in a browser, word processor, or other document reader is not as sophisticated as an Internet search engine. If you're searching for the name of a German composer, it's best to search for either "German" or "composer" in the hopes of finding who you're looking for. (If you were to search for "German composer," you would be successful only if the two words occurred consecutively in the text.) Once the Find tool has you in the right ballpark (and it may take several attempts), you can do treetop skimming to find precisely what you're looking for.

How do you do a ballpark search through multiple documents on the Internet?

Doing a ballpark search on the Internet. Although the Find tools you can use to search the pages in a single electronic document are limited, if you're searching several documents and they are all available on the Internet, then you should be able to do more sophisticated searches. Search engines allow you to refine your search by combining several searches into one. This approach, known as Boolean searching, allows you to establish a relationship between two or more search terms (see Figure 7.1). The rules for particular search engines may vary slightly, but in general, if you search using the words "German" and "composer," the search engine will return all the documents that contain "German," all the documents that contain "composer," and, most important (and normally at the top of the list), all the documents that contain "German" *and* "composer."

**Figure 7.1
How Boolean
Searching Works**
Boolean searching can refine your searches by providing the intersection of two or more sets of data.

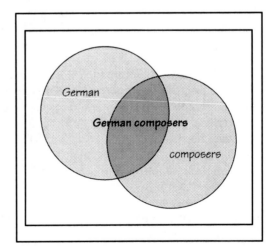

Decide Whether Information Is Important

How does important information differ from relevant information?

IT'S YOUR Q

What happens when you find an answer to the question?

How do you determine what's important?

Of course, just because information is relevant doesn't necessarily mean it's something you want to hold on to. Valuable information is normally both relevant *and* important. Even if you've managed to discard irrelevant information, you may still be left with information of different weights competing for your time and attention. For example, if you had a to-do list that listed "Empty garbage" and "Complete research paper," both tasks would be relevant but they clearly wouldn't have the same weight or importance.

The most important information is the information that responds most directly to a particular question. If you ask, "How do I get to the Statue of Liberty from midtown Manhattan?" the most important information is "To get to the Statue of Liberty from midtown Manhattan, take the subway to the South Ferry station and then catch the Liberty Ferry at Battery Park." But if you asked instead, "Where did the Statue of Liberty come from?" information about the subway and ferry routes would no longer be important. In fact, it wouldn't even be relevant. The most important information would be that "The Statue of Liberty was created by Frederic Auguste Bartholdi and was presented to the United States in 1865 as a gift from France."

Few answers mark an automatic end point. Every answer has the potential to generate new questions. An answer such as "The Statue of Liberty was created by Frederic Auguste Bartholdi and was presented to the United States in 1865 as a gift from France" might prompt you to ask "Who was Bartholdi?" and "Why did France give the United States a statue?" If the authors have anticipated your questions, the sentences or paragraphs that follow may answer them. Or it may turn out that you and the authors hit a fork in the road and move in different directions.

To find what's important, ask questions and then seek to answer them. You can be driven by the engine of the author's questions or by questions of your own.

Answer the Author's Questions

QUESTIONING

Where do you find the author's questions?

A book can be thought of as the answers to a series of invisible questions. Granted, you can't usually see these questions, but they're there. If this sounds like some sort of fairy tale, think again. Questions are actually built in to the unit that organizes almost everything we read. What unit is that? The paragraph. According to its definition, a paragraph "typically deals with a single thought or topic."[3] Everything in a paragraph points

---

[1]David Shenk, *Data Smog: Surviving the Information Glut* (New York: HarperCollins, 1997), p. 22.

[2]Edward V. Rickenbacker, *Rickenbacker* (Englewood Cliffs, NJ: Prentice-Hall, 1967), pp. 31–32.

[3]*The American Heritage Dictionary of the English Language*, 4th ed. (Boston: Houghton Mifflin, 2000), p. 1274.

to that thought or topic. All the other sentences in that paragraph are there to support it. If you read a paragraph and ask, "What's important here?" your answer will be the controlling idea and that should lead you to the invisible question.

> The Empire State Building is an impressive symbol of early twentieth century industrial achievement. At 1,454 feet, this massive two-acre office building is the tallest in New York City and the ninth tallest in the world. Started in 1930, it took a total of 7,000,000 work-hours and a little more than a year of almost nonstop work to complete. It weighs 365,000 tons, has 6,500 windows, and boasts a total of 1,860 steps leading from the street level to the 102nd floor.

How are the controlling ideas arranged?

Most information is organized hierarchically. A chapter or an article has a single controlling idea or "thesis," which answers the question, "What's the point?" All other ideas grow out of that idea. On a smaller scale, each individual paragraph has its own controlling idea, with the rest of the paragraph acting to support it. Just as the controlling idea of the article answers the question "What's the point?" for the article, *these* controlling ideas answer a similar question, but for each individual paragraph this time.

How do the chapter maps show the controlling idea relationships?

The maps that open each of the chapters in this book provide a good example of how this arrangement works. Each idea, like each node in the map, is supported by the ideas beneath it. The controlling idea provides the answer to a question; the ideas beneath provide examples and evidence to support it. This pattern of questions, answers, and support is repeated from article to section to paragraph. With more space, the maps could be expanded to include every paragraph in a chapter. The maps would be much bigger, of course, but the basic arrangement would be the same.

How do you find the most important information in an article or chapter?

To find the most important information in an article or chapter, look for the controlling ideas in each paragraph. These ideas in turn are likely to cluster around a controlling idea for a particular section. And those ideas should all support the chapter or article's controlling idea. Often, the first paragraph of each section provides the controlling idea for that section, and the introductory paragraph for the chapter provides the controlling idea for the entire chapter. Some articles or chapters are better organized than others, but in many cases you should be able to create a framework of controlling ideas that resembles the maps that begin each chapter in this book.

Answer Your Own Questions

QUESTIONING

What if what you think is important differs from what the author thinks is important?

Of course, your view of what's important may differ from the author's view. Just as the Empire State Building was built around a steel framework, an article or chapter is constructed by the author around a framework of controlling ideas. But these important ideas don't necessarily have to be *your* important ideas.

www.cengage.com/success/Pauk/HowTOStudy10e

How do you find what's important to you?

The way to find the information that is important to you is by asking a focused question and then zeroing in on the area that provides the answer. Depending on the scope of your question, that area might be a sentence, a paragraph, a section, a chapter or article, or even an entire book. The next most important information will be the information that directly supports your original answer.

How can you be sure what you've found is the most important?

Unlike relevance, which has to do with whether a connection exists or doesn't, importance is a relative thing. It has to do with the scope of your topic or question. If relevance can be seen as where the camera lens is pointed, importance is influenced by how far you zoom in or zoom out. The larger something is relative to the other facts around it, the more important it's likely to be. So, if your question asks, "How tall is the Empire State Building?" then its height is likely to be the most important piece of information in your answer. If, on the other hand, your question asks, "How big is the Empire State Building?" then its height would presumably compete with its other dimensions for importance.

What happens to information that is interesting but not important?

Keep in mind that what is important is not always the same as what is interesting. A lot of information (such as the number of steps in the Empire State Building) falls under the general heading of *trivia*. Trivia fascinates some students and bores others. Regardless, it's rarely important. At best it provides support for a controlling idea. If you think trivia is interesting, you may find this motivates you to remember it. It's still better to focus your attention on the important ideas though. When you do, the details that interest you will often remain in the picture. If, on the other hand, you focus on trivia instead, the controlling ideas may be pushed out of frame.

Determine Whether Information Is Reliable

How can you tell whether information is reliable?

Questions activate your learning and help you to determine which information is relevant and which information is important. But they play one more especially vital role. They help you put the reliability of information to the test. Compared to finding information that's relevant or deciding which information is important, determining whether information is reliable can be a real challenge. It helps to beware of things that can frequently distract from your ability to determine whether information is reliable and to arrive at some guidelines you can use consistently to analyze information for its overall reliability.

Beware of Reliability Distractors

QUESTIONING

Most of us would like to think that we can determine the reliability of information. However, certain factors such as the echo chamber, confirmation bias, and logical fallacies can sometimes distort our perception of reliability.

10

The Echo Chamber

What is the echo chamber?

The echo chamber describes a situation in which information is amplified by constant repetition. If the information is false, it may be mistaken as true. If the information is true, it may appear to be more relevant or important than it actually is. The satirist H. L. Mencken's "bathtub hoax" offers an interesting insight into the echo chamber run amok, whereas urban legends provide more commonplace examples. And because the echo chamber isn't just for false information, it helps sometimes to take a good look at the "news" that everyone is buzzing about.

What was the bathtub hoax?

The Bathtub Hoax   In 1917, the reporter and satirist Henry Louis Mencken wrote a whimsical, entirely fictional piece for the *New York Evening Mail* called "A Neglected Anniversary," a meticulously fabricated history of the evolution of the bathtub in America and its introduction in the White House during the Millard Fillmore administration in 1850. Unfortunately, many of the people who read the piece must not have been active learners because the joke was lost on them. Soon, Mencken's fictional account of the first White House bathtub made its way into respectable history and reference books. Once the "fact" was available in other sources, the echo chamber effect took hold and the story of the first White House bathtub started popping up in numerous books as though it were the truth. Mencken, who had a distinctly mischievous side, claimed to be astonished by the longevity of his hoax, but given his temperament, he was probably amused by the impact of his stunt, which was an especially colorful illustration of the echo chamber effect.

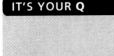

IT'S YOUR Q

Urban Legends   Urban legends are modern myths that once depended almost entirely on word of mouth for their dissemination but have gotten an extra boost with the advent of e-mail. Either method of communication provides the echo chamber. Classic urban legends include the fancy sports car that gets sold for $50, the unsuspecting tourist in Mexico who buys what he or she thinks is a Chihuahua but once home discovers that the little dog is actually a rat, the well-meaning but absent-minded woman who tragically tries to dry off her wet poodle in a microwave, and the passing motorist who picks up a hitchhiker in a prom dress but learns later that the girl he drove home died several years before on that very night. None of these stories is true, and yet you're likely to hear many of them told again and again as true, albeit with some variations that either bring them up to date or associate them with local landmarks.

What makes urban legends convincing?

What makes urban legends convincing, among other things, is that they are usually told by someone you know who insists that he or she knows someone who knows the person the incident actually happened to. For this reason, urban legends are sometimes called FOAF or "friend of a friend" stories. Ironically, the same thing that initially makes urban legends seem convincing is what ultimately gives them away as false.

How can you detect an urban legend?

If you hear a story from someone who knows someone who has a friend the story "really happened to," that's usually a dead giveaway. Urban legends almost never hold up to scrutiny if you try to trace them back to the source. Even in those situations in which the legend is based on truth, it inevitably gets distorted or exaggerated. Although e-mail has done a lot to increase the spread of urban legends, the Internet has made it easier to debunk them. Several websites, including snopes.com, track urban legends. The websites provide regularly updated listings of legends and, in most cases—although not always—proof that they aren't true. This can be valuable because people who unwittingly pass on an urban legend can often get quite irritable if the reliability of their story is questioned. Actual evidence instead of unsubstantiated disbelief is usually enough to convince most people.

The Dangers of Summer   Not all information that gets amplified in the echo chamber is false. Sometimes stories are true but they get blown out of proportion. A good example was the widespread fear of shark attacks and the spread of the West Nile virus in the summer of 2003. From the nervous reactions of some vacationers, you might've gotten the impression that if "Jaws" didn't get them, then the West Nile would. Were the fears of ferocious sharks and a mosquito-borne virus justified? Not according to an article and graphic in the *New York Times* that compared the relative dangers of what it called "The Real Dangers of Summer."[4] The greatest risks, according to the piece, were skin cancer and food poisoning. The former would strike one in 200 people, the latter one in 800. But what of the West Nile virus and sharks? The *Times* statistics showed that these were actually the lowest risks of all summertime hazards, affecting one in 68,500 and one in 6 million, respectively. So why the hysteria? Additional statistics in the same graphic provided a clue. Whereas only 359 newspaper articles had been written the previous summer about the dangers of skin cancer and food poisoning, during the same period a whopping 2,516 articles had dealt with either the West Nile virus or the hungry sharks.

Margin note: How does the echo chamber affect information that is true?

Confirmation Bias

Some information that's unreliable may be embraced while other information that's reliable may be overlooked. Why? It's called confirmation bias.

Have you ever had the experience of learning the meaning of a word, only to find that suddenly everyone around you seems to be using that same word? Of course, if the word you learned actually *is* a new word (also known as a *neologism*), then it may well be that the number of people using that word is increasing. But if it's a word that's only new for you, it's unlikely that others have suddenly decided to use it more often on your account. What's more plausible is that you've just become more attuned to that word. As we move through our daily lives, the sheer magnitude of information we confront means it's almost inevitable that we will tune in some

Margin note: What happens with confirmation bias? What influences whether we tune in or tune out information?

[4]David Ropeik and Nigel Holmes, "Never Bitten, Twice Shy: The Real Dangers of Summer," *New York Times* (August 9, 2003), p. A11.

12

information and tune out some other. When the information relates to something you already know or believe, you're more likely to tune it in. And if the information doesn't relate to something you already know or believe, you're more likely to tune it out.

When is selectivity harmful?

In the case of learning a new word, this tendency is relatively harmless. But the same phenomenon can act to reinforce your particular viewpoint or bias at the expense of other information that may actually contradict or modify your beliefs. This is known as confirmation bias. In the journal *Review of General Psychology*, psychologist Raymond S. Nickerson defines confirmation bias as "the unwitting selectivity in the acquisition and use of evidence."[5] So, although selectivity is an essential tool in reducing the glut of information you're exposed to, it can also have a negative effect by shielding you from vital information or depriving you of the complete picture.

What did Forer's experiment show?

One of the most famous demonstrations of confirmation bias was an experiment conducted by a psychology professor named Forer, who administered a personality profile test to his students. When Forer received the completed tests, he promptly threw them all out and instead, unbeknownst to the students, returned the identical personality profile to each member of his class, asking each student to read his or her profile and then rate its accuracy on a scale of 0 to 5, with 5 meaning "excellent" and 4 meaning "good." Incredibly, the personality profile, even though it was written without any of the students in mind, still received a cumulative average of 4.26 for accuracy. What the students didn't realize—until he told them—is that Forer had clipped the profile out of a newspaper horoscope column. The profile was ambiguous but vaguely complimentary. The criticisms were mild. Thanks to confirmation bias, most of the students who read the profile related to its positive elements, ignored those elements that were too negative or didn't relate specifically to them, and then concluded that it was an accurate assessment of their particular personality traits![6]

What can you do to avoid confirmation bias?

All of us are susceptible to confirmation bias. It's important to be aware of this tendency and to keep your mind open for differing evidence and information that might change your viewpoint. Also, it doesn't hurt to have a set of consistent guidelines that you use to gauge the validity of information.

Why is it risky to make decisions based on your "gut"?

Many people make a decision whether or not to trust information based on their "gut." And it's true that our hunches and instincts do seem to provide us with clues, although there is very little scientific data to support this. Unfortunately, emotional appeals have a way of short-circuiting common sense. It happens to nearly all of us at times. Articulate, charismatic liars can sometimes trigger a positive response while honest but awkward writing or speaking can sometimes put us on guard.

[5]Raymond S. Nickerson, "Confirmation Bias: A Ubiquitous Phenomenon in Many Guises," *Review of General Psychology* 2, no. 2 (1998): pp. 175–220.

[6]Robert Todd Carroll, "Forer Effect," *The Skeptics Dictionary*, available at http://www.skepDic.com/forer/html.

Logical Fallacies

What are logical fallacies?

Although your own biases can affect the way you select and interpret information, there are also elements embedded in some arguments that can lead you to unknowingly accept a false conclusion as fact. Usually there is a flaw in an otherwise reasonable argument that renders it invalid. These are commonly known as logical fallacies and are used by writers and speakers sometimes accidentally but often on purpose to lead you to a desired conclusion.

What is an example of a logical fallacy?

One of the best-known logical fallacies has to do with ice cream sales. It suggests that because an increase in ice cream sales seems to correspond with an increase in crime, ice cream must cause crime. What's tricky about a fallacy is that it's usually made up of a true premise or premises that reach a false conclusion. Therefore, a person who isn't listening or reading critically may notice the true statements but overlook the logical leap that leads to a false outcome. It's true that ice cream sales and crime often increase at the same time. But it's not true that one causes the other. (It's more likely that hot weather is the cause for the increase in both.)

IT'S YOUR Q

Another common fallacy is known as the straw man. That's a situation in which the writer or speaker uses an opposing example that is either weak or imaginary in order to make his argument appear to gain legitimacy or strength. The straw man is often called "some" or "some people" to present the appearance of a real opposition without ever naming it. So, if the authors of a study skills textbook wanted to appear more courageous and defiant than they actually are, they might write: "Although there are some who may want to do away with study skills textbooks altogether, we were determined to make sure that our book was published." A person who read this might feel increased respect and admiration for these brave authors and might even be tempted to purchase an additional book or two just to spite those who want to do away with study skills textbooks altogether. But there's only one problem. The enemy is never specified. It's a phantom. And that is how the straw man fallacy works.

Where can you learn more about fallacies?

There are several books and websites devoted to fallacies. All of them are informative, and many are quite entertaining.

Books

Capaldi, Nicholas. *The Art of Deception: An Introduction to Critical Thinking: How to Win an Argument, Defend a Case, Recognize a Fallacy, See Through a Deception.* Prometheus Books, 1987.

Damer, T. Edward. *Attacking Faulty Reasoning: Practical Guide to Fallacy-Free Arguments,* 5th ed. Wadsworth, 2004.

Engel, S. Morris. *With Good Reason: An Introduction to Informal Fallacies,* 6th ed. St. Martins, 1999.

Gula, Robert J. *Nonsense: A Handbook of Logical Fallacies.* Axios, 2002.

Whyte, Jamie. *Crimes Against Logic.* McGraw-Hill, 2004.

Websites

Fallacies: The Internet Encyclopedia of Philosophy. http://www.iep.utm.edu/fallacy/.
Fallacies: The Nizkor Project. http://www.nizkor.org/features/fallacies/.
Logical Fallacies: The Fallacy Files. http://www.fallacyfiles.org/.
Logical Fallacies and the Art of Debate. http://www.csun.edu/~dgw61315/fallacies.html.

Follow a Set of Guidelines for Analysis

`PLANNING`

How can you avoid being swayed by unreliable information?

Given all the potential ways in which information can be misleading, how do you establish what's reliable and what isn't? One of the most effective ways to guard against being swayed by unreliable information in one instance but unaffected by it in another is to consistently apply standards that allow you to subject everything to the same analysis or test. You can use a test for analyzing all types of information or tailor your analysis for a specific area, such as Internet sites. What's important in either case is to keep your approach systematic and consistent.

Evaluate Information

What are the four steps for Ruggiero's comprehensive thinking strategy?

Critical thinking authority Vincent Ruggiero has defined a four-step "comprehensive thinking strategy."[7]

1. *Identify facts and opinions.* If the information is common knowledge or easily verifiable, it's likely to be factual. If not, treat it as opinion.
2. *Check the facts and test the opinions.* If the information is factual, can you verify it? Did the author or speaker seem to leave out anything important? If it's opinion, do the speaker's views stand up to scrutiny or are they easily refuted?
3. *Evaluate the evidence.* If the author or speaker has offered support for any opinions, is this support reasonable and sufficient?
4. *Make your judgment.* Based on the facts and the evidence, rather than your gut feelings or preferences, decide whether you consider the information reliable.

Evaluate Internet Sites

What special challenge does Internet information create?

The proliferation of online news, opinion, and reference sites has led some to question the reliability of Internet information. One of the Internet's greatest strengths—its wide-open, inclusive nature—is also a potential weakness. With a few days' work and very little money, a talented person can put together a website that superficially resembles one of the top professional news and information sites and yet ignores the standards for quality and accuracy that traditional news organizations live by. Although

[7]Vincent Ryan Ruggiero, *Becoming a Critical Thinker,* 5th ed. (Boston: Houghton Mifflin, 1999), pp. 26–27.

www.cengage.com/success/Pauk/HowTOStudy10e

the following questions may be especially important to ask about Internet sites, they can also apply to traditional TV, radio, magazines, and newspapers.

1. *Who owns them?* More and more news and information operations are owned by companies whose emphasis is on something other than news. This may affect their tone or approach. Others aren't news organizations at all but lobbies or think tanks organized to promote a particular product or viewpoint but whose publications are designed to look like news. With newspapers, magazines, and websites, you can usually find information about the ownership in the paper or magazine or on the site. With television or radio stations, it can take a little more digging. Most news operations try to maintain a wall (see #3) between their business and editorial operations, but it isn't always possible.

2. *How do they make their money?* A key rule of investigative journalism is to "follow the money," and to some degree these special journalists are professional critical thinkers. Almost no publication or website relies solely on money from subscribers to exist. As disillusioning as it is to realize, financial obligations to owners or advertisers can sometimes influence what a publication or broadcaster does and doesn't cover. For example, a newspaper that relies heavily on automobile ads may be reluctant to cover a scandal at a car dealership, whereas a magazine that runs ads for a local restaurant may feel pressure to give that restaurant a good review. Advertisements are usually pretty easy to notice and the nature of the advertising can sometimes be illuminating. It can tell you something about the viewers, readers, or listening audience and may give you an idea of what topics could test the organization's editorial independence.

3. *Can you tell the difference between news, opinion, and advertising?* In the past, publications and broadcasters have gone to great lengths to distinguish between news and paid advertising, feeling that it serves the public better to make sure that this distinction is clear. In newspapers, this is commonly known as "the wall." Journalists are normally well aware of this wall and are proud of its existence. The wall between news and opinion isn't always as clear, and that can be a problem when one is mistaken for the other.

4. *Where do they get their information?* Some small news operations rely heavily on national and international news wires for most or even all of their information. Larger operations have their own staffs of reporters and columnists. Over time, if you pay attention, you should be able to get a sense of a particular news service or journalist's track record for reliability.

5. *How well presented is the information?* Crudely written or clumsily delivered words can occasionally pack a wallop, but, in general, sloppy writing or speaking should set off alarm bells in your head.

6. *What other information is presented?* You can sometimes learn about the reliability of an article from the company it keeps. This is especially true on the Internet. If someone sends you a link to an Internet news story, see if you can navigate back to the

homepage of the site where the story came from. The "mix" of a site's stories can be a tip-off. For example, a White House exclusive may not look very reliable if you discover that it's running alongside a story about a dog with two heads and an article about a miracle weight-loss product.

What is a simpler way for determining whether something is reliable?

A simpler way to determine whether information is reliable or not is basically no different than the strategy for zeroing in on all valuable information: Stay alert, think about your thinking, and above all, ask questions!

FINAL WORDS

What surprising result can zeroing in on valuable ideas sometimes produce?

Not only will zeroing in on what's valuable enable you to extract the most relevant, important, and reliable information from what you read and hear and make it a part of your personal web of knowledge, but it will also produce a result that may surprise you: It will help you to derive real pleasure out of thinking!

CHAPTER CHECKUP

SENTENCE COMPLETION

Complete the following sentences with one of the three words listed below each sentence.

1. Author David Shenk calls the glut of information _____.

   data mining   **databases**   **data smog**

2. Information in an article or chapter is usually organized _____.

   hierarchically   **collectively**   **repeatedly**

3. In newspapers, the distinction between news and advertising is commonly known as _____.

   "the gap"   **"the tower"**   **"the wall"**

MATCHING

In each blank space in the left column, write the letter preceding the phrase in the right column that matches the left item best.

_____ 1. Ballpark

_____ 2. Socrates

_____ 3. Fallacy

_____ 4. Mencken

_____ 5. Forer

_____ 6. Boolean

_____ 7. Bull's-eye

_____ 8. Questions

a. Used questions and answers to promote understanding

b. Wrote a fictional story that was adopted as historical fact

c. The engine that drives the whole understanding process

d. Method of searching for information when you're not exactly sure what you're looking for

e. Method of searching when you know exactly what you're looking for

f. Conducted an experiment with his class that demonstrated confirmation bias

g. Method that lets you define a logical relationship between two or more search terms

h. A flaw in an otherwise logical argument

TRUE-FALSE

Circle T beside the true *statements and F beside the* false *statements.*

1. T   F   In the process of understanding, questions are the engine.
2. T   F   Questions change you from an active learner to a passive one.
3. T   F   Sharks and West Nile virus are the greatest summertime hazards.

18

4. T F Math instructors are careful to keep irrelevant information out of the word problems they assign.

5. T F Most programs that read electronic documents have a Find command.

MULTIPLE CHOICE *Choose the word or phrase that completes each sentence most accurately, and circle the letter that precedes it.*

1. Valuable information should be
   a. relevant.
   b. important.
   c. reliable.
   d. all of the above.

2. Many books can be thought of as a series of
   a. answers to invisible questions.
   b. clues to unsolvable mysteries.
   c. episodes from timeless stories.
   d. conclusions to unspoken introductions.

3. The most important information in a paragraph is
   a. the controlling idea.
   b. a question.
   c. the last sentence.
   d. a detail.

4. The story of the Chihuahua that turned out to be a rat is an example of
   a. confirmation bias.
   b. an urban legend.
   c. a logical fallacy.
   d. a controlling idea.

5. A key rule of investigative journalism is
   a. know thyself.
   b. trust but verify.
   c. follow the money.
   d. none of the above.

REFLECTION

Think about the ideas outlined in this chapter and then draw upon your own opinions and experiences to answer each question fully.

1. Explain the distinction between relevant, reliable, and important information. Which of the three poses the biggest challenge for you? Why?
2. Do you use particular tricks or shortcuts to improve your Internet searching? If so, explain your approach in a way that would be useful for others. If not, suggest ideas you've gleaned from this chapter that may help improve your searching in the future.
3. Cite an example of an urban legend, a case of confirmation bias, or an instance of the echo chamber that fooled you at first and then explain how you eventually realized that it was unreliable.

IT'S YOUR Q

The Q System uses marginal questions to encourage active reading. You'll notice that most but not all paragraphs in this chapter are accompanied by marginal questions. Now it's your Q. Scan the chapter for any paragraph that is missing a question, reread the paragraph, establish the main idea, and then arrive at a question that elicits it. Use the questions in the surrounding paragraphs as models for your own marginal questions.

VOCABULARY IN ACTION

To expand the horizons of your understanding and to refine the precision of your thought, the three exercises that follow are designed to help you grow, strengthen, and maintain your own vocabulary.

SAY WHAT?

From the three choices beside each numbered item, select the one that most nearly expresses the meaning of the italicized word in the quote. Make a light check mark (√) next to your choice.

When strangers start acting like neighbors, communities are *reinvigorated*.

—Ralph Nader (1934–), American lawyer, consumer advocate, and presidential candidate

1. *reinvigorated*   given new   given old   given
                         leaders   standards   new life

It's *stasis* that kills you off in the end, not *ambition*.

—Bono (1960—), Irish musician

2. *stasis*   apathy   inactivity   paralysis

3. *ambition*   drive   enthusiasm   greed

Diplomacy is the art of saying "nice doggie" until you can find a rock.

—Will Rogers (1879–1935), American actor and humorist

4. *diplomacy*   trickery   cleverness   tact

The gambling known as business looks with *austere* disfavor upon the business known as gambling.

—Ambrose Bierce (1842–1914), American author

5. *austere*   stern   enormous   particular

VOCAB-U-LADDER

Use your knowledge of word synonyms and roots to connect the word at the top rung to the word at the bottom rung, using the words listed below.

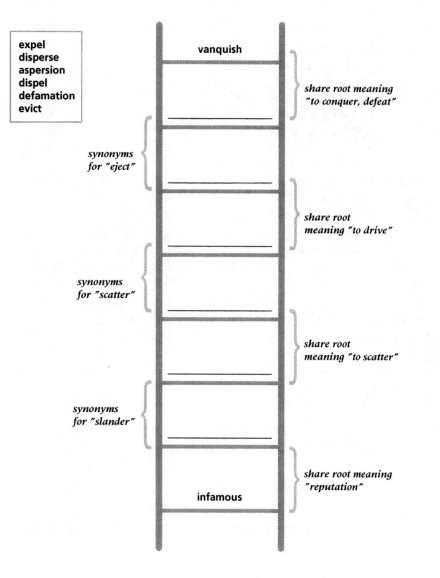

expel
disperse
aspersion
dispel
defamation
evict

vanquish

share root meaning
"to conquer, defeat"

synonyms
for "eject"

share root
meaning "to drive"

synonyms
for "scatter"

share root
meaning "to scatter"

synonyms
for "slander"

share root meaning
"reputation"

infamous

Here's the story behind a word that figures prominently in the chapter you've just read.

Critical Critical words aren't always critical words

critical crit′ ĭ-kəl. *adj*. 1. Inclined to judge severely and find fault. 2. Characterized by careful, exact evaluation and judgment. 3. Of, relating to, or characteristic of critics or criticism. 4. Forming or having the nature of a turning point; crucial or decisive.*

"May I be critical?" Ask someone that, and you're apt to be faced with a frown or maybe even a full-fledged "fight or flight" response. These days, that question can be about as welcome as a punch in the solar plexus. It's a confusing world as far as words are concerned. In some circles, *bad* can mean "good," *cool* can mean "hot," and calling something *sick* can be seen as a compliment. The English language is in an almost constant state of flux. When architect Christopher Wren completed St. Paul's Cathedral in 1710, the Queen told him she thought it was awful. In other words, she loved it. *Awful* meant "awe-inspiring" in Wren's day but now it generally means "*horrid.*" Although somewhere along the way the word critical has acquired a primarily negative connotation, it hasn't always been this way. The words critical and criticism come from the Greek word *krīnein*, which means "to separate, judge, or decide." Both of these words in turn are descendants of crisis, which has met a similar fate. A *crisis* is a crossroads, a critical point where paths may separate or when it's time to judge or decide. The welcome end to a high fever is a crisis; a thoughtful, detailed analysis of a novel is criticism; and a large supply of water can be *critical* on a long hike. But a hurricane is a *crisis*, insults can be *criticism*, and if you thoughtlessly fail to bring water on that hike, the person who scolds you may be accurately described as *critical*. Yes, English words can have slippery meanings. And *critical* is a classic example. A lot depends on the time, the context, and the intentions of the person who uses them. So the next time that someone asks, "May I be critical?" hold your fire, take a deep breath, and think critically before you answer.**

* Adapted from "critical." *The American Heritage Dictionary of the English Language*, 4th ed. Boston: Houghton Mifflin, 2000. http://dictionary.reference.com/browse/critical (accessed May 26, 2009).
** Based on information from "critical." *The American Heritage Dictionary of the English Language*, 4th ed. Boston: Houghton Mifflin, 2000. http://dictionary.reference.com/browse/critical (accessed May 26, 2009).; "critical." *Online Etymology Dictionary*. Douglas Harper, Historian. http://www.etymonline.com/index.php?search=critical (accessed May 26, 2009).; "critical, *a.*" *Oxford English Dictionary*, 2nd ed. 20 vols. Oxford: Oxford University Press, 1989.; "critical, *a.*" *OED Online*. Oxford University Press. http://sc-www2.santacruzpl.org:2062/cgi/entry/50054175 (accessed May 26, 2009).

UNIT TWO

CRITICAL COMPREHENSION

Ariel Skelley/Blend Images/Jupiter Images

Unit Two builds on what you learned in Unit One. A look at the comprehension triangle on the next page shows what you learned about literal comprehension and what you will learn about critical comprehension in this unit. As you work through this unit, you will continue to develop your ability to read at the literal level while learning to develop your ability to read critically.

What Is Critical Comprehension?

Critical comprehension is that level of understanding that entails distinguishing fact from opinion; recognizing an author's intent, attitude, or bias; drawing inferences; and making critical judgments. It's the second branch on the comprehension triangle explained in Unit One. Critical comprehension is a more sophisticated level of understanding than literal comprehension. A well-known reading expert, Dr. Francis Triggs, says, "Critical reading requires a contribution by both the author and the reader and an interplay which usually results in a new understanding." For instance, Jonathan Swift's *Gulliver's Travels* appeals to young people because

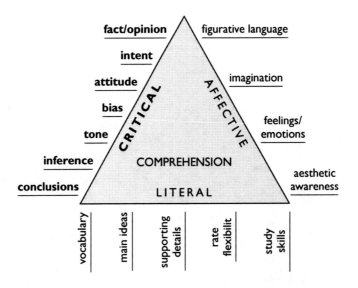

at the literal level it reads like a fairy-tale adventure story about a man who lives with giants and miniature people. However, when the story is read at a more critical level of understanding, it is a very bitter satire on mankind. In other words, an understanding beyond the literal level is necessary for thorough comprehension.

What Does This Unit Cover?

There are four chapters in this unit, each one covering a different facet of critical comprehension. Chapter Four deals with separating fact from opinion. Exercises will call your attention to how we think we are dealing with fact when often we are accepting opinion.

Chapter Five provides exercises for developing the ability to recognize an author's intent or real purpose in writing. Sometimes authors "disguise" their true purpose or thesis by the use of metaphor, satire, irony, or humor. Other times, authors use propaganda or present their evidence in a biased way. Chapter Five should help you analyze an author's actual intention and evaluate bias.

Chapter Six contains practices for discovering how both the author and the reader often draw inferences. Rather than coming right out and saying what they mean, authors sometimes imply or suggest what they want the reader to understand. Likewise, readers often draw inferences about what an author says. When you hear students talking about the "hidden meaning" of a work, or when you hear the statement "Read between the lines," drawing inferences is what is meant. This chapter also provides an opportunity to react to quoted statements, advertisements, and short articles, using what you learned in previous chapters to help you make critical judgments and draw conclusions.

Chapter Seven provides information on developing computer reading skills. Many college classes, as well as a variety of jobs, require not only the ability to read "hard copy," but also the ability to make use of the World Wide Web. More and more information is becoming available on the Internet making it necessary to learn your way around the Web and how to critically evaluate valid information sites. All the reading skills in this unit need to be applied to reading sources found on the Internet.

A comment regarding reading rate is in order here. As you learned in Unit One, speed of reading is not as important as good comprehension. By now you should have realized that although you can increase your overall speed, your reading rate fluctuates with your interest in the topic, the length of the reading selection, your knowledge of the subject, the level of difficulty, and even how you feel on a certain day. That is natural. Some reading selections in this section of the book are timed, mostly for your own concern; most students developing their reading versatility like to have some idea of how fast they are reading. That's fine. Go ahead and practice reading faster. Just remember not to let speed be your goal. As you get to be a better reader, your reading speed also will increase.

What Should You Know after Completing This Unit?

Here are six objectives to work toward in this unit. By the time you complete this unit, you should be able to:

1. Distinguish fact from opinion.
2. Recognize an author's intent, attitude, and tone.
3. Recognize an author's bias and use of propaganda.
4. Recognize inferences being made by an author and make your own inferences from what you read.
5. Make critical judgments and draw conclusions by analyzing the author's diction, style, and use of figurative language.
6. Be familiar with some Internet search engines and how to apply critical reading skills to information found on the World Wide Web.
7. Write a definition of critical comprehension.

If you have any objectives of your own, write them down below and share them with your instructor.

Personal reading objectives for Unit Two:

_____

_____

_____

_____

_____

_____

_____

For now, concentrate on objective 1, distinguishing fact from opinion, which is covered in the next chapter.

CHAPTER ONE

Distinguishing Fact from Opinion

Distinguishing fact from opinion is not always easy. A fact is usually defined as a truth, something that can be tested by experimentation, observation, or research and shown to be real. But even that is an elusive definition. For example, in 1930 it was generally accepted as fact that the atom was the smallest particle of an element and could not be split. With the advent of atomic power in the 1940s, scientists split the atom, making what was once thought to be a fact a fallacy. Today, physicists are just beginning to understand subatomic particles and refer to many of their findings as theory rather than fact. The point is that facts are sometimes "slippery."

An opinion, on the other hand, is often easier to distinguish. Your belief, feeling, or judgment about something is an opinion. It is a subjective or value judgment, not something that can be objectively verified. Even though you base your opinion on fact, others may not agree; an opinion cannot be proven to everyone's satisfaction. For instance, you may be of the opinion that George Clooney is the greatest actor of our time, but there is no way to make your opinion fact. Others have their own favorite actors, while still others do not know who George Clooney is. The only fact that you can prove is that Clooney is an actor.

Test your skill in recognizing fact from opinion by placing an *F* in the blank next to each of the following statements that you believe to be fact.

1. Harry S. Truman was the president of the United States.

2. Truman was one of the best presidents the United States has had.

3. Generally speaking, movies are more entertaining than books. *value judgement*

4. *TIME* is a better magazine than *Newsweek*.

5. Columbus, in 1492, was the first person to discover America.

Now see how well you did. You should have marked the first one as a fact. It is a fact that can be verified objectively. The second statement, however, is not a fact. It is a subjective statement claiming "Truman was one of the best." This claim is a value judgment; although we can prove that Truman was a president, historians may never agree that he was one of the best, even though he might have been. Words that give something value, such as *great, wonderful, beautiful, ugly, intelligent,* or *stupid,* make statements subjective opinions, not verifiable facts.

The third statement is not fact; it is a value judgment. To say something is "more entertaining" or "better" or "worse" is to place a personal value on something. Value judgments may be based on facts, but they are opinions nonetheless.

The fourth statement is not a fact. You may believe one magazine is better than another, but the use of the word "better" needs clarification. Better in what way? Editorial content? News coverage? Critical reviews? Again, "better" implies a value judgment. *TIME* may have a larger circulation than does *Newsweek*, but that in itself does not make it a better magazine.

The fifth statement is one of those "slippery" facts. According to many sources, Columbus did discover America in 1492. Yet, factually, he never actually landed on the continent; Vikings are said to have explored America long before Columbus, and evidence indicates that Native Americans inhabited America more than 25,000 years before Columbus. Obviously, he wasn't the first person to discover America. It is a European viewpoint that many history books continue to express, yet many textbooks are now changing wording to clarify this historical point. As stated, the fifth statement is not an opinion; it is more an erroneous statement than anything else.

On the other hand, if someone claimed that Columbus sailed to the New World in 1592 rather than 1492, it would be easy enough to consult historical records to show that the correct date was 1492. Knowledge that we share and agree upon as a society is called *shared knowledge*. Agreed-upon facts, then, are generally referred to as objective. If we argue that Columbus was a better sailor than Magellan, we get into the subjective realm of opinion. Unless we can find objective evidence that one was better than the other, we can't speak factually.

Which of the following statements are based on objective evidence?

_O_ **1.** Coca-Cola tastes better than Pepsi-Cola.

_F_ **2.** The capital of Illinois is Springfield.

_F_ **3.** The moon revolves around the earth.

_O_ **4.** Italians make great lovers.

Both statements 1 and 4 are based on subjective evidence. You might get fifty people to say Coke tastes better than Pepsi, but you can get another fifty to say the opposite. The same goes for Italians as great lovers. These statements are opinions, not facts. Statements 2 and 3 can be verified by checking agreed-upon information; thus they are facts based on objective evidence until such time as Springfield is no longer the capital and the moon quits revolving around the earth.

Just as our purpose for reading affects our speed and comprehension needs, it also affects the degree to which we must be aware of the differences in objective and subjective statements. When we read the paper for the news of the day, we want facts based on objective reporting. If we want to read someone's interpretation of the facts and what implications that news may have for us, we read editorials and columnists' opinions to see how they subjectively interpret the news. When we read a recipe, we want factual measurements, not opinions on how the finished product will taste. When we read an encyclopedia, we want the facts. But when we read a critic's opinion or interpretation of the importance of those facts, we are looking for a subjective reaction, an opinion.

As a critical reader of all kinds of writing, you need to be able to discern between objective and subjective statements and then draw your own conclusions. The following drills will help you develop your ability to distinguish facts, opinions, and erroneous-sounding statements. If some of the answers seem "picky," just remember that the point is to sharpen your reading versatility.

A.   Fact-Finding

PRACTICE **A-1:** Fact-Finding

Directions: Read each of the following statements and place an *F* in the blank next to each statement that you feel is *mostly* fact and an *O* in the blank next to each statement that is *mostly* opinion.

_F_ 1.   A world auction record for a single piece of furniture—$415,800 for a Louis XVI table—was set today at a sale of the French furniture collection of the late Mrs. Anna Thomson Dodge of the Detroit auto fortune. (From a United Press International release.)

_O_ 2.   The junior college is a <u>better</u> place to attend school for the first two years than is a university or four-year school. This is so primarily because classes are <u>smaller</u> at a junior college and more individualized attention can be given to students.

_F_   3. Medsker and Trent found that four-year colleges draw approximately three-fourths of their freshmen from the upper 40 percent of the high school graduating class, whereas about half the junior college transfer students were in the upper 40 percent of their high school graduating classes. (From K. Patricia Cross, *The Junior College Student: A Research Description*, Educational Testing Service, 1968.)

_F_   4. A black person can expect to live, on the average, seven years less than a white person of the same sex, to enjoy a little more than half the income—even if he has more education than his white brothers—and to suffer about twice the unemployment rate. (From Robert K. Carr et al., *Essentials of American Democracy*, 1968.)

_F_   5. Not since the frontier days have Native Americans faced greater threats to their existence than they do today. Malnutrition, disease, and despair are rampant. Their school dropout rate is 50 percent greater than the national average. Unemployment is ten times the rate of other Americans. The Native American today has the shortest life expectancy of any group in the country.

_O_   6. Eric Larnabee's *Commander in Chief* is a bold, fresh, and utterly convincing portrait of FDR as a war leader.

_O_   7. Adolf Hitler's mistress, Eva Braun, was a pudgy, middle-class blonde who gloomed more than she glittered. Yet her name will go down in history alongside such famous and glamorous kept women as Lola Montez, Madame de Pompadour, Nell Gwyn, and Du Barry.

_O_   8. America's Favorite Cigarette Break—Benson & Hedges 100s. (From a Benson & Hedges advertising slogan.)

_F_   9. The president is the only official who represents every American—rich and poor, privileged and underprivileged. He represents…also the great, quiet, forgotten majority—the non-shouters and the non-demonstrators, the millions who ask principally to go their own way in decency and dignity. (From a 1968 campaign speech by Richard M. Nixon.)

_O_   10. Businessmen, especially big-businessmen, do whatever they want to you: They set outrageously high prices on their products, bombard you with advertising so that you'll buy something you don't want and don't even need, and then make sure that what you've bought falls apart just when you get it home. (From Angus Black, *A Radical's Guide to Economic Reality*, Holt, Rinehart and Winston, 1970.)

PRACTICE A-2: More Fact-Finding

Directions: Read each of the following statements. Circle the number of any that you think are primarily factual or can be objectively proven. Then underline any words in the statements that you feel are too subjective to be verified as factual.

1. In the first seven months of 1988, once-private companies raised $17.4 billion through initial public offerings, or two-thirds more than in the same period of 1987.

2. There are still young people who read for pleasure and who do well in school, but their number dwindles. The middle range of children muddle through high school and some go through college, but the general level of their academic achievement is significantly below what it was thirty years ago.

3. In the presidential election of 1828, Andrew Jackson defeated John Quincy Adams with a popular vote of 647,286 votes over 508,064 for Adams.

4. Take the plunge into the splashiest resort on the most spectacular beach on the most exquisite island in Hawaii—the new Willoughby Maui Hotel. Join in the dreamlike atmosphere of waterfalls, tropical lagoons, and lush tiered gardens—or simply soak up the sun.

5. While grammar usage offers the most immediate clues to a person's educational background, another important clue is vocabulary. The writer or speaker who uses words appropriately and accurately is probably well educated. One who often mis-uses words or phrases is not soundly educated, because a major purpose of educa-tion is to teach people to use their native tongue with accuracy.

6. Since 1957, writes Ben J. Wattenberg in his *The Birth Dearth*, the average American woman's fertility rate has dropped from 3.77 children to 1.8—below the 2.1 size needed to maintain the present population level. Meanwhile, he argues, Commu-nist-bloc countries are producing at a rate of 2.3 children per mother, while the Third World rate is rising so fast that within fifty years its population may be ten times that of the West.

7. But specific challenges to Wattenberg's data have been raised. Some demographers question his projections, because he gathered his information from population trends with little or no regard for such unpredictable factors as wars, epidemics, famines, and baby booms.

8. Scientific data show that, although the Sahara desert moved south between 1980 and 1984, it went north in 1985 and 1986. In 1987 the Sahara's border shifted south, north in 1988, and south again in 1989 and 1990. To find any long-term trends in these annual fluctuations, the researchers say, data would have to be taken for several decades.

PRACTICE A-3: Fact versus Opinion

Directions: Each sentence is lettered in the following statements. On the line below each state-ment, write the letter of each sentence you think can be accepted as a statement of fact. The first one has been done for you.

1. (a) The last great Greek astronomer of antiquity was Claudius Ptolemy (or Ptole-meus), who flourished about a.d. 140. (b) He compiled a series of thirteen volumes on astronomy known as the *Almagest*. (c) All of the *Almagest* does not deal with Ptolemy's own work, for it includes a compilation of the astronomical achieve-ments of the past, principally of Hipparchus. (d) In fact, it is our main source of information about Greek astronomy. (e) The *Almagest* also contains accounts of the contributions of Ptolemy himself. (From George Abell, *Exploration of the Uni-verse*, Saunders College Publisher, 1982.)

(a). although the phrase last great may not be fact (b). (c). (d). (e)

2. (a) The July 1987 Almanac states that there are four West Coast species of salmon. This is incorrect. (b) There are five species. (c) The West Coast species belong to the genus *Oncorhynchus*. (d) Their common names are chinook, also called the spring or king salmon; the chum or dog salmon; the coho or silver salmon; the pink salmon; and the sockeye or red salmon.

a, b,   c, d

false   *false*

3. We hold these truths to be self-evident, (a) that all men are created equal; (b) that they are endowed by their Creator with certain unalienable rights; (c) that among these are life, liberty, and the pursuit of happiness; (d) that to secure these rights, governments are instituted among men. (From the Declaration of Independence.)

   a - truths to be Self-evident, b, c, d.

4. (a) If the American political system is to survive without repression, it will be because of positive political leadership that faces up to the problems and convinces both private citizens and public officials that these problems are serious and interrelated; (b) that they must be attacked, attacked immediately, and attacked together by coordinated and probably expensive programs. (c) As we have said so many times...if there is to be positive leadership in American politics, it can only come from the president. (d) Even then the Madisonian system may stalemate. (e) But without presidential leadership there is no hope that the system can move with any speed or controlled direction.

5. (a) *The Glass Bead Game* by Hermann Hesse appeared in Switzerland in 1943. (b) It was his last major work of any importance. (c) It is also the best of all his novels, an "act of mental synthesis through which the spiritual values of all ages are perceived as simultaneously present and vitally alive." (d) It was with full artistic consciousness that Hesse created this classic work.

   a, b, c - best of his novels, d.

6. (a) Although over 500 ruins are recorded within the Grand Canyon National Park, we know only the outline of this area's prehistory. (b) Most ruins are small surface pueblos in and along the north and south rims of the canyon. (c) No large communal centers have been found. (d) Small cliff dwellings and numerous granaries occupy caves and niches in the canyon walls. (e) A few early pit houses, some ruins of late Havasupai houses, and occasional hogans and sweat lodges left by the Navajos complete the roster. (From Joe Ben Wheat, *Prehistoric People*, Grand Canyon Natural History Association, 1959.)

   a, e.

PRACTICE A-4: Interpreting "Facts"

Directions: Read the following two paragraphs. They are accounts of the same historical event written by two different historians. Notice how they both use facts and how they interpret these facts.

When anarchy visited Nicaragua, Coolidge had no choice but to act unilaterally First, in 1925, he withdrew a token force of marines from that nation, which then seemed capable of servicing its foreign debt and preserving its internal stability. But the appearance was deceptive. Almost at once revolution broke out, and Coolidge again landed the marines, in time some five thousand. Regrettably, in its quest for order, the United States chose to support the reactionary faction, whose identification with large landowners and foreign investors had helped provoke the revolution in the first place. (From John Blum et al., *The National Experience*, Harcourt Brace Jovanovich, 1963, p. 617.)

The United States, despite the current anti-war sentiment, was reluctantly forced to adopt warlike measures in Latin America. Disorders in Nicaragua, perilously close to the Panama Canal jugular vein, had jeopardized American lives and property and in 1927 President Coolidge felt compelled to dispatch over 5,000 troops to this troubled banana land. His political foes, decrying mailed-fist tactics, accused him of waging a "private war," while critics south of the Rio Grande loudly assailed *Yanqui* imperialism. (From Thomas A. Bailey, *The American Pageant*, 2nd edition, Heath, 1961, p. 503.)

1. Underline the main idea in each paragraph, and be ready to justify your answer.

2. List two supporting details that support the main idea in *each* of the paragraphs.

   _____

   _____

   _____

3. What facts reported in the first passage are also reported in the second one? Are there any differences in the reporting of facts? _____

   _____

   _____

4. Explain whether the two authors agree on the reason Coolidge sent troops to Nicaragua. _____

   _____

5. Do the two authors agree on the reactions to Coolidge's action? Explain.

   _____

   _____

PRACTICE A-5: Comparing "Facts"

Directions: In 2003, the U.S. Court of Appeals for the Ninth Circuit in California declared unconstitutional the phrase "one nation under God" in the Pledge of Allegiance. At the time of this writing, the ruling has been sent to the Supreme Court on appeal. Two essays on the issue are presented here. One author believes the phrase should not be in the pledge; the other author believes it belongs there.

Before you read the essays, check one of the following statements:

____ 1. I believe the phrase "one nation under God" belongs in the pledge.

____ 2. I believe the phrase "one nation under God" does not belong in the pledge.

____ 3. I don't know.

Now read both of the following essays. As you read them, underline any statements you think are factual.

DO WE NEED GOD IN THE PLEDGE?

JAY SEKULOW

Fact

IT'S A STATEMENT OF PATRIOTISM, NOT RELIGION

1   As our nation battles terrorism—at home and abroad—there is a very real threat that millions of students in the western United States will no longer have an opportunity to express their patriotism by voluntarily reciting the Pledge of Allegiance with the phrase "one nation under God."

2   That phrase has been declared unconstitutional by the U.S. Court of Appeals for the 9th Circuit in California. The full appeals court refused to reconsider an earlier ruling by a three-judge panel of the appeals court that determined the phrase "one nation under God" violates the separation of church and state. Now, the only recourse rests with the Supreme Court.

3   The Supreme Court is being asked to take the case and ultimately uphold the constitutionality of a phrase that has become a time-honored tradition—an integral part of the Pledge for nearly 50 years.

4   The Pledge first appeared in print in 1892 as a patriotic exercise expressing loyalty to our nation. Congress added the phrase "under God" in 1954. That phrase first appeared in President Lincoln's Gettysburg Address, which concluded that "this nation, under God, shall have a new birth of freedom—and that the government of the people, by the people, shall not perish from the earth."

5   While the Supreme Court has never ruled directly on the constitutionality of the Pledge, there are numerous cases over the years where justices concluded that the phrase "one nation under God" is not an establishment of religion, but merely a way for the government to acknowledge our religious heritage.

6   In 1962, in *Engel v. Vitale*, Justice Potter Stewart referred to the Pledge of Allegiance as an example of governmental recognition when he quoted a 1952 finding by the court (*Zorach v. Clauson*) that Americans "... are a religious people whose institutions presuppose a Supreme Being."

7   In *Abington v. Schempp*, Justice William Brennan wrote in 1963 that such patriotic exercises like the Pledge do not violate the Establishment Clause of the First Amendment because such a reference, as he put it, "may merely recognize the historical fact that our nation was believed to have been founded 'under God.' Thus reciting the pledge may be no more of a religious exercise than the reading aloud of Lincoln's Gettysburg Address."

8   In 1984, the court in *Lynch v. Donnelly* recognized "there is an unbroken history of official acknowledgement by all three branches of government of the role of religion in American life." Among the many examples of our government's acknowledgement of our religious heritage, according to the court, is the phrase "one nation, under God."

9   And in 1985, Justice Sandra Day O'Connor, quoting herself from *Lynch v. Donnelly*, argued in *Wallace v. Jaffree* that the inclusion of the words "under God" in the Pledge is not unconstitutional because they "serve as an acknowledgement of religion with 'the legitimate secular purpose of solemnizing public occasions, and expressing confidence in the future.'"

10   The California appeals court relied on faulty legal reasoning in reaching a troubling conclusion that can now only be overturned by the Supreme Court. There is no guarantee that the high court will hear the case. But it should. The Pledge is a patriotic expression—not an affirmation of a particular faith.

11   As the Supreme Court considers what to do, it's important to note that the decision will not be made in a vacuum. After all, the court has its own time-honored tradition at stake. Each session begins with the sound of a gavel—and a dramatic call to order that concludes with these words: "God save the United States and this honorable court."

12   The Supreme Court should take the case and keep the Pledge intact.

Now answer the following questions.

1. Is this essay mostly fact or opinion? ___Fact_____

_____

2. What is the author's thesis or main idea? _____

_____

3. Is the thesis or main argument based on facts? Explain. _____

___Under god Sr_____

_____

4. Did the author convince you of his position? _____

_____

5. Do you think the Supreme Court should take the case and keep the Pledge intact?

_____

The following essay offers the opposite opinion regarding the pledge. As you read, underline any statements you feel are factual.

GOVERNMENT SHOULDN'T IMPOSE RELIGION ON CITIZENS

BARRY W. LYNN

1   A federal appeals court decision declaring school-sponsored recitation of the Pledge of Allegiance unconstitutional has generated tremendous confusion, to say nothing of downright hysteria.

2   Contrary to popular belief, the use of the phrase "under God" in the Pledge does not have a long history in America. The Pledge was written in 1892 by a clergyman, and it was originally secular. "Under God" was inserted by Congress in 1954 at the behest of conservative religious pressure groups.

3   To hear some tell it, removing "under God" from the Pledge would all but ensure America's downfall. In fact, the United States won two world wars, survived the Great Depression, and became a world economic and military powerhouse with a non-religious Pledge.

4   Under the Constitution, our laws are supposed to have a secular purpose. What is the secular purpose of having schoolchildren recite a pledge with religious content everyday? It can't be to foster love of country and respect for democracy. Those goals could be—and in the past were—met with a non-religious pledge.

5   No, the politicians who altered the Pledge in 1954 by adding "under God" knew exactly what they were doing. They wanted to make a religious statement. They wanted to send the message that belief in God is an essential part of being a good American. "God and country" was their motto.

6   The problem with this is that not everyone believes in God. Some Americans believe in no God, others believe in many gods.

7   For them, "under God" in the Pledge and "In God We Trust" on our money are a constant slap in the face, a daily reminder that they are different, that they are indeed not full members of the American experiment. That they're out of step—and wrong.

8   But it isn't just atheists and polytheists who are offended by government's use of generic religiosity. Many devoutly religious people are offended by the emptiness of such "God and Country" rhetoric. Real devotion to God, they argue, is not enhanced by the endless repetition of a phrase.

9   Some courts have upheld government's use of generic religious language, calling it "ceremonial deism." It's all right for the government to employ ceremonial deism, the argument goes, because it's not really that religious, and the government's constant use of a phrase like "under God" drains it of religious meaning.

10   As a minister, I find this argument bizarre and offensive. Religious terminology does not lose its sacred meaning just because people use it a lot, no more so than a prayer becomes non-religious through frequent repetition.

11   If that argument were true, it should be all the more alarming to the devout because it suggests that the state may promote religion as long as it first drains it of all meaning and power. In other words, we can have an official, government-supported religion in the United States—as long as it is bland, watered-down, generic, and ultimately meaningless.

12   In fact, the U.S. Constitution allows for no establishment of religion, specific or generic. The U.S. Congress lost sight of that fact in 1954 when it altered the Pledge of Allegiance. It has taken nearly 50 years for a federal court to recognize Congress' mistake. It shouldn't take another 50 for people to realize that "ceremonial deism" is a fraudulent myth that offends both church and state.

Now answer the following questions.

1. Is this essay mostly fact or opinion? _____

   _____

2. What is the author's thesis or main idea? _____

   _____

   _____

3. Is the thesis or main argument based on facts? Explain. _____

   _____

   _____

4. Did the author convince you of his position? _____

   _____

5. Have you changed your opinion after reading these two essays? Explain why or why not? _____

_____

_____

As a point of information, the Supreme Court did hear the case and overturned the 2002 ruling by California's 9th Circuit Court.

B.   Reading Opinions of Others

PRACTICE B-1

Directions: Take a few seconds to survey the following selection. Referring to the title, the headings, and your brief survey, write in the space below what you think the article will cover.

Probable coverage _____

Now read the article, underlining factual statements.

HOW GOOD ARE YOUR OPINIONS?

VINCENT RYAN RUGGIERO

1   "Opinion" is a word that is often used carelessly today. It is used to refer to matters of taste, belief, and judgment. This casual use would probably cause little confusion if people didn't attach too much importance to opinion. Unfortunately, most do attach great importance to it. "I have as much right to my opinion as you to yours" and "Everyone's entitled to his opinion" are common expressions. In fact, anyone who would challenge another's opinion is likely to be branded intolerant.

2   Is that label accurate? Is it intolerant to challenge another's opinion? It depends on what definition of opinion you have in mind. For example, you may ask a friend "What do you think of the new Buicks?" And he may reply, "In my opinion, they're ugly." In this case, it would not only be intolerant to challenge his statement, but foolish. For it's obvious that by opinion he means his *personal preference*, a matter of taste. And as the old saying goes, "It's pointless to argue about matters of taste."

3   But consider this very different use of the term. A newspaper reports that the Supreme Court has delivered its opinion in a controversial case. Obviously the justices did not state their personal preferences, their mere likes and dislikes. They stated their *considered judgment*, painstakingly arrived at after thorough inquiry and deliberation.

4   Most of what is referred to as opinion falls somewhere between these two extremes. It is not an expression of taste. Nor is it careful judgment. Yet it may contain elements of both. It is a view or belief more or less casually arrived at, with or without examining the evidence.

5   Is everyone entitled to his opinion? Of course. In a free country this is not only permitted, but guaranteed. In Great Britain, for example, there is still a Flat Earth Society. As the name implies, the members of this organization believe that the earth is not

spherical, but flat. In this country, too, each of us is free to take as creative a position as we please about any matter we choose. When the telephone operator announces "That'll be 95¢ for the first three minutes," you may respond, "No, it won't—it'll be 28¢." When the service station attendant notifies you "Your oil is down a quart," you may reply "Wrong—it's up three."

6   Being free to hold an opinion and express it does not, of course, guarantee you favorable consequences. The operator may hang up on you. The service station attendant may threaten you with violence.

7   Acting on our opinions carries even less assurance. Some time ago in California a couple took their eleven-year-old diabetic son to a faith healer. Secure in their opinion that the man had cured the boy, they threw away his insulin. Three days later the boy died. They remained unshaken in their belief, expressing the opinion that God would raise the boy from the dead. The police arrested them, charging them with manslaughter. The law in such matters is both clear and reasonable. We are free to act on our opinions only so long as, in doing so, we do not harm others.

OPINIONS CAN BE MISTAKEN

8   It is tempting to conclude that, if we are free to believe something, it must have some validity. But that is not so. Free societies are based on the wise observation that since knowledge often comes through mistakes and truth is elusive, every person must be allowed to make his own path to wisdom. So in a way, free societies are based on the realization that opinions can be wrong.

9   In 1972 a British farmer was hoeing his sugar beet field when he uncovered a tiny statue. It looked to him like the figure of a man listening to a transistor radio. In his opinion, it was a piece of junk. Yet it turned out to be a work of art made of gilt bronze in the twelfth century and worth more than $85,000. He was free to have his opinion. But his opinion was wrong.

10   For scores of years millions of people lit up billions of cigarettes, firm in their opinion that their habit was messy and expensive, but harmless. Yet now we know that smoking is a significant factor in numerous diseases and even does harm to nonsmokers who breathe smoke-polluted air and to unborn babies in the wombs of cigarette addicts. Those millions of people were free to believe smoking harmless. But that didn't make them right. Nor did it protect their bodies from harm.

KINDS OF ERROR

11   There are four general kinds of error that can corrupt anyone's beliefs. Francis Bacon classified them as follows: (1) errors or tendencies to error common among all people by virtue of their being human; (2) errors that come from human communication and the limitations of language; (3) errors in the general fashion or attitude of an age; (4) errors posed to an individual by a particular situation.

12   Some people, of course, are more prone to errors than others. John Locke observed that these people fall into three groups. He described them as follows:

- Those who seldom reason at all, but do and think according to the example of others, whether parents, neighbors, ministers, or whoever else they choose or have implicit faith in, to save themselves the pain and trouble of thinking and examining for themselves.
- Those who are determined to let passion rather than reason govern their actions and arguments, and therefore rely on their own or other people's reasoning only so far as it suits them.

- Those who sincerely follow reason, but lack sound, overall good sense, and so do not have a full view of everything that relates to the issue. They talk with only one type of person, read only one type of book, and so are exposed to only one viewpoint.

INFORMED VERSUS UNINFORMED OPINION

13   In forming our opinions it helps to seek out the views of those who know more than we do about the subject. By examining the views of informed people, we broaden our perspective, see details we could not see by ourselves, consider facts we were unaware of. No one can know everything about everything. It is not a mark of inferiority but of good sense to consult those who have given their special attention to the field of knowledge at issue.

14   Each of us knows something about food and food preparation. After all, most of us have eaten three meals a day all our lives. But that experience doesn't make us experts on running a restaurant or on the food packaging industry. Many of us have played varsity sports in high school. But it takes more than that experience to make us authorities on a particular sport.

15   Some years ago the inmates of Attica prison in New York State overpowered their guards and gained control of the prison. They took a number of hostages and threatened to kill them if their demands were not met. Negotiations proceeded for a time. Then they were at an impasse. The situation grew tense. Finally lawmen stormed the prison and, before order was restored, a number of the hostages were killed. In the wake of the tragedy were two difficult questions: Had the prisoners' demands been reasonable? And who was responsible for the breakdown in negotiations?

16   A number of people in public and private life offered their opinions. One newspaper editorial stated that the main fault lay with the prisoners, that they had refused to negotiate reasonably. A letter to the editor explained that the prisoners were unquestionably in the wrong simply because they were prisoners, and thus had forfeited all rights and privileges. A U.S. senator from another state declared that the blame lay with American life in general. "We must ask," he said, "why some men would rather die than live another day in America."

17   The governor of New York State issued this statement: "The tragedy was brought on by the highly-organized, revolutionary tactics of militants who rejected all efforts at a peaceful settlement, forcing a confrontation, and carried out cold-blooded killings they had threatened from the outset."

18   In a much less publicized statement, a professor at a small liberal arts college, an expert in penology (the study of prison systems), expressed sympathy with the prisoners, criticized the terrible conditions in the nation's prisons, agreed fully with many of the prisoners' demands, rejected a few as absurd, and explained some of the underlying causes of prison unrest.

19   Now all those opinions deserved some consideration. But which was most helpful in coming to an understanding of the issue in all its considerable complexity? Certainly the most informed opinion. The opinion of the expert in penology.

20   For all of us, whether experts or amateurs, it is natural to form opinions. We are constantly receiving sensory impressions and responding to them first on the level of simple likes and dislikes, then on the level of thought. Even if we wanted to escape having opinions, we couldn't. Nor should we want to. One of the things that makes human beings vastly more complex and interesting than trees or cows is their ability to form opinions.

21   This ability has two sides, though. If it can lift man to the heights of understanding, it can also topple him to the depths of ludicrousness. Both the wise man and the fool have opinions. The difference is, the wise man forms his with care, and as time increases his understanding, refines them to fit even more precisely the reality they interpret.

Comprehension Check

Part A

Directions: Answer the following questions. Don't look back unless you are referred to a particular paragraph for an answer.

1. Circle the letter of the statement that best expresses the thesis of the article:

   a. We need to form our opinions with care.

   b. It is natural to form opinions.

   c. The word *opinion* is used carelessly today.

   d. Everyone has a right to his or her own opinion.

2. T/F The statement "Being free to hold an opinion and express it does not, of course, guarantee you favorable consequences" is a fact.

3. T/F Paragraph 9 is mostly factual in content.

4. Which of the following are mentioned as the kinds of error that can corrupt anyone's beliefs?

   a. errors posed to an individual by a particular situation

   b. errors or tendencies to error common among all people by virtue of being human

   c. errors in the general fashion or attitude of an age

   d. errors that come from limitations of language

5. T/F In forming our opinions, it helps to seek out the views of those who do not know more than we do about the subject.

6. T/F "No one can know everything about everything" is an opinion.

7. In paragraph 19, the author claims that the expert in penology was the most helpful in coming to an understanding of the prison riot issue. Why would this opinion be better than the others mentioned? _____

   _____

8. What is the difference between personal preference and considered judgment?

   _____

   _____

   _____

9. "One of the things that makes human beings vastly more complex and interesting than trees or cows is their ability to form opinions," says the author. Is this a statement of fact or opinion? _____ Explain. _____

   _____

   _____

10. Is the article mostly fact or opinion? _____ ___ Explain. _____

    _____

    _____

Part B

Directions: The preceding questions can be answered objectively. The following questions require subjective responses. Be ready to explain your answers in class discussion.

1. "We are free to act on our opinions only as long as, in doing so, we do not harm others," says the author. Is this a good rule to follow?_____ Explain.

_____

_____

_____

_____

2. The author refers to a couple who took their diabetic son to a faith healer as an example of how acting on our opinions can be dangerous. Give an example of an opinion you hold or held at one time that could be dangerous in certain circumstances. _____

_____

_____

_____

3. Reread paragraph 12. In your opinion, do you fit any one of the three groups? Explain. _____

_____

_____

_____

4. Give an example of an opinion you once held but no longer do. Explain why you changed your viewpoint. _____

_____

_____

_____

_____

Vocabulary Check

Part A

Directions: Define the following underlined words from the selection.

1. their considered judgment

_____

2. it must have some validity

_____

3. errors posed to an individual

_____

4. some are more <u>prone</u> to errors

_____

5. they have <u>implicit</u> faith in themselves

_____

Part B

Directions: Write each word from the following list in the appropriate blank.

overpowered   inmates   tense   impasse   proceeded

"Some years ago the **(6)** _____ of Attica prison in New York State **(7)** _____ their guards and gained control of the prison. Negotiations **(8)** _____ for a time. Then they were at an **(9)** _____. The situation grew **(10)** _____."

Record the results of the comprehension (Part A only) and vocabulary checks on the Student Record Chart in the Appendix. Each correct answer is worth 10 points, for a total of 100 points possible for comprehension and 100 points for vocabulary. Discuss any problems or questions with your instructor before you continue.

PRACTICE B-2: Evaluating Differing Opinions

Part A

According to the organization called Law Enforcement Against Prohibition (LEAP), the so-called "War on Drugs" costs the United States an estimated $69 billion a year and does not see law enforcement ever winning the war. They and others call for the legalization of drugs and taxing them as we do alcohol and tobacco. Opponents feel that ending the prohibition of drugs would cause a rise in drug use and create enormous costs in accidents and productivity loss. Still others feel that only marijuana should be legalized. The subject produces many opinions and calls for substantial facts.

Directions: Following are two differing arguments on the subject of legalizing and taxing drugs, especially marijuana. Before you read them, use the space below to write why you would or would not support legalizing drugs presently illegal.

_____

_____

_____

The following selection was written by Brian O'Dea, one of the biggest marijuana smugglers in U.S. history and author of *High: Confessions of an International Drug Smuggler*. He presently produces film and television projects in Toronto, Canada. As you read, use what you have learned to distinguish between facts and opinions.

AN EX-DRUG SMUGGLER'S PERSPECTIVE

BRIAN O'DEA

1   I was one of the "masterminds" behind the importation and sale of approximately 75 tons of pot from Southeast Asia to the U.S. in 1986 and 1987. It was the culmination of a 20-year career as a drug smuggler, a deal that netted in excess of $180 million wholesale. And the only thing the government got out of those drug hauls was the sales tax from the cash my gang spent. There were, of course, some financial forfeitures once my gang was finally rounded up some years later. However, had rational minds prevailed over the past 70-plus years, the U.S. government would have reaped huge benefits from organizations like ours.

2   But no. Rather than accept the fact that some 30 million Americans cannot possibly be criminals, our society has squandered almost a trillion dollars in a futile effort to stop drug use.

3   We're hearing a lot about drug-related violence in Mexico these days. But listening to the news recently, I heard of a police sweep in Toronto—where I live some months out of the year. The operation involved more than 1,000 police officers and netted, among other things, a vast quantity of firearms, including loaded AK-47s, sawed-off shotguns and 34 handguns, none of which were obtained legally. These weapons came from the United States and were smuggled north. Here is how it works (I know firsthand): Canadian gangs grow pot in apartment buildings, putting everyone who lives there in danger. Once harvested, the pot is traded to U.S. gangs for cocaine and guns. America's arcane drug laws provide the currency for these gangs to exist.

4   South of the border, it's even worse. Some analysts say Mexico is on the slipperiest of slopes toward becoming a failed state, and illegal drugs are playing a huge part. Drug traffickers are able to operate only because they have currency. Take away the currency, you take away the drug traffickers.

5   In my days in that business, guns were nowhere to be found. Now, however, I cannot imagine anyone being in the trade without a gun. It has to stop, but how?

6   Steve Lopez, a Los Angeles Times columnist, recently wrote, "I'm sitting in Costa Mesa with a silver-haired gent who once ran for Congress as a Republican and used to lock up drug dealers as a federal prosecutor, a man who served as an Orange County [California] judge for 25 years. And what are we talking about? He's begging me to tell you we need to legalize drugs in America."

7   A judge is saying this. Say it ain't true, baby, but it is. And he's not the only one saying it. Former Seattle Police Chief Norm Stamper (in whose jurisdiction I was sentenced to 10 years in prison) says the same thing. That's why he is involved with Law Enforcement Against Prohibition, a group of former and current police officers, government agents and other law-enforcement agents who oppose the war on drugs.

8   According to LEAP, "After nearly four decades of fueling the U.S. policy of a war on drugs with over a trillion tax dollars and 37 million arrests for non-violent drug offenses, our confined population has quadrupled, making building prisons the fastest growing industry in the United States." More than 2.3 million U.S. citizens are in jail, and every year we arrest 1.9 million more, guaranteeing prisons will be busting at their seams. Every year, the war on drugs will cost U.S. taxpayers another $69 billion.

9   While the U.S. has only 5 percent of the world's population, it has 25 percent of the world's known prison population. This startling number is due to one major factor: our arcane drug laws. It is time we stopped treating a medical condition with law enforcement.

10   Ultimately, does the fact that people smoke pot make them criminals? Is the struggling heroin addict a criminal? If he is, it is only because we are not treating the root of the problem.

11   It is time to legalize marijuana. The tax revenue generated could then be used to help addicts. I work with these folks every day, in one way or another, and not one of them wants to live the way they do, but they don't know how to stop. They need help, not punishment.

12   Back in the 1920s, America saw one of the most violent organized criminal elements in history. Who can forget the tommy guns, the blood on the street and names like Luciano and Capone? Well, they exist today, it's just that the names have been changed to Escobar and Huerta Rios. As LEAP so succinctly puts it: Alcohol prohibition, drug prohibition, same problem, same solution.

Now answer the following questions:

1. What is the main idea of the essay? _Whether legal or not, people will do drugs._

2. Is the essay mostly fact or opinion? _fact_

3. What is the author's main argument for legalizing marijuana? _____

4. What factual support does the author use in favor of his opinion? _____

5. Did the author convince you of his argument? _____ Explain._____

Part B

Directions: The next essay offers the opposite view on legalizing marijuana and other illegal drugs. As you read, apply what you have learned about separating facts from opinions.

SHOULD WE TAX POT?

PATT MORRISON

1   Barack Obama is probably getting more letters than Santa Claus this year.

2   The transition office's mailbox must be full of pleas: "Dear President-elect Obama: I realty want a My Little Pony Pinkie Pie – Love. Susie." and "Dear President-elect

Obama: I really want a Mustang hybrid model that will sell half a million units in the first year – Love, Alan Mulally."

3   In Philadelphia this week, the nation's governors did everything but climb into Obama's lap with their wish lists for money to build roads and bridges and schools. Gov. Arnold Schwarzenegger's list alone runs to about $28 billion. Americans want healthcare reform and safe pensions and, truly, world peace.

4   But who's coming up with the money for this? Do we think we can stick our bicuspids under the pillow and the national tooth fairy will leave $800 billion? No? Then what about legalizing and taxing one of our biggest, oldest vices?

5   That notion arose because Friday is the 75th anniversary of the end of a nation-wide ban on a substance that millions of Americans broke the law and bought anyway: liquor. Criminalizing it turned out to have complications so enormous and expensive that in 1933 a new president, faced with a profound economic crisis, wanted it legal-ized and taxed again.

6   Now, as we're desperately trying to reinvent the economy, should we consider marijuana?

7   We've dipped a toe in those waters already in California. Sales of medical mari-juana are taxable – $11.4 million worth for 2005–2006, the most recent (though admit-tedly murky) figures available.

8   How much more might we raise from the tons of now-illegal marijuana? When we tried to tax it decades ago, it wasn't so much about raising money as about cutting the demand for dope. In 1937, a new federal tax added so much cost and red tape to purveying marijuana that even doctors were priced out of legally prescribing the stuff. Once pot was banned outright, the tax became a double-dipping opportunity for law-men. They got you for possessing or selling and for not paying the tax too. In 1968, the feds busted a Santa Barbara couple with 600 pounds of marijuana – and gave them a tax bill for $1,622,000.

9   Of course, by paying the tax, you would be confessing to breaking the law. Timothy Leary was busted for not paying a marijuana "transfer" tax, but the Supreme Court said the law amounted to self-incrimination and threw his case out.

10   However, if we keep charging a tax – something above and beyond a sales tax – but take away the criminality, we'd be win-win, right? We don't mind paying "sin" taxes, or levying them, like Schwarzenegger's plan to help beat the deficit with a new 5-cent-a-drink tax.

11   Marijuana is a huge component of the nation's underground economy. A couple of years ago, the legalize-it forces estimated that the U.S. marijuana crop was worth $35 billion a year. California's share of that was $13.8 billion.

12   If the number is even half that, any tax windfall, on top of money saved by not prosecuting marijuana crimes, would mean a bonanza, wouldn't it?

13   Sacramento would be doing the backstroke in black ink. With all the new parks and health clinics, we'd have more ribbon-cuttings than a baby shower. Is this just a pipe dream?

14   Rosalie Pacula says that in all likelihood, yes. She's a senior economist at the Rand Corp. and co-director of its drug policy research center. Here's how she burst my bubble:

15   First, you have to consider that legalizing it would have its own costs. Recent research, Pacula says, shows marijuana to be more addictive than was thought. Because marijuana is illegal, and because its users often smoke tobacco or use other drugs, teas-ing out marijuana's health effects and associated costs is almost impossible. And more people would smoke it regularly if it were legal – Pacula estimates 60% to 70% of the population as opposed to 20% to 30% now – and the social costs would rise.

16   She takes issue with figures from Harvard's Jeffrey Miron, among others, who says that billions spent on enforcing marijuana laws could all be saved by legalization. Rand's research, Pacula says, finds that many marijuana arrests are collateral – say, part of DUI checks or curfew arrests – and many arrestees already have criminal records, meaning they might wind up behind bars for something else even if marijuana were legal.

17   Legalization also wouldn't do away with pot-related crime entirely. There would likely be a black market, just as there is in other regulated substances, such as cigarettes and liquor. That means police and prosecution, which cost money.

18   As to the tax benefit, that's partly a function of the price point for legalized pot. If everyone could legally grow and consume dope, then the crop probably wouldn't be worth $35 billion and the taxes wouldn't be anything to write home about.

19   "I have a hard time believing the tax revenue would offset the full cost of regulating and enforcing the legal market," Pacula concludes.

20   No golden pot tax in the pot at the end of the rainbow, then? Pacula left me thinking that the unintended consequences of legalizing marijuana in 2009 might match the unintended consequences of outlawing liquor in 1919.

21   I'm sorry to let you down, President-elect Obama.

22   I think I'll go have a drink. Here's your tax nickel, Arnold. Oh heck – I want to do my bit for California. Here's a dime.

Now answer the following questions.

1. What is the main idea of the essay? _____
    _____
    _____

2. Is the essay mostly fact or opinion? Mostly _____

3. What facts does the author give in support of her thesis? _____
    _____
    _____

4. Is the main argument based mostly on facts? _____ Explain _____
    _____
    _____
    _____

5. Did the author convince you of Pacula's argument? _____ Explain._____
    _____
    _____
    _____

6. Reread your stated opinion on the subject (page 181). Then explain why you have or have not changed your mind after reading these two essays. _____
    _____
    _____
    _____

7. What would it take to change your opinion? _____

_____

_____

_____

Optional Exercise

Directions: If you are interested in the pros and cons of legalizing drugs, you may wish to go online and type in *legalizing drugs* in a search engine. Exploring some of the listings, you will find many more pro and con opinions and facts on the subject.

PRACTICE B-3: Quick Quiz on Fact/Opinion

Part A

Directions: Place an *O* in the blank next to each statement of opinion; place an *F* in the blank next to each statement that is fact or can be verified.

___F___ 1. Fifty-seven items in the L. L. Bean Women's Outdoor Catalog are offered in various shades of pink.

___O___ 2. We can no longer get along in our present society without telephones.

___O___ 3. It is important for college students to have good study skills if they are to succeed in the academic world.

___F___ 4. The Tobacco Institute donated $70,000 to help underwrite the antidrug booklet *Helping Youth Say No.*

___O___ 5. The two most interesting things in the world, for our species, are ideas and the individual human body, two elements that poetry uniquely joins together.

___F___ 6. Last year, as a result of the worldwide collapse of oil prices, the Mexican economy shrank 5 percent, and underemployment reached 50 percent. Things are worse in El Salvador.

___F___ 7. The United States is a nation of immigrants, and of immigration policies—policies designed to facilitate the orderly entry of people into the country, but also to keep them out.

___F___ 8. War against the Plains Indians in the early nineteenth century was a hopeless proposition for Europeans armed with swords, single-shot pistols, and breech-loading rifles. The Indians were infinitely better horsemen and could loose a continuous fusillade of arrows from beneath the neck of a pony going at full tilt.

___O___ 9. Mark Hunter's comments on the lack of spirit and spontaneity found in contemporary rock music are accurate. But his attack on MTV is misguided and his assertion that rock music is no longer worth listening to is absurd.

___F___ 10. Your jeweler is the expert where diamonds are concerned. His knowledge can help make the acquisition of a quality diamond of a carat or more a beautiful, rewarding experience.

Part B

Directions: In the space provided, explain what kind of evidence you would have to gather to prove each statement as fact.

1. The viewing of violence on television has created a more violent society. _____
   _____
   _____
   _____
   _____

2. City slums breed crime. _____
   _____
   _____
   _____
   _____

3. Solar energy is the most efficient way to heat homes in some parts of the United States. _____
   _____ How it work _____
   _____
   _____
   _____

4. A college education provides better job opportunities. _____
   _____
   _____
   _____
   _____

5. If you are rich, you probably won't get convicted of a crime as easily as you will if you are poor. _____
   _____
   _____
   _____

Discuss your answers in class.

C.   Detecting Propaganda

Before you begin this section on propaganda, answer the following questions.

1. Define *propaganda*: _____
   _____
   _____

2. Does the word *propaganda* have a positive or negative connotation for you? Explain. _____

_____

_____

3. Give some examples of the use of propaganda. _____

_____

_____

_____

4. Do you think you are always aware of propaganda when it is being used? Explain.

_____

_____

_____

Now read the following information, comparing your definition and examples of propaganda with those provided here.

Propaganda is the deliberate attempt on the part of a group or an individual to sway our opinions in their favor. Contrary to what some think, propaganda is not merely a tool used by dictatorial governments. We are exposed to various propaganda techniques nearly every day of our lives. Politicians use propaganda, along with other devices, to get us to accept their opinions and vote for them. Newspapers and magazines use propaganda techniques to influence our opinions on political and social issues. Religious leaders use propaganda to influence our opinions on morality. Advertisers, through television, radio, newspapers, magazines, and the Internet, use propaganda techniques to get us to buy things we often don't need or to change the brand of soap we use.

Propaganda techniques usually appeal to our emotions or our desires rather than to our reason. They cause us to believe or do things we might not believe or do if we thought and reasoned more carefully. When we are too lazy to think for ourselves, we often become victims of propaganda. Propagandists are usually not concerned with good or bad, right or wrong. They are more concerned with getting us to believe what they want us to believe. The techniques they use can range from outright lies to subtle truths.

The power of propaganda cannot be overrated. While some propaganda may be socially beneficial, it can also be harmful. Through propaganda techniques, our opinions can be changed to be "for" or "against" certain nations, political rulers, races, moral values, and religions. What we must guard against is having our opinions formed for us by others. We must not let ourselves be used or fooled, even for good causes.

The Institute for Propaganda Analysis identified seven of the most frequently used propaganda techniques:

1. *Name calling*: an attempt to arouse people with emotionally charged words that appeal to our fears or hatred. The technique is used with the hope that we will reject a person or idea on the basis of a negative symbol or word. Labeling someone as a *terrorist*, *fascist*, *fag*, or *radical* is done with the intent of creating a negative response to that person. However, sometimes name calling is done in reverse. The government changed the name of the War Department to the Department of

Defense. The MX missile, a weapon of destruction, is called the *Peacekeeper*. The term *shell shock* was changed to *combat fatigue*, then later to *post-traumatic stress disorder* in an attempt to lose its connection to war.

The institute suggests that we ask these questions when we spot name calling being used:

    a. What does the name mean?

    b. Is there a real connection between the name and the person or idea being labeled?

    c. Leaving the name out of it, what are the merits of the idea or person?

2. *Glittering generalities*: using words such as *justice, founding fathers, freedom, love of country, loyalty, the American way,* and *patriot* that are vague but have positive connotations that appeal to our emotions; propagandists often use them because they know we will be touched by such words. *Defending democracy* has a nice ring to it, but what is being planned or done in the name of *defending democracy* may be wrong when the concept is examined beyond the glittering generality. It is name calling in reverse.

When you spot this technique being used:

    a. Consider the merits of the idea itself when separated from specific words.

    b. Ask whether you are being manipulated by the use of your feelings toward the words being used.

3. *Transfer*: linking something we like or respect to some person, cause, or product; symbols are frequently used. If we respect the flag or the Christian cross, our respect for the symbol is transferred to whatever use it is being associated with. While at war in Iraq, people transfer their support by wearing pins of the American flag or by placing yellow ribbons on their cars saying "Support Our Troops." Cartoons of Uncle Sam smiling or frowning are used to reflect the government's approval or disapproval on an issue. Those referred to as the enemy, on the other hand, burn the American flag in protest using the symbol to transfer their feelings. Transfer is often used in politics to transfer the blame or bad feelings from one politician to another or from one political party to another. Transfer, then, can be used for or against causes and ideas.

When you spot this method being used:

    a. Consider whether the symbol being used really applies to the person, product, or cause.

    b. Ask whether you are being manipulated by the use of the symbol.

4. *Testimonial*: using well-known people to testify that a certain person, idea, or product is "the best." Famous or respected people are used to sell us ideas or products, because we transfer our positive feelings for them to the product or idea being sold. Look at advertisements in magazines or on television and you will see how many actors and athletes give testimonials for products, hoping we will transfer that respect to the product. This technique is closely connected to the transfer technique.

When you spot this method being used:

    a. Ask yourself whether the person giving the testimonial has any knowledge about the subject or product.

    b. Ask yourself whether you are being convinced by the person or by the facts of the testimonial.

    c. Ask how factual the content of the testimonial is.

5. *Plain folks*: an attempt to convince the public that the propagandist's views reflect those of the common person and that he or she is working in their best interests. A politician speaking to a blue-collar audience may roll up his sleeves, undo his tie, and attempt to use the specific idioms of the crowd. He may even use language incorrectly on purpose to give the impression that he is "just one of the folks." This technique usually also employs the use of glittering generalities to give the impression that the politician's views are the same as those of the crowd being addressed. Labor leaders, businesspeople, ministers, educators, and advertisers have used this technique to win our confidence by appearing to be just plain folks like ourselves.

   When you spot this method being used:

   a. Ask what the propagandist's ideas are worth when separated from his or her personality.

   b. Ask what the plain folks approach is covering up.

   c. Check for the facts, not the hype.

6. *Card stacking*: including only the information that is for or positive about a certain person or position and omitting evidence to the contrary. This technique stacks the evidence against the truth by omitting, changing, or evading facts; telling half-truths; or stating things out of context. This technique is very effective in convincing the public because most people don't bother to examine the other side of the issue being exploited, especially if the information is being offered by someone whom we admire or who we feel is serving our best interests. This is often used in advertising, in which a product might claim it "helps stop bad breath," leading us to think it *does* stop bad breath.

   When you see this method at work:

   a. Evaluate what is being presented as fact.

   b. Get more information about the subject before making up your mind.

7. *The bandwagon*: an appeal to join in, come aboard, follow the crowd. This technique appeals to our desire to be on the winning side, to be like or better than everyone else, and to be "one of the gang." It is an attempt to make us believe that we will be in the minority if we don't join or believe what's being offered. The propagandist directs the appeal to groups held together by common ties, such as religion, sex, race, and nationality, and uses the fears, hatreds, prejudices, ideals, and convictions of a group to join in or lose what you hold dear. In 2006, public figures found it difficult to criticize the Bush administration's foreign policies because the bandwagon mentality asserts that everyone must unite in the fight against terrorism, weapons of mass destruction, and those opposed to freedom and democracy. On the other hand, the United States has more weapons of mass destruction, sells more arms to other countries than any other nation in the world, and seems willing to destroy countries in order to bring them democracy.

   When you see this method at work:

   a. Ask yourself what the propagandist's program is.

   b. Ask yourself if there is evidence for or against the program.

   c. Ask whether the program really serves or undermines your own interests.

Propaganda, for good or bad, tries to manipulate us. As Paul R. Lees-Haley reminds us:

> Manipulators strive to divorce us from the facts. Rather than encouraging
> us to examine the evidence and reasoning of people who appear to disagree

with us, they block communications and openly or indirectly try to persuade us that people who disagree with their views are dishonest, not trustworthy, incompetent, biased, racist, only concerned with money, insulting our intelligence, corrupt, betrayers of the American dream, and so on. The subtext is: "Do not consider alternative points of view. Do what we tell you, without realizing that we are controlling you." Like cult leaders, manipulators encourage us to close ranks and form an in-group suspicious of those who question the party line. (From Paul R. Lees-Haley, "Propaganda Techniques Related to Environmental Scares," Quackwatch, http://www.quackwatch .org/01QuackeryRelatedTopics/propa.html.)

Most of these devices work because they appeal to our emotions, our fears, our ignorance, or our desire to do the "right thing." But by sorting facts from opinions, and by recognizing these propaganda techniques when used, we won't become victims, but rather thoughtful readers and thinkers who see these techniques for what they are.

PRACTICE C-1: Detecting Propaganda Techniques

Directions: Read each of the following items and in the space provided write in the propaganda technique or techniques being used and why you think so.

1. "My opponent, Senator Glick, has a record of being soft on crime at a time when we need to be strong." *name calling*

2. "Senator Cluck cares what happens to the farmers; he cares for the future of the American tradition of prosperity. He'll put this country back on track!" *general generalities,*

3. "Jerry Seinfeld. Cardmember since 1986" (American Express ad). *testimonial*

4. "M Lotion helps skin keep its moisture … discourages tired-looking lines under eyes." *card stacking*

5. "Over 8,000,000 sold! Why would anyone want to buy anything else?" *bandwagon*

6. "Buy Banhead. It contains twice as much pain reliever." *card stacking*

7. "Mayor Naste has shown time and again he's for the little guy. You don't see him driving a big limo or wearing fancy suits. No, sir. You'll find him out talking to us folks to see how he can serve us better." _____ *Plain folk*

   _____

8. "Buy the Sportsman's Shaving System, appointed the exclusive skin care system for the Winter Olympics." _____ *transfer, testimony*

   _____

9. "Yes, I lied. But I did it for my country. As God is my witness, I felt in my heart—and still do—that what I did was right, and the people of this country who want to preserve its freedom will thank me some day." _____ *appeal general glittery*

   _____

10. "Drive to class reunions in the new Hummer 3 and even Mr. Most-Likely-to- Succeed will be envious." _____ *name calling*

    _____

PRACTICE C-2

Directions: Survey the following passage from a textbook titled *Preface to Critical Reading* by reading the opening paragraph, some of the first sentences in selected paragraphs, and the questions that follow the reading. Then use the information from the survey to read the selection, marking key points.

DETECTING PROPAGANDA

RICHARD D. ALTICK and ANDREA A. LUNSFORD

1   All of us, whether we admit it or not, are prejudiced. We dislike certain people, certain activities, certain ideas—in many cases, not because we have reasoned things out and found a logical basis for our dislike, but rather because those people or activities or ideas affect our less generous instincts. Of course we also have positive prejudices, by which we approve of people or things—perhaps because they give us pleasure or perhaps because we have always been taught that they are "good" and never stopped to reason why. In either case, these biases, irrational and unfair though they may be, are aroused by words, principally by name-calling and the use of the glittering generality. Both of these techniques depend on the process of association, by which an idea (the specific person, group, proposal, or situation being discussed) takes on emotional coloration from the language employed.

2   *Name-calling* is the device of arousing an unfavorable response by such an association. A speaker or writer who wishes to sway an audience against a person, group, or principle will often use this device.

> The bleeding-heart liberals are responsible for the current economic crisis.
> The labor union radicals keep honest people from honest work.
> Environmental extremists can bankrupt hard-pressed companies with their fanatical demands for unnecessary and expensive pollution controls such as chimney-scrubbers.

3   Name-calling is found in many arguments in which emotion plays a major role. It rarely is part of the logic of an argument but instead is directed at personalities. Note how the speakers here depend on verbal rock throwing in their attempt to win the day:

> He's no coach, but a foul-mouthed, cigar-chomping bully who bribes high-school stars to play for him.
> The Bible-thumping bigots who want to censor our books and our television shows represent the worst of the anti-intellectual lunatic fringe.
> Mayor Leech has sold the city out to vested interests and syndicates of racketeers. City Hall stinks of graft and payola.

4   The negative emotional associations of the "loaded" words in these sentences have the planned effect of spilling over, onto, and hiding, the real points at issue, which demand—but fail to receive—fair, analytical, objective judgment. Generating a thick emotional haze is, therefore, an affective way for glib writers and speakers to convince many of the unthinking or the credulous among their audience.

5   The *glittering generality* involves the equally illogical use of connotative words. In contrast to name-calling, the glittering generality draws on traditionally positive associations. Here, as in name-calling, the trouble is that the words used have been applied too freely and thus are easily misapplied. Many writers and speakers take advantage of the glitter of these words to blind readers to real issues at hand. *Patriot, freedom, democracy, national honor, Constitution, God-given rights, peace, liberty, property rights, international cooperation, brotherhood, equal opportunity, prosperity, decent standard of living*: words or phrases like these sound pleasant to the listener's ear, but they can also divert attention from the ideas the speaker is discussing, ideas which are usually too complex to be fairly labeled by a single word.

> The progressive, forward-looking liberal party will make certain that we enjoy a stable and healthy economy.
> The practical idealists of the labor movement are united in supporting the right of every person to earn an honest living.
> Dedicated environmentalists perform an indispensable patriotic service for us all by keeping air-polluting industries' feet to the fire.
> He's a coach who is a shining light to our youth. He believes that football helps to build the character, stamina, and discipline needed for the leaders of tomorrow.
> The decent, God-fearing people who want to protect us from the violence and depravity depicted in books and on television represent the best of a moral society.
> Mayor Leech has stood for progress, leadership, and vision at a time when most cities have fallen into the hands of the corrupt political hacks.

6   The effectiveness of name-calling and the glittering generality depends on stock responses. Just as the scientist Pavlov, in a classic experiment, conditioned dogs to

increase their production of saliva every time he rang a bell, so the calculating persuader expects readers to react automatically to language that appeals to their prejudices.

7   The abuse of authority is one of the *transfer devices* which exploit readers' willingness to link one idea or person with another, even though the two may not be logically connected. The familiar *testimonials* of present-day advertising provide an instance of this device. In some cases, the "authority" who testifies has some connection with the product advertised. The problem to settle here is, when we try to decide which brand of sunburn cream is best, how much weight may we reasonably attach to the enthusiastic statements of certain nurses? When we are thinking of buying a tennis racket, should we accept the say-so of a champion who, after all, is well paid for telling us that a certain make is the best? In other cases, the testifying authorities may have no formal, professional connection with the products they recommend. An actor, who may very well be a master of his particular art, praises a whiskey, a coffee, or an airline. He likes it, he says. But, we may ask, does the fact that he is a successful actor make him better qualified than any person who is not an actor to judge a whiskey, a coffee, or an airline? Competence in one field does not necessarily "transfer" to competence in another.

8   Furthermore, advertisers often borrow the prestige of science and medicine to enhance the reputation of their products. Many people have come to feel for the laboratory scientist and the physician an awe once reserved for bishops or statesmen. The alleged approval of such people thus carries great weight in selling something or inducing someone to believe something. Phrases such as "leading medical authorities say ..." or "independent laboratory tests show ..." are designed simply to transfer the prestige of science to a toothpaste or deodorant. Seldom are the precise "medical authorities" or "independent laboratories" named. But the mere phrases carry weight with uncritical listeners or readers. Similarly, the title "Dr." or "Professor" implies that the person quoted speaks with all the authority of which learned people are capable— when, as a matter of fact, doctoral degrees can be bought from mail-order colleges. Therefore, whenever a writer or speaker appeals to the prestige that surrounds the learned, the reader should demand credentials. Just *what* "medical authorities" say this? Can they be trusted? What independent laboratories made the tests—and what did the tests actually reveal? Who are the people who speak as expert educators, psychologists, or economists? Regardless of the fact that they are "doctors," do they know what they are talking about?

9   Another closely related form of transfer is the borrowing of prestige from a highly respected institution (country, religion, education) or individual (world leader, philosopher, scientist) for the sake of enhancing something else. Political speakers sometimes work into their speeches quotations from the Bible or from secular "sacred writings" (such as a national constitution). Such quotations usually arouse favorable emotions in listeners, emotions which are then transferred to the speaker's policy or subject. When analyzing an appeal that uses quotations from men and women who have achieved renown in one field or another, the chief question is whether the quotation is appropriate in context. Does it have real relevance to the point at issue? It is all very well to quote George Washington or Abraham Lincoln in support of one's political stand. But circumstances have changed immensely since those statements were first uttered, and their applicability to a new situation may be dubious indeed. The implication is, "This person, who we agree was great and wise, said certain things which 'prove' the justice of my own stand. Therefore, you should believe I am right." But to have a valid argument, the writer must prove that the word of the authorities is really applicable to the present issue. If that is true, then the speaker is borrowing not so much their prestige as their wisdom—which is perfectly justifiable.

10   Another version of the transfer device is one which gains prestige not through quotations or testimonials of authorities but from linking one idea to another. Here is an advertisement that illustrates how this device works.

THE TELEPHONE POLE THAT BECAME A MEMORIAL

The cottage on Lincoln Street in Portland, Oregon, is shaded by graceful trees and covered with ivy.

Many years ago, A. H. Feldman and his wife remodeled the house to fit their dreams ... and set out slips of ivy around it. And when their son, Danny, came along, he, too, liked to watch things grow. One day, when he was only nine, he took a handful of ivy slips and planted them at the base of the telephone pole in front of the house.

Time passed... and the ivy grew, climbing to the top of the pole. Like the ivy, Danny grew too. He finished high school, went to college. The war came along before he finished—and Danny went overseas. And there he gave his life for his country.

Not very long ago the overhead telephone lines were being removed from the poles on Lincoln Street. The ivy-covered telephone pole in front of the Feldman home was about to be taken down. Its work was done.

But, when the telephone crew arrived, Mrs. Feldman came out to meet them. "Couldn't it be left standing?" she asked. And then she told them about her son.

So the pole, although no longer needed, wasn't touched at all. At the request of the telephone company, the Portland City Council passed a special ordinance permitting the company to leave it standing. And there it is today, mantled in ivy, a living memorial to Sergeant Danny Feldman.

11   What did the telephone company wish to accomplish by this ad? Readers are not urged to install a telephone, equip their homes with extra telephones, or use any of the various new services the company has developed. Nor are they told how inexpensive and efficient the telephone company thinks those services are. Instead, this is what is known as an "institutional" advertisement. Its purpose is to inspire public esteem, even affection, for the company.

12   How do such advertisements inspire esteem and respect? Simply by telling an anecdote, without a single word to point up the moral. In this ad, every detail is carefully chosen for its emotional appeal: the cottage ("home, sweet home" theme), the ivy (symbol of endurance through the years; often combined, as here, with the idea of the family home), the little boy (evoking all the feelings associated with childhood), the young man dying in the war (evoking patriotic sentiment). Thus at least four symbols are combined—all of them with great power to touch the emotions. Then the climax: Will the company cut down the ivy-covered pole? To many people, *company* has a connotation of hardheartedness, impersonality, coldness, which is the very impression this particular company, one of the biggest in the world, wants to erase. So the company modestly reports that it went to the trouble of getting special permission to leave this one pole standing, "mantled in ivy, a living memorial."

13   The writer of this advertisement has, in effect, urged readers to transfer to the telephone company the sympathies aroused by the story. The ivy-covered pole aptly symbolizes what the writer wanted to do—"mantle" the pole (symbolizing the company) with the ivy that is associated with home, childhood, and heroic death. If it is possible to make one feel sentimental about a giant corporation, an advertisement like this one—arousing certain feelings by means of one set of objects and then

transferring those feelings to another object—will do it. But the story, although true enough, is after all only one incident, and a sound generalization about the character of a vast company cannot be formed from a single anecdote. The company may well be as "human" as the advertisement implies, but readers are led to that belief through an appeal to their sympathies, not their reason.

14   A third kind of fallacy involves *mudslinging*, attacking a person rather than a principle. Mudslingers make personal attacks on an opponent (formally known as *ad hominem* arguments, those "against the man"), not merely by calling names, but often by presenting what they offer as damaging evidence against the opponent's motives, character, and private life. Thus the audience's attention is diverted from the argument itself to a subject which is more likely to stir up prejudices. If, for example, in denouncing an opponent's position on reducing the national debt, a candidate refers to X's connection with certain well-known gamblers, then the candidate ceases to argue the case on its merits and casts doubt on the opponent's personal character. The object is not to hurt X's feelings but to arouse bias against that person in the hearer's mind. Critical readers or listeners must train themselves to detect and reject these irrelevant aspersions. It may be, indeed, that X has shady connections with underworld gamblers. But that may have nothing to do with the abstract right or wrong of his stand on the national debt. Issues should be discussed apart from character and motives. Both character and motives are important, of course, since they bear on any candidate's fitness for public office and on whether we can give him or her our support. But they call for a separate discussion.

15   A somewhat more subtle kind of personal attack is the *innuendo*, which differs from direct accusation roughly as a hint differs from a plain statement. Innuendo is chiefly useful where no facts exist to give even a semblance of support to a direct charge. The writer or speaker therefore slyly plants seeds of doubt or suspicion in the reader's or listener's mind, as the villainous Iago does in the mind of Shakespeare's *Othello*. Innuendo is a trick that is safe, effective—and unfair. "They were in the office with the door locked for four hours after closing time." The statement, in itself, may be entirely true. But what counts is the implication it is meant to convey. The unfairness increases when the doubts that the innuendo raises concern matters that have nothing to do with the issue anyway. An example of the irrelevant innuendo is found in the writings of the historian Charles A. Beard. In assailing the ideas of another historian, Admiral Alfred T. Mahan, Beard called him "the son of a professor and swivel-chair tactician at West Point," who "served respectably, but without distinction, for a time in the navy" and "found an easy berth at the Naval War College." Actually, the occupation of Mahan's father has nothing to do with the validity of the son's arguments. But observe the sneer—which is meant to be transferred from father to son—in "professor" and "swivel-chair tactician." Beard's reference to Mahan's naval record is a good elementary instance of damning with faint praise. And whether or not Mahan's was "an easy berth" at the Naval War College (a matter of opinion), it too has no place in a discussion of the man's ideas or intellectual capacities.

16   Newspapers often use this device to imply more than they can state without risking a libel suit. In reporting the latest bit of gossip about celebrated members of the "jet set" or the "beautiful people" (what do the terms suggest about the habits and tastes of the people referred to?), a paper may mention the fact that "gorgeous movie actress A is a frequent companion of thrice-divorced playboy B" or that they "are seen constantly together at the Vegas night spots" or that they are "flitting from the Riviera to Sun Valley together." The inference suggested, however unfounded it may be, is that their relationship is not just that of good friends who happen to be in the same place at the same time. Similarly, newspapers which value sensationalism more than responsibility may describe an accused "child slayer" or "woman molester" as "dirty

and bearded" (implication: he is a suspicious-looking bum). His face may, in addition, be "scarred" (implication: he is physically violent). Such literal details may be true enough. But how much have they to do with the guilt or innocence of the person in this particular case? The effect on the reader is what courts of law term "prejudicial" and therefore inadmissible. Unfortunately the law does not extend to slanted writing, however powerfully it may sway public opinion.

17   Another instance of the way in which emotionally loaded language can be combined with unproved evidence to stir up prejudice may be taken from the field of art. A modern critic condemned certain paintings as "a conventional rehash of cubist patterns born among the wastrels of Paris forty years ago." In so doing, the critic attacked the art through the artist. The artistic merit of paintings has nothing to do with the private lives of the people who paint them. The painters referred to may well have been wastrels. But that fact—if it is a fact—has no bearing on the point at issue. The assumed connection between the personal virtues or shortcomings of artists and the artistic value of their productions has resulted in a great deal of confused thinking about literature, music, and the other arts.

18   Another diversionary tactic which introduces an irrelevant issue into a debate is the *red herring*. It too may involve shifting attention from principles to personalities, but without necessarily slinging mud or calling names. Since neither relaxing at a disco nor having a taste for serious books is yet sinful or criminal, a political party slings no mud when it portrays the other party's candidate as a playboy or an intellectual. Still, such matters are largely irrelevant to the main argument, which is whether one or the other candidate will better serve the interests of the people. The red-herring device need not involve personalities at all; it may take the form simply of substituting one issue for another. If a large corporation is under fire for alleged monopolistic practices, its public relations people may start an elaborate advertising campaign to show how well the company's workers are treated. Thus, if the campaign succeeds, the bad publicity suffered because of the assertions that the company has been trying to corner the market may be counteracted by the public's approval of its allegedly fine labor policy.

19   Unfortunately, most of us are eager to view questions in their simplest terms and to make our decisions on the basis of only a few of the many elements the problem may involve. The problem of minority groups in North America, for instance, is not simply one of abstract justice, as many would like to think. Rather, it involves complex and by no means easily resolvable issues of economics, sociology, politics, and psychology. Nor can one say with easy assurance, "The federal government should guarantee every farmer a decent income, even if the money comes from the pocketbooks of the citizens who are the farmer's own customers" or "It is the obligation of every educational institution to purge its faculty of all who hold radical sympathies." Perhaps each of these propositions is sound; perhaps neither is. But before either is adopted as a conviction, intelligent readers must canvass their full implications. ... After the implications have been explored, more evidence may be found *against* the proposition than in support of it.

20   Countless reductive generalizations concerning parties, races, religions, and nations, to say nothing of individuals, are the result of the deep-seated human desire to reduce complicated ideas to their simplest terms. We saw the process working when we touched on stereotypes ... and in our discussion of rhetorical induction. ... Unfortunately, condemning with a few quick, perhaps indefensible assumptions is easier than recognizing the actual diversity in any social group. But every man and woman has an urgent obligation to analyze the basis of each judgment he or she makes: "Am I examining every aspect of the issue that needs to be examined? Do I understand the problem sufficiently to be able to make a fair decision? Or am I taking the easiest and simplest way out?"

Now answer the following questions. You may look back if necessary.

1. What two propaganda devices are used to stir up our prejudices? _____

_____

_____

2. What part do our emotions play in the effectiveness of some propaganda techniques? _____

_____

_____

3. What do the authors mean when they say that "advertisers often borrow the prestige of science and medicine to enhance the reputation of their products"?

_____

_____

_____

4. What is meant by the term *transfer device*? Give some examples. _____

_____

_____

_____

5. Name the three devices or methods frequently used to attack a person rather than a principle. _____

_____

_____

6. Define the following terms: _____

   a. transfer devices _____

   _____

   b. testimonials _____

   _____

   c. mudslinging _____

   _____

   d. innuendo _____

   _____

   e. red herring _____

   _____

   f. oversimplification _____

   _____

7. Why is it important to recognize and understand how propaganda is used? _____

_____

_____

_____

Optional Exercise

To learn more about propaganda and its uses, type in *propaganda techniques* in a search engine and explore some of the sites listed.

Application I: Recognizing Propaganda at Work

Find an example of one of the seven propaganda techniques used in a current magazine or newspaper advertisement or essay. Write a brief explanation of how the technique is being used, attach it to the advertisement or essay, and share it in class.

D. Putting It All Together

The next two practices give you the opportunity to use what you have learned about critical comprehension to distinguish fact from opinion, read opinions of others, and detect propaganda. Review your scores on the Student Record Sheet in the Appendix and try to match or do better than your scores for the previous reading selections. If you make mistakes, analyze errors and figure out how to improve the next time. The first practice follows an introduction to the author Ishmael Reed; the second practice is timed.

Now read about the following author, Ishmael Reed, to understand more about how an author's life affects his opinions. His views on reading and literacy may inspire you to develop different views. Another way to find current information, quotations, or pictures of this author is to use the World Wide Web. Type in the author's name in a search engine such as Google or AltaVista.

Introducing Ishmael Reed

Ishmael Reed has been called one of the most innovative and outspoken voices in contemporary literature. His work embodies seven novels, four books of poetry, three plays, several collections of essays, and book reviews. In addition

to these works, Reed is a songwriter, television producer, and magazine editor. Reed has taught at Harvard, Yale, Dartmouth, and the University of California–Berkeley.

Reed is a strong advocate of literacy and its power. In an essay that first appeared in the *San Francisco Examiner* and was later reprinted in his collection *Writin' Is Fightin'*, Reed spoke out against illiteracy:

If you're illiterate, people can do anything they want to you. Take your house through equity scams, cheat you, lie to you, bunko you, take your money, even take your life. …

As you go through life *X*-ing documents, unable to defend yourself against forces hostile to you, people can deprive you of your voting rights through ger-rymandering schemes, build a freeway next to your apartment building or open a retail crack operation on your block, with people coming and going as though you lived next door to Burger King—because you're not articulate enough to fight back, because you don't have sense enough to know what is happening to you, and so you're shoveled under at each turn in your life; you might as well be dead.

One of the joys of reading is the ability to plug into the shared wisdom of mankind. One of my favorite passages from the Bible is "Come, and let us reason together"—Isaiah 1:18. Being illiterate means that you often resort to violence, during the most trivial dispute...because you don't have the verbal skills to talk things out....

I'm also convinced that illiteracy is a factor contributing to suicide becoming one of the leading causes of death among white middle-class youngsters, who allow their souls to atrophy from the steady diet of spiritual Wonder Bread: bad music and bad film, and the outrageous cheapness of superficial culture. When was the last time you saw a movie or TV program that was as good as the best book you've read, and I don't mean what imitation elitists call the classics. I'd settle for Truman Capote, John A. Williams, Cecil Brown, Lawson Inada, Paule Marshall, Xam Wilson Cartier, Victor Cruz, Howard Numerov, William Kennedy, Paula Gunn Allen, Margaret Atwood, Diane Johnson, Edward Field, Frank Chin, Rudolfo Anaya, Wesley Brown, Lucille Clifton, Al Young, Amiri Baraka, Simon Ortiz, Bob Callahan, David Metzer, Anna Castillo, Joyce Carol Oates and Harryette Mullen, a group of writers as good as any you'd find anywhere....(From Ishmael Reed, "Killer Illiteracy," *Writin' Is Fightin'*, Atheneum, 1988, pp. 185–186.)

Reed's essay "America: The Multinational Society" offers his reasons for dis-agreeing with those who believe the United States "is part of Western civilization because our 'system of government' is derived from Europe."

PRACTICE D-1: Timed Reading

Directions: Before reading the following article, take a minute to survey it and the questions. Then time yourself as you begin to read the article. As you read, discover why the author believes America is a multinational society.

Begin timing: _____

AMERICA: THE MULTINATIONAL SOCIETY

ISHMAEL REED

1   At the annual Lower East Side Jewish Festival yesterday, a Chinese woman ate a pizza slice in front of Ty Thuan Duc's Vietnamese grocery store. Beside her a Spanish-speaking family patronized a cart with two signs: "Italian Ices" and "Kosher by Rabbi Alper." And after the pastrami ran out, everybody ate knishes.

—*New York Times*, 23 June 1983

2   On the day before Memorial Day, 1983, a poet called me to describe a city he had just visited. He said that one section included mosques, built by the Islamic people who dwelled there. Attending his reading, he said, were large numbers of Hispanic people, forty thousand of whom lived in the same city. He was not talking about a fabled city located in some mysterious region of the world. The city he'd visited was Detroit.

3   A few months before, as I was leaving Houston, Texas, I heard it announced on the radio that Texas's largest minority was Mexican American, and though a foundation recently issued a report critical of bilingual education, the taped voice used to guide the passengers on the air trams connecting terminals in Dallas Airport is in both Spanish and English. If the trend continues, a day will come when it will be difficult to travel through some sections of the country without hearing commands in both English and Spanish; after all, for some western states, Spanish was the first written language and the Spanish style lives on in the western way of life.

4   Shortly after my Texas trip, I sat in an auditorium located on the campus of the University of Wisconsin at Milwaukee as a Yale professor—whose original work on the influence of African cultures upon those of the Americas has led to his ostracism from some monocultural intellectual circles—walked up and down the aisle, like an old-time southern evangelist, dancing and drumming the top of the lectern, illustrating his points before some serious Afro-American intellectuals and artists who cheered and applauded his performance and his mastery of information. The professor was "white." After his lecture, he joined a group of Milwaukeeans in a conversation. All of the participants spoke Yoruban, though only the professor had ever traveled to Africa.

5   One of the artists told me that his paintings, which included African and Afro-American mythological symbols and imagery, were hanging in the local McDonald's restaurant. The next day I went to McDonald's and snapped pictures of smiling youngsters eating hamburgers below paintings that could grace the walls of any of the country's leading museums. The manager of the local McDonald's said, "I don't know what you boys are doing, but I like it," as he commissioned the local painters to exhibit in his restaurant.

6   Such blurring of cultural styles occurs in everyday life in the United States to a greater extent than anyone can imagine and is probably more prevalent than the sensational conflict between people of different backgrounds that is played up and often encouraged by the media. The result is what the Yale professor, Robert Thompson, referred to as a cultural bouillabaisse, yet members of the nation's present educational and cultural Elect still cling to the notion that the United States belongs to some vaguely defined entity they refer to as "Western civilization," by which they mean, presumably, a civilization created by the people of Europe, as if Europe can be viewed in monolithic terms. Is Beethoven's Ninth Symphony, which includes Turkish marches, a part of Western civilization, or the late nineteenth- and twentieth-century French paintings, whose creators were influenced by Japanese art? And what of the cubists, through whom the influence of African art changed modern painting, or the surrealists, who were so impressed with the art of the Pacific Northwest Indians that, in their map of North America, Alaska dwarfs the lower forty-eight in size?

7   Are the Russians, who are often criticized for their adoption of "Western" ways by Tsarist dissidents in exile, members of Western civilization? And what of the millions of Europeans who have black African and Asian ancestry, black Africans having occupied several countries for hundreds of years? Are these "Europeans" members of Western civilization, or the Hungarians, who originated across the Urals in a place called Greater Hungary, or the Irish, who came from the Iberian Peninsula?

8   Even the notion that North America is part of Western civilization because our "system of government" is derived from Europe is being challenged by Native American historians who say that the founding fathers, Benjamin Franklin especially, were actually influenced by the system of government that had been adopted by the Iroquois hundreds of years prior to the arrival of large numbers of Europeans.

9   Western civilization, then, becomes another confusing category like Third World, or Judeo-Christian culture, as man attempts to impose his small-screen view of political and cultural reality upon a complex world. Our most publicized novelist recently said that Western civilization was the greatest achievement of mankind, an attitude that flourishes on the street level as scribbles in public restrooms: "White Power," "Niggers and Spics Suck," or "Hitler was a prophet," the latter being the most telling for wasn't Adolph Hitler the archetypal monoculturalist who, in his pigheaded arrogance, believed that one way and one blood was so pure that it had to be protected from alien strains at all costs? Where did such an attitude, which has caused so much misery and depression in our national life, which has tainted even our noblest achievements, begin? An attitude that caused the incarceration of Japanese-American citizens during World War II, the persecution of Chicanos and Chinese Americans, the near-extermination of the Indians, and the murder and lynchings of thousands of Afro-Americans.

10   Virtuous, hardworking, pious, even though they occasionally would wander off after some fancy clothes, or rendezvous in the woods with the town prostitute, the Puritans are idealized in our schoolbooks as "a hardy band" of no-nonsense patriarchs whose discipline razed the forest and brought order to the New World (a term that annoys Native American historians). Industrious, responsible, it was their "Yankee ingenuity" and practicality that created the work ethic. They were simple folk who produced a number of good poets, and they set the tone for the American writing style, of lean and spare lines, long before Hemingway. They worshiped in churches whose colors blended in with the New England snow, churches with simple structures and ornate lecterns.

11   The Puritans were a daring lot, but they had a mean streak. They hated the theater and banned Christmas. They punished people in a cruel and inhuman manner. They killed children who disobeyed their parents. When they came in contact with those whom they considered heathens or aliens, they behaved in such a bizarre and irrational manner that this chapter in the American history comes down to us as a late-movie horror film. They exterminated the Indians, who taught them how to survive in a world unknown to them, and their encounter with the calypso culture of Barbados resulted in what the tourist guide in Salem's Witches' House refers to as the Witchcraft Hysteria.

12   The Puritan legacy of hard work and meticulous accounting led to the establishment of a great industrial society; it is no wonder that the American industrial revolution began in Lowell, Massachusetts, but there was the other side, the strange and paranoid attitudes toward those different from the Elect.

13   The cultural attitudes of that early Elect continue to be voiced in everyday life in the United States: the president of a distinguished university, writing a letter to the *Times*, belittling the study of African civilizations; the television network that promoted its show on the Vatican art with the boast that this art represented "the finest achievements of the human spirit." A modern up-tempo state of complex rhythms that depends upon contacts with an international community can no longer behave as if it dwelled in a "Zion Wilderness" surrounded by beasts and pagans.

14   When I heard a schoolteacher warn the other night about the invasion of the American educational system by foreign curriculums, I wanted to yell at the television

set, "Lady, they're already here." It has already begun because the world is here. The world has been arriving at these shores for at least ten thousand years from Europe, Africa, and Asia. In the late nineteenth and early twentieth centuries, large numbers of Europeans arrived, adding their cultures to those of the European, African, and Asian settlers who were already here, and recently millions have been entering the country from South America and the Caribbean, making Yale Professor Bob Thompson's bouillabaisse richer and thicker.

15   One of our most visionary politicians said that he envisioned a time when the United States could become the brain of the world, by which he meant the repository of all of the latest advanced information systems. I thought of that remark when an enterprising poet friend of mine called to say that he had just sold a poem to a computer magazine and that the editors were delighted to get it because they didn't carry fiction or poetry. Is that the kind of world we desire? A humdrum, homogeneous world of all brains but no heart, no fiction, no poetry; a world of robots with human attendants bereft of imagination, of culture? Or does North America deserve a more exciting destiny? To become a place where the cultures of the world crisscross. This is possible because the United States is unique in the world: The world is here.

Finish Timing: Record time here_____ and use the Timed Reading

Conversion Chart in the Appendix to figure your rate:_____wpm.

Comprehension Check

Directions: Answer the following questions without looking back.

1. List one fact about Detroit. _____
   _____
   _____

2. Is the following statement fact or opinion? "If the trend continues, a day will come when it will be difficult to travel through some sections of the country without hearing commands in both English and Spanish." _____
   _____
   _____

3. What is Reed's main argument about "Western civilization"? _____
   _____
   _____

4. List one of the facts he gives to support his argument. _____
   _____
   _____

5. List another fact he gives to support his argument. _____
   _____
   _____

6. According to Reed, what are some of the problems in the United States because of the attitude that Western civilization is the greatest achievement of mankind? ___

_____

_____

7. What is Reed's overall opinion of the Puritans? _____

_____

_____

8. List one or two of the facts he uses to support this opinion. _____,_____

_____

_____

9. Are Reed's arguments in this article based more on fact or opinion? Explain. ____

_____

_____

10. Did the author convince you of his argument? Explain. _____

_____

_____

Vocabulary Check

Directions: Define the following underlined words from the selection.

1. has led to his <u>ostracism</u> _____

_____

2. from some <u>monocultural</u> intellectual circles _____

_____

3. Afro-American <u>mythological</u> symbols _____

_____

4. referred to as a cultural <u>bouillabaisse</u> _____

_____

5. as if Europe can be viewed in <u>monolithic</u> terms _____

_____

6. and what of the <u>cubists</u> _____

_____

7. Hitler, the <u>archetypal</u> monoculturist _____

_____

8. the <u>incarceration</u> of Japanese-American citizens _____

_____

9. simple structures and <u>ornate</u> lecterns _____

_____

10.   those whom they considered <u>heathens</u> _____

Record your rate and the results of the comprehension and vocabulary checks on the Student Record Chart in the Appendix. Each correct answer is worth 10 points, for a total of 100 points possible for comprehension and 100 points for vocabulary. An average score is around 250 wpm with 70 percent comprehension. Discuss any problems, concerns, or questions you have with your instructor.

PRACTICE D-2: Timed Reading

Directions: Before reading the following article, take a minute to survey it and the questions. Then time yourself as you begin to read the article. As you read, notice the authors' opinion on the draft.

Begin timing : _____

BRING BACK THE DRAFT

WILLIAM L. HAUSER and JEROME SLATER

1   In the ongoing struggle between radical Islamism and Western democracy, military intervention by the United States may again be judged necessary as a last resort against particularly dangerous states or organizations. Although presidential candidate Barack Obama made drawing down U.S. forces in Iraq the centerpiece of his national security agenda, so as to focus on the "real fight" in Afghanistan, President Obama will find that even with a complete withdrawal from Iraq, the United States' current all-volunteer forces will be inadequate for accomplishing its worldwide national security goals. Regarding Afghanistan in particular, even the planned reinforcement of 20,000 to 30,000 troops will not begin to match the 1 to 10 troop-to-population ratio generally acknowledged to be necessary for success in counterinsurgency.

2   Moreover, as a result of the repetitive stresses of Afghanistan and Iraq, the human-resources quality of the U.S. military appears to be declining: recruitment and retention rates (by pre-Iraq standards) are slipping, forcing the armed services to lower their physical, educational, and psychological standards; to soften the rigors of initial training; and even to expand the moral waivers granted to some volunteers with criminal records. Generous inducements have also been needed to retain junior officers beyond the length-of-service payback requirements of their academy or ROTC educations. The economic downturn might help temporarily, but the problem cannot be resolved by continuing the present system. There will have to be a reinstitution, albeit in a significantly modified version, of universal military service—a "draft."

3   Our proposal is to combine a revived military draft with a broader public-service program as already practiced in some European states—a "domestic Peace Corps." Indeed, a crucial component of our proposal is that draftees be allowed to

William I. Hauser and Jerome Slater, "Bring Back the Draft," Foreign Policy.com, February 2009, http://www.foreignpolicy.com/story/cms.php?story_id=4659. Permission to reprint.

choose between military and nonmilitary service. A program structured along those lines would simultaneously increase the political appeal of conscription, defuse the opposition of those who disapprove of the use of military force, and serve such valuable national purposes as public health, public works, and the alleviation of shortages of teachers and social workers in disadvantaged regions of the country.

4   To be sure, an enlarged military can give rise to its own dangers, particularly an expansion of what some already consider excessive presidential power. It will be essential, therefore, that the creation of larger forces by means of conscription be accompanied by legal safeguards to prevent presidential unilateralism. First, Congress should use its constitutionally mandated role in decisions to go to war. Second, Congress should employ its appropriations powers—"the power of the purse"—to prohibit, limit, or end U.S. participation in unwise wars or military interventions by refusing to fund them. Third, to reduce political opposition to a revived draft as well as to provide another constraint against presidential unilateralism, a law establishing conscription should include a provision that draftees cannot be sent into combat without specific congressional authorization.

5   Of course, reinstating the draft will generate opposition from all parts of the political spectrum, on the left by civil libertarians and opponents of any use of force, in the center by classic libertarians and those who would regard conscription as an unfair "tax on youth," and even by some on the political right, who (as noted earlier) would correctly perceive that the modified draft proposed here would inherently constrain presidential unilateralism. The professional military, traditionally conservative, might initially resist such fundamental change, though we are confident the professional military will come to value its significant advantages.

6   The benefits of universal national service, however, far outweigh these resolvable objections. Aside from the strictly military advantages—larger and better-educated armed forces—there would be a number of positive social consequences. Conscription will enable the forces to reflect the full spectrum of American pluralism, in terms of both socioeconomic classes and racial/ethnic groups. It is unacceptable that less than 1 percent of the country's eligible population serves in the armed forces, with almost no war-relevant sacrifice being asked from the rest of society. It ought to be axiomatic that the hardships and dangers of military service be more widely shared.

7   A draft could also increase responsibility on the part of political decision-makers. There would surely be a greater likelihood of sound foreign and military policies if the sons and daughters of the United States' political and business elites also served in uniform—as so many did in the past, but so few do today.

8   These arguments would constitute a strong case for reinstating the draft at any time. But at the moment, the United States simply has no other option. The U.S. mission in Afghanistan, crucial in the global fight against Islamist terrorism, simply cannot be accomplished with current force levels. Looking beyond Afghanistan toward the long-term struggle with radical Islamism, the United States is going to need larger standing forces of considerable quality, with the educational, cultural, linguistic, and technical skills needed for modern military operations in foreign lands.

9   In the event of new terrorist attacks on U.S. soil on the scale of 9/11, let alone the unimaginable consequences if American cities were struck by nuclear or biological weapons, the arguments against conscription would vanish overnight, and there would be a crash program to build up the armed forces, similar to the aftermath of attack on Pearl Harbor. The country would be in a far stronger position if it put these forces in place now, rather than waiting until a catastrophe occurred. Moreover, if the United States had such larger standing forces, they would provide a credible deter-

rent against states that currently support, tolerate, or ineffectively suppress terrorist groups. Indeed, the reinstatement of the draft is not an invitation for more war; it may be the best chance for peace.

Finish Timing: Record time here _____ and use the Timed Reading Conversion Chart in the Appendix to figure your rate: _____ wpm.

Comprehension Check

Directions: Answer the following questions without looking back.

1. What type of draft system do the authors propose? _____
   _____
   _____

2. Why do the authors believe a draft system is needed at this time? _____
   _____
   _____

3. Which of the following do the authors believe has occurred because of the stresses of fighting in Afghanistan and Iraq?
   a. Recruitment and retention rates in the military are slipping
   b. A lowering of physical, educational, and psychological enlistment standards
   c. A softening of initial military training
   d. Granting induction waivers to some criminals
   e. All of the above

4. What type of service would non-military draftees perform? _____
   _____
   _____

5. What dangers can arise from an enlarged military establishment? _____
   _____
   _____

6. Which of the following are proposed safeguards against a president misusing his power as commander-in-chief?
   a. Congress should use its constitutionally mandated role in decisions to go to war.
   b. Congress should use its "power of the purse" to prohibit participation in unwise wars or military intervention.
   c. A law should be passed establishing a provision that draftees cannot be sent into combat without specific congressional authority.
   d. All of the above.
   e. None of the above.

7. Reinstating the draft, according to the authors, will generate opposition from which of the following:

    a. Opponents of any use of force

    b. Those who would consider the draft as an unfair "tax on youth"

    c. Conservative professional military personnel

    d. All of the above

    e. None of the above

8. T/F According to the authors, there would be a greater likelihood of sound foreign and military policies if the children of political and business elites had to serve in the military.

9. Why do the authors believe that the draft should be instituted now rather than wait for a large scale attack or sudden emergency? _____

    _____

    _____

10. Is the article based mostly on fact or opinion? _____

    _____

    _____

Vocabulary Check

Directions: Define the following underlined words from the selection.

1. necessary for success in <u>counterinsurgency</u>

    _____

2. generous <u>inducements</u> have been needed

    _____

3. increase the political appeal of <u>conscription</u>

    _____

4. the <u>alleviation</u> of shortages of teachers

    _____

5. safeguards to prevent presidential <u>unilateralism</u>

    _____

6. use its <u>mandated</u> role in decisions

    _____

7. it ought to be <u>axiomatic</u> things be shared

    _____

8. similar to the <u>aftermath</u> of attack on Pearl Harbor

_____

_____

9. employ its <u>appropriation</u> powers

_____

10. a credible <u>deterrent</u> against states that support terrorism

_____

Record your rate and the results of the comprehension and vocabulary checks on the Student Record Chart in the Appendix. Each correct answer is worth 10 points, for a total of 100 points possible for comprehension and 100 points for vocabulary. An average score is around 250 wpm with 70 percent comprehension. Discuss any problems, concerns, or questions you have with your instructor.

Questions for Group Discussion

1. Divide your group in two, one group arguing for conscription, the other group against. How much of each argument is based on facts and opinion?

2. As a group, discuss your opinions on the legalization of drugs. Make a list of facts expressed and a list for opinions expressed. Where might you go to research the subject for factual information?

3. As a group, see how many of you can use the following words in a sentence. Make certain you learn the ones you still may not be able to use or recognize by writing the definition in the blank space.

a. monolithic _____

b. archetypal _____

c. ornate _____

d. heathens _____

e. conscription _____

f. incarceration _____

g. ethical _____

h. deterrent _____

i. axiomatic _____

On Your Own

Pick ten new words you learned in this chapter, not necessarily those listed in question 4, and on a separate sheet of paper write a sentence for each word, using it correctly in context. Turn in the paper to your instructor.

ABOUT THIS READING

Writer Michele Simon is author of *Appetite for Profit: How the Food Industry Undermines Our Health and How to Fight Back* (2006) and founder and director of the Center for Informed Food Choices. This reading appeared in *At Issue: Fast Food*, edited by Roman Espejo (2009).

Even the "Healthy" Choices at Fast-Food Restaurants Are Unhealthy

By MICHELE SIMON

In response to sharpening criticism from nutrition advocates, fast-food franchises have added supposedly "healthy" options to their menus. For instance, McDonald's has launched a line of "premium" salads and now offers apple slices and apple juice or milk with its Happy Meals as alternatives to fries and sodas. However, these new menu items are anything but healthy. Besides being labeled with misleading dietary information, one of the worst-offending McDonald's salads has as many calories and grams of fat as a Big Mac. Also, the new Happy Meal option, which includes a sugar-loaded caramel dipping sauce, does nothing to offset the high calories and dismally low nutritional value of McDonald's hamburgers, cheeseburgers, and Chicken McNuggets. Moreover, the profits from the more-healthy fast-food options do not add up to those of the millions of burgers served every day, and so the more-healthy choices are often discontinued.

Let's be honest. McDonald's french fries taste good. Really good. Founder Ray Kroc didn't turn the fast-food chain into such a phenomenal success by selling lettuce. Good nutrition was about the last thing on the milkshake salesman's mind. Kroc's 1950s vision of dining has since spread to thirty thousand restaurants in 120 countries, serving fifty million customers a day and counting. That's a lot of burgers and fries. But this rapacious business model is not stopping McDonald's from trying to claim that it has the answer to America's health problems.

Years ago, the environmental movement coined the term "greenwashing" to describe how corporations use public relations [PR] to make themselves appear environmentally friendly. Today, nutrition advocates need their own moniker for a similar trend among major food companies—I like to call it "nutriwashing." As the food industry finds itself increasingly under attack for promoting unhealthy foods, one of its major defense strategies is to improve, or promise to improve, the nutritional content of its food.

McDonald's wants its customers to associate the *idea* of health lifestyles with its brand.

Among the major peddlers of fast food, McDonald's has borne the brunt of the criticism from nutrition advocates, many of whom are especially troubled by the company's shameless marketing to children. In response, the corporation has developed a massive PR campaign aimed at convincing us that it really does care. But before believing the spin, we should ask whether these moves have any positive impact on the nation's health, or if, worse, the campaign could actually encourage people to eat more of the wrong foods. . . .

Ulterior Motives

By the time the obesity debate started heating up, McDonald's was already a company in need of serious spin control. So, in April 2004, with then U.S. secretary of Health and Human Services (HHS) Tommy Thompson at its side, McDonald's announced "an unprecedented, comprehensive balanced lifestyles platform to help address obesity in America and improve the nation's overall physical well-being." Sounds very impressive, until you bother to scratch the surface. The major news outlets focused largely on the initiative's "Go Active! Adult Happy Meal" component, which included a "premium salad," bottled water, and a pedometer. Other "highlights" of the plan included how McDonald's promised to take an "industry-leading role" in working with HHS to determine the best way to "communicate" nutrition information to consumers. (Are the folks who invented the Big Mac really the best candidates for this job?)

An important concept in brand marketing is the "halo effect," which is the generalization of a positive feeling about a brand from one good trait. In other words, if you think that a food company is selling healthy products, this can generate an overall good feeling about the company's brand. Whether or not the items are actually any healthier is beside the point.

Mary Dillon is responsible for McDonald's global marketing strategy and brand development, as well as the company's Balanced, Active Lifestyles initiative. Here is how Dillon describes the effort: "McDonald's cares about the well-being of each of its guests throughout the world, and by making balanced, active lifestyles an integral part of the brand we aim to make a difference in this area of their lives." In other words, McDonald's wants its customers to associate the *idea* of healthy lifestyles with its brand—a classic halo effect maneuver.

An Unhealthy Salad

In 2003, the nonprofit Physicians Committee for Responsible Medicine (PCRM) conducted a nutritional analysis of thirty-four salads served at fast-food chains, and the results, to put it mildly, were dismal. The group awarded only two menu items (from Au Bon Pain and Subway) an "outstanding" rating for being high in fiber and low in saturated fat, cholesterol, sodium, and calories. McDonald's salads were among the worst offenders. PCRM noted that all of the corporation's salad entrees contain chicken (which has virtually as much cholesterol as beef) and concluded that the salads "may very well clog up your arteries." The group also awarded the Bacon Ranch Salad with Crispy Chicken and Newman's Own Ranch Dressing "the dubious distinction of having the most fat of any salad rated. At 661 calories and 51 grams of fat, this salad is a diet disaster," with "more fat and calories and just as much cholesterol as a Big Mac."

Curiously, when I checked the current data on the Bacon Ranch Salad with Crispy Chicken at the company's Web site, the numbers were different. (The salad is listed at 510 calories and 31 grams of fat.) When I asked dietitian Brie Turner-McGrievy (who conducted the PCRM study) to explain the discrepancy, she said that the site numbers must have changed, since she used data that was posted in 2003. She also noted that right after her group's study was released, McDonald's changed

their nutrition facts to list all of the salads without chicken as an option. (This was not available prior to the survey.) "So we know they went back to look at their nutrition facts after our review. I wouldn't be surprised if they reanalyzed their salads—maybe using less dressing or less chicken—to come up with more favorable ratings," she said.

Whatever the number of calories, merely calling something a salad doesn't make it healthy. Also, calling chicken "crispy" instead of fried is misleading. Essentially what McDonald's has done is taken the contents of its chicken sandwiches, dumped them on top of some lettuce, and served it up with a creamy dressing. As Bob Sandelman—whose market research firm specializes in the restaurant industry—told the press, food chains "have doctored those products up. If people really knew, they would find out that the salads pack more fat and calories. That's why the key word in all this is 'perceived' to be healthy." The Fruit & Walnut Salad is better at 310 calories, but it's unlikely to hold you for a meal since it's just apples, grapes, and a few "candied walnuts," even with the "creamy low-fat yogurt."

McDonald's number-one motivation is to keep its customers addicted to its products, and lettuce covered with fried chicken furthers that goal. But touting its "premium salads" gives the false impression that the company sells healthy items.

Not Happier Meals

In response to charges that it's turning a new generation of young people into loyal Big Mac and McFlurry fans, McDonald's now offers "Happy Meal Choices." The new and improved Happy Meal gives parents the option of replacing high-fat french fries with "Apple Dippers" (sliced apples and caramel dipping sauce). Instead of a Coke, kids can now have apple juice or milk. There is, however, no substitute for the hamburger, cheeseburger, or Chicken McNuggets.

But is this any real improvement? Probably not. For a toddler who needs about 1,000 calories per day, a Happy Meal consisting of four Chicken McNuggets, small french fries, and low-fat chocolate milk totals 580 calories, or more than half of a child's daily recommended calorie intake. This of course says nothing about the dismal nutritional quality of these foods, which are devoid of fiber as well as vitamins and minerals that are especially important for growing children. And while it's true that the "Apple Dippers" in the Happy Meal contain fewer calories than french fries, this "improvement" hardly compensates for the heavy dose of sugar delivered by the dipping sauce that kids are sure to love. . . .

A Small Fraction Are Healthier

In 2005, McDonald's conceded that despite all the hoopla around its new salad offerings, only a tiny fraction of its customers actually orders them. While the company loudly trumpets the sale of 400 million premium salads since their introduction in 2003, that number is dwarfed by the total body count. McDonald's serves 23 million people a day in the United States alone, or roughly 16.8 billion people in the two-year period since the salads' introduction. As the *Washington Post* calculated, this means that in mid-2005 just 2.4 percent of McDonald's customers had ordered salads since they were added to the menu.

[Healthy menu options] make for effective window dressing, helping to keep critics and regulators quiet.

We need look no further than the fast-food king itself to confirm these stats: McDonald's spokesperson Bill Whitman explained, "The most popular item on our menu continues to be the double cheeseburger, hands down." McDonald's isn't alone in this regard. Data from NPD Foodworld indicate that the number-one entree ordered by men in America is a hamburger and the number-one selection among women is french fries, followed by hamburgers. Also, a typical Burger King outlet sells only 4 or 5 of its allegedly healthier Veggie Burgers in a day compared to 300 to 500 of any other sandwich or burger on the menu.

Burgers More Profitable

Fast-food-chains are faced with unavoidable food-related obstacles when it comes to serving truly healthy alternatives. For example, produce is much harder to store than, say, frozen hamburger patties. Other challenges include standardization and mass production of messy, perishable fruits and vegetables. Such annoyances of nature add up to

more complexity and higher costs. As Matthew Paull, McDonald's chief financial officer candidly explained to the *Economist* magazine, "There is no question that we make more money from selling hamburgers and cheeseburgers."

As a result, one of the basic tenets of fast-food economics is the so-called 80-20 rule, which holds that 80 percent of a fast-food company's revenue derives from 20 percent of its products, usually its flagship line of burgers and fries. As *Forbes* magazine writer Tom Van Riper explains, so-called healthier fare at fast-food chains serves only a narrow fraction of the population while conveniently deflecting attention away from the remainder of the unwholesome menu.

Certainly, soups and salads have added incremental revenue, since they serve that segment that has made a commitment to healthier eating. They also make for effective window dressing, helping to keep critics and regulators quiet. But a fast-food fixture that has measured its success in terms of "billions served" can't live on lightweight salads that people can get anywhere. It must beef up sales of Big Macs and Quarter Pounders. Given the 80-20 rule, a 5% drop in burger and fries sales, coupled with a 10% gain in "new menu" items, would net out to a 2% drop in revenue. For a $20 billion company like McDonald's, that's a $400 million hit. . . .

Game Over

Getting products (any products) into the mouths of cash-carrying customers is of course the top priority for food marketers. So when one of their creations fails to "show them the money," it gets swept into the dustbin of failed ideas. Such was the fate of the apparently less than popular Go Active! Adult Happy Meal, which was jettisoned by McDonald's after it had dutifully delivered the desired halo effect following the 2004 press conference. A nice McDonald's "customer satisfaction representative" apologized when I asked if it was still available, explaining that it was a "limited-time promotion." Other "well-intentioned" menu innovations have also met their untimely demises at the hands of major restaurant chains. For example, in 2004 Ruby Tuesday reduced some portion sizes and added healthier items. However, when slumping sales threatened quarterly returns, the company soon returned to its roots, aggressively promoting its biggest burgers and restoring its larger portions of french fries and pasta. Similarly, while Wendy's garnered great press in February 2005 for its "bold" decision to add fresh fruit to its menu, that resolution was rescinded as soon as corporate headquarters reviewed the disappointing sales figures a few months later. As the *Washington Post* explained in 2005, "Fast-food and casual dining chains are slowly going back to what they do best: indulging Americans' taste for high-calorie, high-fat fare."

ANALYZE THIS READING

1. What is "nutriwashing"? What is its connection to "greenwashing"?

2. What is a "halo effect," and how does the writer apply it to McDonald's? What research does the writer bring in to debunk McDonald's PR claims?

3. According to the writer, what is the intention of fast-food restaurants like McDonald's offering salads and other presumably healthy items?

RESPOND TO THIS READING

1. What is the role of fast food in your life? Is the convenience it offers worth the nutritional hazards? Explain.

2. What issues do you associate with fast food? Consider the many issues that fall within the topics of beef production, transportation, nutrition, and ecological sustainability. What single issue might you argue on, and what would you claim?

ABOUT THIS READING

In this reading, writer and former editor of the *Paris Review* Oliver Broudy interviews Peter Singer. Singer is the DeCamp Professor of Bioethics at Princeton University and author of *Animal Liberation* (1975), a book many consider to be at the center of the animal rights movement. This interview originally appeared in the May 8, 2006, edition of *Salon.com*, a daily online magazine that focuses on liberal politics.

The Practical Ethicist: "The Way We Eat" Author Peter Singer Explains the Advantage of Wingless Chickens, How Humans Discriminate Against Animals, and the Downside of Buying Locally Grown Food

By OLIVER BROUDY

Oliver Broudy: One of the things that distinguishes your new book [The Way We Eat: Why Our Food Choices Matter] is all the field research that went into it. What most shocked you, over the course of doing this research?

Peter Singer: Probably this video I saw of this kosher slaughterhouse, *AgriProcessors*. I guess

I had this idea that kosher slaughter is more strictly controlled than normal slaughter, and when you see that video and you see these cattle staggering around with their throats cut, and blood pouring out—by no stretch of the imagination is this just a reflex movement. It goes on and on. And this happens repeatedly, with many different animals.

How are kosher animals supposed to be slaughtered?

They are supposed to be slaughtered with a single blow of a sharp knife across the throat. There's a virtually instant loss of consciousness, because the brain loses blood so quickly. That's the idea, anyway. But when you see this video, it's so far from that, I really did find it quite shocking.

You mention in your book that cows today produce three times as much milk as they did 50 years ago. That's a great advance, isn't it?

It is an advance, but you have to consider how this has been achieved. Fifty years ago, cows were

Oliver Broudy, "The Practical Ethicist: 'The Way We Eat' Author Peter Singer Explains the Advantage of Wingless Chickens, How Humans Discriminate Against Animals, and the Downside of Buying Locally Grown Food," Salon, May 8, 2006. This article first appeared in Salon .com, at www.salon.com. An online version remains in the Salon archives. Reprinted with permission.

basically fed on grass. They walked around and selected their food themselves, food that we can't eat, chewing it up and producing milk that we *can* eat. Now cows are confined indoors, and a lot of their food supply is grown specifically for them, on land that we could have used to grow food for ourselves. So it's actually less efficient, in that we could have gotten more food from the land if we didn't pass it through the cow.

[Even in an organic farm] there were no hens outside at all. The hens were all in these huge sheds, about 20,000 hens in a single shed, and they were pretty crowded.

Most of us have an idealized notion of what an organic farm is like. You visited an organic chicken farm in New Hampshire. Did it meet your expectations?

I have to say that it didn't. I guess I was expecting some access to pasture for the hens. When I got to this place, although it was in a beautiful green valley in New Hampshire, and it was a fine, sunny fall day, there were no hens outside at all. The hens were all in these huge sheds, about 20,000 hens in a single shed, and they were pretty crowded. The floor of the shed was basically a sea of brown hens, and when we asked about access to outdoors, we were shown a small dirt run which at the best of times I don't think the hens would be very interested in. In any case the doors were closed, and when we asked why, we were told that the producer was worried about bird flu. So, yes, it was not really what I expected. It was still a kind of a factory farm production— although undoubtedly it was much better than a caged operation.

How much space are birds allotted in caged operations?

In the U.S., birds have as little as 48 square inches, a six- by eight-inch space. The United Egg Producers' standards are gradually increasing over the next five years. We'll get up to 67 square inches. But that's still not the industry average, and even 67 square inches is just [the size of] a sheet of standard letter paper. In a cage, the birds are unable to stretch their wings. The wingspan of the bird is about 31 inches, so even if you lined one bird up on the diagonal, she wouldn't be able to spread her wings. And there's not just one bird in these cages,

there are four or five. The weaker birds are unable to escape from the more aggressive birds. They end up rubbing against the wire and getting pecked, so they lose a lot of feathers, and they can't lay their eggs in the nesting box.

Requiring a hen to lay in an open space [is like] asking a human to shit in public. They don't like it.

One good thing about this organic farm in New Hampshire is that there was this row of nesting boxes. It's been shown that hens have a strong instinct to lay in this kind of sheltered area. Conrad Lawrence, the science fiction writer and author of *The Council to Save the Planet*, once compared requiring a hen to lay in an open space to asking a human to shit in public. They don't like it.

What if it were possible to genetically engineer a brainless bird, grown strictly for its meat? Do you feel that this would be ethically acceptable?

It would be an ethical improvement on the present system, because it would eliminate the suffering that these birds are feeling. That's the huge plus to me.

What if you could engineer a chicken with no wings, so less space would be required?

I guess that's an improvement too, assuming it doesn't have any residual instincts, like phantom pain. If you could eliminate various other chicken instincts, like its preference for laying eggs in a nest, that would be an improvement too.

It seems to come down to a trade-off between whether the bird has wing space or whether you can fit more birds in your shed, and therefore have to pay less heating costs. How does one go about weighing these alternatives? How does the ethicist put a price on the impulse of a chicken to spread its wings?

We ought to be prepared to pay more for eggs so that the chicken can enjoy its life, and not be frustrated and deprived and miserable.

We recognize the chicken as another conscious being. It's different from us, but it has a life, and if something is really important for that chicken, if it would work hard to try to get it, and if we can give it without sacrificing something that's really important to us, then we should. If it's a big burden on us, that's surely different, but if it's a question of paying a few more cents for eggs, when we pay just as much if not more for a brand label we like, then we ought to be prepared to pay more for eggs so that the chicken can enjoy its life, and not be frustrated and deprived and miserable.

What constitutes a big burden? Doubtless the chicken farmer would say that building a larger shed or paying a bigger heating bill is a big burden.

It's only a burden to him if it harms his business, and it only harms his business if he can't sell the eggs he produces because other producers who don't follow those standards are selling eggs more cheaply. So, there's two ways around that: Either you have ethically motivated consumers who are prepared to pay a somewhat higher price for humanely certified eggs, or you cut out the unfair competition with regulations. Prohibiting cages, for example. And that's been done already, in Switzerland. And the entire European Union is already saying you can't keep hens as confined as American hens; it's on track to require nesting boxes, and areas to scratch, by 2012. So you can do it, and it doesn't mean that people can no longer afford to eat eggs.

In your book you discuss this in terms of the right of the chicken to express its natural behavior.

I tend not to put it in terms of rights, because philosophically I have doubts about the foundations of rights. But yes, I think these animals have natural behaviors, and generally speaking, their natural behaviors are the ones they have adapted for. And if we prevent them from performing those natural behaviors, we are likely to be frustrating them and making them miserable. So, yes, I think we ought to try to let them perform those natural behaviors.

We have, over centuries of history, expanded the circle of beings whom we regard as morally significant.

Could you explain your position on "speciesism," and what this has to do with your call to "expand the circle"?

The argument, in essence, is that we have, over centuries of history, expanded the circle of beings whom we regard as morally significant. If you go back in time you'll find tribes that were essentially only concerned with their own tribal members. If you were a member of another tribe, you could be killed with impunity. When we got beyond that

there were still boundaries to our moral sphere, but these were based on nationality, or race, or religious belief. Anyone outside those boundaries didn't count. Slavery is the best example here. If you were not a member of the European race, if you were African, specifically, you could be enslaved. So we got beyond that. We have expanded the circle beyond our own race and we reject as wrongful the idea that something like race or religion or gender can be a basis for claiming another being's interests count less than our own.

So the argument is that this is also an arbitrary stopping place; it's also a form of discrimination, which I call "speciesism," that has parallels with racism. I am not saying it's identical, but in both cases you have this group that has power over the outsiders, and develops an ideology that says, Those outside our circle don't matter, and therefore we can make use of them for our own convenience.

I don't think we can say that somehow we, as humans, are the sole repository of all moral value, and that all beings beyond our species don't matter.

That is what we have done, and still do, with other species. They're effectively *things*; they're property that we can own, buy and sell. We use them as is convenient and we keep them in ways that suit us best, producing products we want at the cheapest prices. So my argument is simply that this is wrong, this is not justifiable if we want to defend the idea of human equality against those who have a narrower definition. I don't think we can say that somehow we, as humans, are the sole repository of all moral value, and that all beings beyond our species don't matter. I think they do matter, and we need to expand our moral consideration to take that into account.

So you are saying that expanding the circle to include other species is really no different than expanding it to include other races?

Yes, I think it's a constant progression, a broadening of that circle.

But surely there's a significant difference between a Jew, for instance, and a chicken. These are different orders of beings.

Well, of course, there's no argument about that. The question is whether saying that you are not a member of my kind, and that therefore I don't have to give consideration to your interests, is something that was said by the Nazis and the slave traders, and is also something that we are saying to other species. The question is, what is the relevant difference here? There is no doubt that there is a huge difference between human and nonhuman animals. But what we are overlooking is the fact that nonhuman animals are conscious beings, that they can suffer. And we ignore that suffering, just as the Nazis ignored the suffering of the Jews, or the slave traders ignored the suffering of the Africans. I'm not saying that it's the same sort of suffering. I am not saying that factory farming is the same as the Holocaust or the slave trade, but it's clear that there is an immense amount of suffering in it, and just as we think that the Nazis were wrong to ignore the suffering of their victims, so we are wrong to ignore the sufferings of our victims.

But how do you know at what point to stop expanding the circle?

I think it gets gray when you get beyond mammals, and certainly it gets grayer still when you get beyond vertebrates. That's something we don't know enough about yet. We don't understand the way the nervous systems of invertebrates work. . . .

Chickens get some slaughterhouse remnants in their feed,. . .so that could be a route by which mad-cow disease gets. . .into the cattle.

I wanted to list a few factoids that jumped out at me while reading your book, and if you want to comment on them I'd love to hear your thoughts. First, each of the 36 million cattle produced in the United States has eaten 66 pounds of chicken litter?

The chicken industry produces a vast amount of litter that the chickens are living on, which of course gets filled with the chicken excrement, and is cleaned maybe once a year. And then the question is, what [do] you do with it? Well, it's been discovered that cattle will eat it. But the chickens get some slaughterhouse remnants in their feed, and some of that feed they may not eat, so the slaughterhouse remnants may also be in the chicken litter. So that could be a route by which mad-cow disease gets from these prohibited slaughterhouse products into the cattle, through this circuitous route.

Second factoid: 284 gallons of oil go into fattening a 1,250-pound cow for slaughter?

That's a figure from David Pimentel, a Cornell [University] ecologist. The fossil fuel goes into the fertilizer used to fertilize these acres of grain, which are then harvested and processed and transported to the cattle for feed. We get back, at most, 10 percent of the food value of the grain that we put into the cattle. So we are just skimming this concentrated product off the top of a mountain of grain into which all this fossil fuel has gone.

So even if we all started driving Priuses we'd still have these cows to worry about.

Yes. In fact, there's a University of Chicago study that shows that if you switch from driving an American car to driving a Prius, you'll cut your carbon-dioxide emissions by one ton per year. But if you switch from a typical U.S. diet, about 28 percent of which comes from animal sources, to a vegan diet with the same number of calories, you'll cut your carbon-dioxide emissions by nearly 1.5 tons per year.

Third factoid: We have more people in prison in the United States than people whose primary occupation is working on a farm?

A local chicken farm was getting rid of hens at the end of their laying period by throwing them by the bucketload down a wood chipper.

Isn't that amazing? Just as an example, when I wrote *Animal Liberation* 30 years ago or so, there were more than 600,000 independent pig farms in the U.S. Now there are only about 60,000. We're still producing just as many pigs, in fact more pigs, but there has been such concentration that we are now producing more pigs with a tenth as many pig farms. The same has happened in dairy and many other areas.

And finally, it turns out that a wood chipper is not the best way to dispose of 10,000 spent hens?

Yes, this also came to mind when you asked me what most shocked me. This was in San Diego County, in California. Neighbors noticed that a local chicken farm was getting rid of hens at the end of their laying period by throwing them by the bucketload down a wood chipper. They complained to the Animal Welfare Department, which investigated, and the chicken farmer told them that this was a recommendation that had been made by their vet, a vet who happens to sit on the Animal Welfare Committee of the American Veterinary Medical Association. The American Veterinary Medical Association, I should say, does not condone throwing hens down a wood chipper, but it is apparently done. We've also had examples of hens being taken off the conveyor belt and simply dumped into a bin, where by piling more hens on top, the hens on the bottom were suffocated. These old hens have no value, that's the problem, and so people have been killing them by whatever means is cheapest and most convenient.

So if you were stuck with 10,000 spent hens, what would you do with them?

I think you have a responsibility. Those hens have been producing eggs for you for a year or 18 months. You have a responsibility to make sure they are killed humanely. And you can do that. You can truck them to a place where there is stunning, or, better still, you can bring stunning equipment to the farm, and you can make sure that every hen is individually stunned with an electric shock and then killed by having its throat cut.

Avoid factory farm products. The worst of all the things. . .is intensive animal agriculture.

I thought you might suggest a retirement program.

That's an ideal that some people would like to see, but if you have to maintain and feed hens when they are no longer laying eggs, that will significantly increase the cost of the egg, and even the organic farms don't do that.

After reading this interview, some readers might be inspired to change their diets. If you could suggest one thing, what would it be?

Avoid factory farm products. The worst of all the things we talk about in the book is intensive animal agriculture. If you can be vegetarian or vegan that's ideal. If you can buy organic and vegan that's

better still, and organic and fair trade and vegan, better still, but if that gets too difficult or too complicated, just ask yourself, Does this product come from intensive animal agriculture? If it does, avoid it, and then you will have achieved 80 percent of the good that you would have achieved if you followed every suggestion in the book.

ANALYZE THIS READING

1. What solutions does Singer offer regarding more humane methods of raising chickens? How does he justify his ideas?

2. What definition does Singer offer for the term "speciesism"? How does the idea of suffering inform Singer's thinking on this term?

3. What advice does Singer offer for changing our diets?

RESPOND TO THIS READING

1. This interview is not a formal argument, but it does contain support that could be used in an argument. Looking at the factoids discussed in the interview, for example, what sort of claim could the factoids serve? Would their appeals be primarily logical? Explain.

2. Singer urges readers who consume chicken, beef, and pork to recognize the suffering that factory farm–raised animals endure. Are you satisfied with Singer's recommendation that we pay more for animal products so that animals can be raised in better conditions? Can you offer recommendations in addition to or apart from Singer's regarding the factory farming of animals? Explain.

3. Imagine building an argument on an issue related to intensive animal agriculture, or factory farming. On what values and philosophical foundation would your argument rest?

CHAPTER TWO

Recognizing Tone, Figurative Language, and Point of View

A.   Recognizing Intent, Attitude, and Tone

In addition to distinguishing fact from opinion, critical reading requires an awareness of an author's *intent, attitude,* and *tone.*

An author's **intent** is not always easy to recognize. Let's say, for instance, that you are reading Jonathan Swift's essay "A Modest Proposal," an essay that appears frequently in English literature anthologies. At the time he wrote this essay in the eighteenth century, many Irish people were dying from famine. To read his essay at the literal level, Swift would seem to be in favor of taking the profusion of children in Ireland and treating them as cattle, fattening up some for slaughter, exporting some to boost the economy, and raising some strictly for breeding. However, to accept his essay on the literal level would be to miss his intent. His essay is a satire, and his intent was to make his readers more aware of a social problem that existed in his day. His real purpose was to ridicule the people in power at the time. He intentionally wrote in a rather cold, uncompassionate way to shock his readers into action. Yet if you were not perceptive enough to understand Swift's intent, you could completely miss his point.

An author's intent may be to satirize a problem or condition; to amuse readers; to make them cry by arousing sympathy, pity, or fear; to argue a point that another writer has made; or to accuse someone of something. But whatever an author's intent may be, you, as a critical reader, need to be absolutely certain that you understand what it is.

An author's treatment of a subject reflects an **attitude** toward it. Swift, for instance, in the essay mentioned here, uses satire, but his attitude is serious. He is not serious about using children as an economic commodity, even though he provides a detailed plan for doing so. He was angry at the people of his day for allowing such deplorable conditions to exist. He was serious about wanting to change these conditions. An author's attitude, then, is the author's personal feeling about a subject. Attitudes can range from sad to happy, angry to delighted, sympathetic to unsympathetic, tolerant to furious.

The language an author uses is frequently a clue to that writer's attitude to both his or her subject and to the reader. In his book *Preface to Critical Reading,* Richard Altick provides a good example of how paying attention to the language a writer uses can reflect intent and attitude:

> Compare the two ways in which a person could express the desire [intent] to borrow some money: (1) "Hey, good buddy, how about loaning me a ten for a few days? I'm in a bind. You'll get it back on Friday." (2) "I'm very sorry to impose on you, but I'm in a bit of a predicament, and I need ten dollars just until payday. I'd be extremely grateful." The language of the first appeal suggests that slang is the normal means of expression for this speaker. The meaning of the second appeal is identical, and the general approach is the same. But whereas the first speaker is forthright and unembarrassed, the other seems hesitant and apologetic. The personalities of the two seem as different as the connotations of bind and predicament. (From Richard Altick, *Preface to Critical Reading,* 5th edition, Holt, Rinehart and Winston, 1960, p. 90.)

In other words, the intent of both appeals is the same; they want to borrow money. But the attitudes are different. Critical reading requires an ability to distinguish such differences.

How an author uses language creates what is called a **tone**. Tone in writing is similar to what we call a tone of voice. For instance, the phrase "Thanks a lot!" can have different meanings based on the tone of voice used to express it. If we are truly grateful, we will say it one way; if we want to be sarcastic, we'll say it another way; and if we are angry or disgusted, we'll say it still another way. When reading, however, we can't hear an author's tone of voice. But as critical readers, we must be able to recognize the true tone intended by the author.

Here are a few words that can be used to describe attitude, intent, and tone, depending on the context. Look up the ones you don't know.

angry	firm	ambivalent
disgruntled	confused	witty
humorous	furious	sad
light	antagonistic	lively
playful	outraged	resentful
positive	annoyed	amusing
negative	irritated	offended
harsh	troubled	disrespectful
sarcastic	somber	tyrannical
sardonic	delighted	compassionate
dismayed	favorable	sniveling
objective	troubled	bombastic
subjective	solemn	thankful
moderate	alarmed	
strident	rude	

The following practices will help you learn to recognize intent, attitude, and tone in various types of writing.

PRACTICE A-1

Directions: Read the following magazine article, looking for fact, opinion, intent, attitude, and tone.

BAN ATHLETES WHO DON'T USE STEROIDS

SIDNEY GENDIN

1   Governments and sports federations are wrong for continuing to ban the use of performance-enhancing drugs like steroids. Steroids are less hazardous to human health than smoking or drinking, and society has traditionally permitted people to engage in risky activities, such as mountain climbing, when the danger posed only affects the individual involved. In addition, ineffective and more costly dietary supplements, which falsely claim to work just like steroids, are legal. Steroid use by athletes should not be considered unnatural or cheating—the drugs simply allow athletes to perform at their very best.

2   Isn't it time for the brainwashed public to know the truth about steroids? In their ideological zeal to ban "performance enhancing" drugs, national governments and the various local and international sports federations have ignorantly and self-righteously declared that steroid use is cheating, dangerous, and stupid. In fact, in general, it is neither dangerous nor stupid and it is cheating only because it has been capriciously commanded to be so.

STEROID DANGERS ARE MINIMAL

3   In the first place, with respect to the alleged danger, people ought to know that there are dozens of steroids and it would be absurd to imagine that their risks are identical. Moreover, steroids come in two broad classes—the orals and the injectables. It is true that most of the orals have associated hazards but not a single one of them is as hazardous as smoking or drinking. The principal dangers of the injectables result from overdosing and, even so, they are mainly such alarming matters as acne and severe headache. Every legally obtainable prescription drug comes with a warning of dozens of worse side effects.

4   But what is that to you and me? Why should we legislate what risks people should run unless they can interfere with the rest of us? In our democratic, capitalist society many persons risk their last few dollars to start up businesses which will probably fail. We do not stop them. If and when they become multimillionaires we congratulate them. We don't permit people to drive without seatbelts because their accidents drive up insurance rates for the rest of us but we let people engage in the far riskier business of climbing mountains since the danger is mainly self-regarding. So enough virtue-parading preaching.

PRODUCT HYPOCRISY

5   As for the so-called cheating, who really are the cheaters? The average steroid user spends about $100–150 per month while the supplement industries grow rich on suckering in the hundreds of thousands, possibly millions, of foolish people spending up to $1,000 per month on a variety of mumbo jumbo: androstenedione, 4-androstenedione, 19-androstenedione, androstenediol and the several 4, 5, 17, and 19 varieties of androstenediol, tribulus terrestris, enzymatic conversion accelerators, growth hormone stimulators, hormone-releasing peptides, testosterone "boosters," dozens of magical herbs and a ridiculous number of "non drugs" with unpronounceable names so they are always abbreviated such as HMB and DHEA. On top of all this, these folks who tend to be more affluent than steroid users are pumping protein powders into their milk—$9 per day—and gobbling down protein candy bars—up to $3 each—while saving a bit of energy for screaming "Foul! Cheater!" at the poor steroid user. They are told by the manufacturers and distributors of these outlandish products that they look like steroids, feel like steroids and work like steroids. So? Why not ban them like steroids?

6   But I say ban them and only them. For one thing, they don't work as well as steroids. More importantly, what care I as a fan that someone sets a remarkable record because he used steroids? I pay money to see sporting events and I am entitled to an athlete's very best. Isaac Stern can afford a violin that few violinists and no high school orchestra player can afford. Is he taking unfair advantage of them? If I pay $60 to hear Stern and learn his tone was not up to par because he was too lazy to bring his own violin and borrowed a $50 one from a high school kid, I justifiably want my money back. What care I that he usually plays upon a $200,000

instrument? I am not bothered by this; I want his very best. Likewise, I want the very best an athlete can give me. I don't want to watch athletes who could have done better if only they had used steroids. Talk of steroid performance as unnatural is as ridiculous as complaining about artificial hearts. As for me I plan to have a T-shirt made for me that will read on its front: "Use steroids or go home. Enough of crying and whining."

Now answer the following questions.

1. (T)/F The main idea of this essay is that athletic use of steroids should not be banned.

2. T/(F) The main idea is based mostly on fact.

3. Which of the following best states the author's foremost intent?

   a. To show that there are dozens of steroids with various risk factors

   b. To show that the public has been brainwashed about the falsehoods of steroid use

   c. To show that the principal danger of steroid use is from overdosing

   d. To convince the reader that we should not make something illegal, like steroids, unless the risk interferes with the public

4. Which of the following best describes the author's attitude toward legislation banning steroid use among athletes?

   a. concerned   c. humorous

   b. open-minded   d. disgruntled

5. The tone of the essay is

   a. objective   c. apologetic.

   b. harsh.   d. respectful.

6. Based on the evidence provided, do you agree with the author? Explain.

   _____

   _____

   _____

Now let's look at your answers. The statement in question 1 is true. The statement in question 2 is false. The answer to question 3 is (d). For question 4, of the words offered, the best answer is (d), disgruntled. For question 5, the best choice is (b), harsh. This is not to say that other words might apply as well, but of the choices given, these are the best.

As to question 6, you've given your opinions; compare and discuss them in class.

PRACTICE A-2

Directions: As you read the following article, apply everything you've learned about main ideas and supporting details, considering especially the author's opinions on her topic, her attitude or point of view toward her topic, her intent in writing the essay, and her tone. Notice how they all work together.

IS HARRY POTTER EVIL?

JUDY BLUME

1   I happened to be in London last summer on the very day *Harry Potter and the Prisoner of Azkaban*, the third book in the wildly popular series by J. K. Rowling, was published. I couldn't believe my good fortune. I rushed to the bookstore to buy a copy, knowing this simple act would put me up there with the best grandmas in the world. The book was still months away from publication in the United States, and I have an 8-year-old grandson who is a big Harry Potter fan.

2   It's a good thing when children enjoy books, isn't it? Most of us think so. But like many children's books these days, the Harry Potter series has recently come under fire. In Minnesota, Michigan, New York, California and South Carolina, parents who feel the books promote interest in the occult have called for their removal from classrooms and school libraries.

3   I knew this was coming. The only surprise is that it took so long—as long as it took for the zealots who claim they're protecting children from evil (and evil can be found lurking everywhere these days) to discover that children actually like these books. If children are excited about a book, it must be suspect.

4   I'm not exactly unfamiliar with this line of thinking, having had various books of mine banned from schools over the last 20 years. In my books, it's reality that's seen as corrupting. With Harry Potter, the perceived danger is fantasy. After all, Harry and his classmates attend the celebrated Hogwarts School of Witchcraft and Wizardry. According to certain adults, these stories teach witchcraft, sorcery and satanism. But hey, if it's not one "ism," it's another. I mean Madeleine L'Engle's *A Wrinkle in Time* has been targeted by censors for promoting New Ageism, and Mark Twain's *Adventures of Huckleberry Finn* for promoting racism. Gee, where does that leave the kids?

5   The real danger is not in the books, but in laughing off those who would ban them. The protests against Harry Potter follow a tradition that has been growing since the early 1980's and often leaves school principals trembling with fear that is then passed down to teachers and librarians.

6   What began with the religious right has spread to the politically correct. (Remember the uproar in Brooklyn last year when a teacher was criticized for reading a book entitled "Nappy Hair" to her class?) And now the gate is open so wide that some parents believe they have the right to demand immediate removal of any book for any reason from school or classroom libraries. The list of gifted teachers and librarians who find their jobs in jeopardy for defending their students' right to read, to imagine, to question, grows every year.

7   My grandson was bewildered when I tried to explain why some adults don't want their children reading about Harry Potter. "But that doesn't make any sense!" he said. J. K. Rowling is on a book tour in America right now. She's probably befuddled by the brouhaha, too. After all, she was just trying to tell a good story.

Judy Blume, "Is Harry Potter Evil?" Reprinted with permission from Judy Blume. From the *New York Times* Op-Ed section, October 22, 1999.

8   My husband and I like to reminisce about how, when we were 9, we read straight through L. Frank Baum's Oz series, books filled with wizards and witches. And you know what those subversive tales taught us? That we loved to read! In those days I used to dream of flying. I may have been small and powerless in real life, but in my imagination I was able to soar.

9   At the rate we're going, I can imagine next year's headline: "*Goodnight Moon* Banned for Encouraging Children to Communicate With Furniture." And we all know where that can lead, don't we?

Now answer the following questions.

1. What is the thesis or main idea of this essay?

   a. Some people believe the Harry Potter books are evil and should not be available to children.

   b. The author has had various books of hers banned in some places.

   c. There is a growing danger that some parents believe they have a right to demand removal of books from schools and libraries for any reason.

   d. Parents should allow their children to read about wizards and witches if it gets them to enjoy reading.

2. T/F The opinions in this article are mostly based on factual accounts and reports.

3. Which of the following best describes the author's attitude toward book censorship?

   a. Concerned   **c.** Angry

   b. Open-minded   **d.** Pleased

4. Looking at the list on page 212, what word or words best describe the author's attitude and tone? _____

5. What is the author's intent?

   a. To caution readers about the growing attempts at book censorship by parents

   b. To show that reading books dealing with the occult are not harmful

   c. To defend the Harry Potter series against those who want it banned

   d. To laugh off those who want to ban certain books they find objectionable

Questions for Group Discussion

In small groups, pick one of the two essays, "Ban Athletes Who Don't Use Steroids" or "Is Harry Potter Evil?" Discuss your reactions to the author's intent, attitude, and tone. How do these reactions aid or hinder your acceptance of the author's thesis?

B. Recognizing Figurative Language

Frequently, writers use **figurative language** to express their tone. Figurative language is used in an imaginative way rather than in a literal sense. For instance, when a writer says, "her eyes flashed fire," the intent is not for us to imagine real fire coming from someone's eyes but to realize that the character is angry. Or, when we read that a lawyer "dropped his client like a hot potato," we are given to understand that the lawyer's actions were quick, just as we'd be quick to drop a hot potato.

Figurative language is familiar to everyone. A great deal of our slang and ordinary speech is based on figurative language, as well as a great many works in literature. For example, many baseball terms have become part of our regular figurative speech:

Keep your eye on the ball.
What he said came out of left field.
The salesman's pitch was off base.
His friend went to bat for him.
If you want to work here, you'll need to play ball with the manager.
He got started right off the bat.
The sales record knocked the ball out of the park.
His bank account holds ballpark figures.

Without figures of speech, our language would be dull and mechanical. It becomes, therefore, important in developing reading comprehension to know the difference between literal and figurative language. It also becomes important to know the difference between literal and figurative language in developing your aesthetic understanding of what you read. More on that in later chapters.

One form of figurative language is the **metaphor**. A metaphor is a comparison of two things without the use of the word *like* or *as*. For instance, when you say someone "clammed up and wouldn't talk," you are comparing the person's closed mouth with the tightness of a closed clam. When you say someone has a "stone face," you are comparing their unchanging expression with the immobility of stone.

Dead metaphors are metaphors that have been used so frequently that we accept them almost literally. Terms such as "a tenderfoot," "hands" on a watch, the "head" of a cane, a "run" in a stocking, or an engine "knocking" are all dead metaphors, yet they help us convey meaning that is seldom misunderstood. S. I. Hayakawa says that metaphors are probably the most important of all the means by which language develops, changes, grows, and adapts itself to our changing needs.

A **simile** is another form of figurative language. It, like a metaphor, compares one thing with another but uses the word *like* or *as*. Examples of similes are "out like a light," "sparkles like a lake," "sounds like a machine gun," "cool as spring water," and "phony as a three-dollar bill."

When metaphors and similes are overused, they turn into **clichés**. Clichés are worn-out figures of speech such as "a blanket of snow covered the hill," "the silence was broken," or "my old lady." Such terms have been used so often in speech and writing that they lose their real effectiveness and seem stale.

Still another type of figurative language is **hyperbole**. Hyperbole is a deliberate exaggeration or overstatement used to emphasize a point being made. For instance, if a friend tells you she can't go to the movies because she has "mountains of homework" to do, she is using hyperbole. If someone tells you that the story was "so funny he almost died laughing," he's using hyperbole. If you "love someone to pieces," know someone who "talked your ear off," or couldn't get your work done because "the phone rang ten thousand times," then you have been dealing with hyperbole. Just as overused similes and metaphors can become clichés, it can happen with hyperbole, too.

Some writers use **puns**, a humorous use of words that involves a word or phrase that has more than one possible meaning. For example:

Two silk worms had a race; they ended in a tie.
No matter how much you push the envelope, it'll still be stationery.
A dog gave birth to puppies near the road and was cited for littering.
Time flies like an arrow. Fruit flies like a banana.
A chicken crossing the road is poultry in motion.

You get the picture.

Recognizing how authors use figurative language helps us clarify whether an author's attitude is serious, playful, sympathetic, outraged, sarcastic, bitter, humorous, and so on. Thus, attitude and tone are closely allied through the use of figures of speech.

PRACTICE **B-1**: Identifying Literal versus Figurative Language

Directions: The following statements are either literal or figurative. Place an *F* in the blank next to each statement that uses figurative speech. If you want more practice with the identification of figurative language, see Chapter Eight, Practice A-1.

_____   **1.** Mr. Timpkin went through the ceiling when his son told him that he had wrecked the car.

_____   **2.** Alyce waited eagerly for the show to start.

_____   **3.** Doreen's checks are bouncing all over town.

_____   **4.** The crowd was getting increasingly angry waiting for the musicians to show up.

_____   **5.** The battery is dead as a doornail.

_____   **6.** Prices are being slashed to rock bottom.

_____   **7.** Mom really stuck her neck out for you this time.

_____   **8.** I find myself out on a limb.

_____   **9.** When Jimmy screamed, her hair stood on end.

_____   **10.** The Giants were defeated 18–4 in the last game.

PRACTICE **B-2**: Recognizing Tone through Figurative Language

Directions: Read the following paragraphs and answer the questions that follow.

1. There is an appalling cloud of illiteracy shadowing America's pride. We would do well to attack some basic causes for the lack of literacy facing us. Instead, we seem to throw more money down the drain for more grants and studies.

   a. The expression "cloud of illiteracy shadowing America's pride" means _____

   _____

b. T/F The literary term for the phrase in question 1(a) is *simile.*

c. T/F Using the phrase "money down the drain" lets us know the author is happy with what efforts are taking place.

d. The tone of this passage is best described as

_____ serious concern.   _____ concerned displeasure.
_____ humorous concern.   _____ sarcastic.

2. My job was really starting to get to me. It seemed a dead end, a treadmill taking me nowhere. If I was to keep from blowing a fuse, I had to somehow shatter my negativity toward my work or go for broke and resign. After what seemed like centuries of indecisiveness, one day I plunked myself down at the typewriter, quickly tossed off my resignation, and boldly signed it with great flair. So I wouldn't chicken out at the last minute, I sailed into my boss's office and slapped it down on her desk.

   a. The tone of this passage is best described as

   _____ one of relief.   _____ frustration.
   _____ fear of losing a job.   _____ indecision.

   b. The phrase "go for broke" here means _____

   _____

   c. T/F "My treadmill job was a dead end" is an example of a metaphor.

   d. T/F It is possible to literally shatter a negative attitude.

3. Out deeper, in cooler water, where trout live, floating on one's back is a kind of free ride, like being fifteen again, like being afloat upon another sky. Perhaps there is a bit of Tom Sawyer's pleasure at watching his own bogus funeral in this, but before we get overly morbid, a fish begins nibbling our toes. Floating on one's back is like riding between two skies. (From Edward Hoagland, "Summer Pond," *New York Times*, August 1, 1979.)

   a. T/F The author mostly uses similes in the preceding passage.

   b. The tone of the paragraph is best described as

   _____ lazy.   _____ morbid.
   _____ pleasant.   _____ sad.

   c. T/F The intent of the passage is to relive the joys of swimming in a pond or lake.

4. "C'mon, we're supposed to be having fun," snaps her companion, a clone. In razor-crease jeans and stiletto heels they stamp into the ladies room, flounce around the corner past the polished washbasins and disappear into the two long rows of toilet stalls. They are the kind of girls who obey their mothers' warnings never to sit on strange toilet seats. Attendants have to nip in after that type, making sure the next woman will have no unpleasant surprises. (From Jane O'Reilly, "In Las Vegas: Working Hard for the Money," *Time*, January 9, 1984.)

   a. T/F The phrase "razor-crease jeans and stiletto heels" reflects a negative attitude toward the girls.

   b. T/F The intent of the passage is to gain sympathy for the two girls.

   c. The tone of the passage can best be described as

   _____ humorous.   _____ sweet.
   _____ sarcastic.   _____ apathetic.

5. There had been some change in the kitchen staff since my last visit and somehow the perfect little salad had become a Plain Jane. The tortilla soup was a bowl of monotone flavor and tasted like tortilla chips thrown into a blender. This soup compared to the previous soup was like comparing a No. 2 pencil against a Mont Blanc pen. The grilled cheese with apple, Gruyere, and whole-grain mustard was disappointing. In trying to be original, a grilled cheese got whiplashed into a sloppy, runny junket of sweet, mustard and cheese flavors, all coming together like a blind date. Worse is the heavy-scented sweet vanilla deodorizer in the gas-station-like loo, which is reminiscent of walking down the candle aisle at Pier 1. (From Arthur von Wiesenberger, "A Mixed Harvest," *Santa Barbara News-Press*, March 10, 2006, p. 33.)

   a. T/F The intent of this passage is to compare the food of a previous restaurant visit with the latest visit.

   b. The tone of the passage is mostly

   _____ humorous.   _____ objective.

   _____ disappointment.   _____ frustration.

   c. What does the author mean by the phrase "Plain Jane"?

   _____

   _____

   d. What effect does the author create with the use of the term "whiplashed"?

   _____

   _____

   e. The author uses several similes. Write down two of them.

   _____

   _____

6. Three decades after bursting into pool halls and living rooms, video games are taking a place in academia.... Traditionalists in both education and the video game industry pooh-pooh the trend, calling it a bald bid by colleges to cash in on a fad. But others believe that video games—which already rival movie tickets in sales—are poised to become one of the dominant media of the new century. Certainly, the burgeoning game industry is famished for new talent. And now, universities are stocked with both students and young faculty members who grew up with joystick in hand. (Seth Schiesel, "Video Games Are Their Major," *New York Times*, November 22, 2005.)

   Explain how these words and phrases are used figuratively:

   a. bursting into

   _____

   b. pooh-pooh

   _____

   c. a bald bid

   _____

d. famished for

_____

e. stocked with

_____

PRACTICE B-3

Directions: Read the following essay, looking for intent, attitude, tone, and figurative language.

THIRST FOR A HERO CAN GET US IN HOT WATER

PHILADELPHIA INQUIRER

1   At a low point of the Iraq war, when unexpected Iraqi opposition seemed to threaten U.S. troops with a morass, America badly needed a hero.

2   And it found one.

3   This was the story, and a compelling one it was. Pfc. Jessica Lynch, a fresh-faced, 19-year-old Army supply clerk from West Virginia, was miraculously rescued from a hospital in Nasiriyah where, gravely injured, she was being held captive.

4   The *Washington Post* quoted unnamed U.S. officials recounting that Ms. Lynch had engaged in a "fierce" firefight after her unit was ambushed following a wrong turn. She shot several enemy soldiers before her ammo ran out and she was captured.

5   "She was fighting to the death" and has multiple gunshot wounds, said an unnamed U.S. official in the story.

6   The most exciting part of the tale came next: Ms. Lynch's rescue.

7   The defense sources described for the *Post* a classic Special Operations raid, with commandos in Black Hawk helicopters engaging Iraqi forces on their way into and out of Ms. Lynch's medical compound.

8   The commandos had been directed there by a heroic Iraqi lawyer who was appalled to see the bedridden Ms. Lynch slapped twice in the face by one of her captors. This account was trumpeted by U.S. print and broadcast outlets far and wide.

9   The story was a balm to American hearts.

10   Except that much of it now appears to be untrue. The British Broadcasting Corp. cast cold water on the tale two weeks ago: Ms. Lynch's injuries were probably caused by a road crash; she had received good treatment at the hospital; there wasn't a single armed opposition soldier in the hospital when the U.S. troops burst in, John Wayne style.

11   Later—too much later—the American media have begun examining the story they had so eagerly swallowed in April.

12   Thursday, a lengthy *Chicago Tribune* story quoted Iraqis on the scene who said that much of the Lynch hero/rescue story was, basically, bunk. (Ms. Lynch herself has no memory of events.)

13   Now this glorious tale must be traded for some complicated questions about the sticky entanglements of a rah-rah Pentagon, a thirsty press, and a public desperate for good news.

14   Those questions don't just concern the story of Jessica Lynch.

15   Early reports of her rescue were, as the saying goes, the first, rough-draft history. But, then, so too are all the accounts so far of this fast-moving war.

16   Stay tuned—perhaps decades from now—for the real story. What really did become of those weapons of mass destruction, if they existed at all? Where is Saddam Hussein? Exactly how many Iraqi civilians suffered and died?

17   It's too easy just to blame a sloppy press for overdramatizing the Jessica Lynch story initially. In the fog of war, most reporting is quick and dirty, with virtually no chance for outside corroboration. Clearly, in this case, at least some in the military were eager to peddle the more heroic narrative. And, to journalism's credit, the original, faulty stories usually get revised when facts finally become clear.

18   Is Pfc. Lynch indeed a hero?

19   For volunteering to serve the way she did, and enduring the way she did, she is. There are no doubt thousands more untold stories about the heroism of individual American and British soldiers in Iraq.

20   But a search for the perfect heroic story—and eager acceptance of any "facts" that enhance the tale—does a disservice to both heroes and the truth.

Comprehension Check

Directions: Answer the following questions without looking back.

1. What is the intent of this article? _____

    _____

2. Which of the following best describes the author's attitude toward the media's coverage of the Jessica Lynch story?

    a. sympathetic

    b. tolerant

    c. furious

    d. alarmed

3. Which of the following best describes the author's attitude toward the U.S. official who gave the story to the press?

    a. praise

    b. disturbed

    c. accepting

    d. can't tell

4. The tone of the essay is mostly

    a. humorous.

    b. nasty.

    c. sarcastic.

    d. troublesome.

5. The tone of paragraph 13 can best be described as

   a. mean.

   b. sarcastic.

   c. serious.

   d. ecstatic.

6. Rewrite paragraph 11 without using any figurative language.

   _____

   _____.

7. T/F The phrases "a rah-rah Pentagon" and "a thirsty press" in paragraph 13 are examples of figurative language.

8. Reread paragraph 10. What, if any, figurative language is being used? _____

   _____

9. What examples of figurative language are used in paragraph 17?

   _____

   _____

10. Why does the author believe that the press reported the Jessica Lynch story without checking on the "unnamed U.S. official"?

   _____

   _____

Vocabulary Check

Directions: Define the following underlined words from the selection.

1. opposition seemed to threaten troops with a <u>morass</u>

   _____

2. and a <u>compelling</u> one it was

   _____

3. was <u>appalled</u> to see

   _____

4. this account was <u>trumpeted</u> by U.S. print and broadcast outlets

   _____

5. perhaps <u>decades</u> from now

   _____

6. about the sticky <u>entanglements</u>

   _____

7. no chance for outside <u>corroboration</u>

   _____

8. <u>enduring</u> the way she did

_____

9. "facts" that <u>enhance</u> the tale

_____

10. a <u>disservice</u> to both heroes and the truth

_____

Record the results of the comprehension and vocabulary checks on the Student Record Chart in the Appendix. Each correct answer is worth 10 points, for a total of 100 points possible for comprehension and 100 points for vocabulary.

PRACTICE B-4

Directions: Read the following essay, looking for intent, attitude, tone, and figurative language.

DO AWAY WITH PUBLIC SCHOOLS

JONAH GOLDBERG

1   Here's a good question for you: Why have public schools at all?

2   OK, cue the marching music. We need public schools because blah blah blah and yada yada yada. We could say blah is common culture and yada is the government's interest in promoting the general welfare. Or that children are the future. And a mind is a terrible thing to waste. Because we can't leave any child behind.

3   The problem with all these bromides is that they leave out the simple fact that one of the surest ways to leave a kid "behind" is to hand him over to the government. Americans want universal education, just as they want universally safe food. But nobody believes that the government should run nearly all of the restaurants, farms and supermarkets. Why should it run the vast majority of the schools—particularly when it gets terrible results?

4   Consider Washington, home of the nation's most devoted government-lovers and, ironically, the city with arguably the worst public schools in the country. Out of the 100 largest school districts, according to _The Washington Post_, the District of Columbia ranks third in spending for each pupil ($12,979) but last in spending on instruction. Fifty-six cents of every dollar go to administrators who, it's no secret, do a miserable job administrating, even though D.C. schools have been in a state of "reform" for nearly 40 years.

5   In a blistering series, the _Post_ has documented how badly the bureaucrats have run public education. More than half of Washington's teenagers spend their days in "persistently dangerous" schools, with an average of nine violent incidents a day in a system with 135 schools. "Principals reporting dangerous conditions or urgently needed repairs in their buildings wait, on average, 379 days...for the problems to be fixed," according to the _Post_. But hey, at least the kids are getting a lousy education. A mere 19 schools managed to get "proficient" scores or better for a majority of students on the district's Comprehensive Assessment Test.

6   A standard response to such criticisms is to say we don't spend enough on public education. But if money were the solution, wouldn't the district, which spends nearly $13,000 on every kid, rank near the top? If you think more money will fix the schools, make your checks out to "cash" and send them to me. Private, parochial and charter schools get better results. Parents know this. Applications for vouchers in the district dwarf the available supply, and home schooling has exploded.

7   As for schools teaching kids about the common culture and all that, as a conservative, I couldn't agree more. But is there evidence that public schools are better at it? The results of the 2006 National Assessment of Educational Progress history and civics exams showed that two-thirds of U.S. high school seniors couldn't identify the significance of a photo of a theater with a sign reading "Colored Entrance." And keep in mind, political correctness pretty much guarantees that Jim Crow and the civil rights movement are included in syllabi. Imagine how few kids can intelligently discuss Manifest Destiny or free silver.

8   Right now, there's a renewed debate about providing "universal" health insurance. For some liberals, this means replicating the public school model for health care. (Stop laughing.) But for others, this means mandating that everyone have health insurance—just as we mandate that all drivers have car insurance—and then throwing tax dollars at poorer folks to make sure no one falls through the cracks.

9   There's a consensus in America that every child should get an education, but as David Gelernter noted recently in *The Weekly Standard*, there's no such consensus that public schools need to do the educating.

10   Really, what would be so terrible about government mandating that every kid has to go to school and providing subsidies and oversight when necessary, but then getting out of the way?

11   Milton Friedman noted long ago that the government is bad at providing services—that's why he wanted public schools to be called "government schools"—but that it's good at writing checks. So why not cut checks to people so they can send their kids to school?

12   What about the good public schools? Well, the reason good public schools are good has nothing to do with government's special expertise and everything to do with the fact that parents care enough to ensure their kids get a good education. That wouldn't change if the government got out of the school business. What would change is that fewer kids would get left behind.

Comprehension Check

Directions: Answer the following questions without looking back.

1. What is the author's thesis or main idea? _____

_____

_____

2. The tone of paragraph 2 is

   a. serious.

   b. playful.

   c. angry.

   d. sarcastic.

3. Explain how paragraph 2 sets up the tone of the essay. _____

_____

_____

4. Which of the following describes Goldberg's attitude toward those in control of public school education and funding?

   a. pleased

   b. angry

   c. favorable

   d. disapproving

5. Goldberg's intent is to

   a. offer ideas that would better serve public schools.

   b. criticize the public school system.

   c. show we don't spend enough on public education.

   d. praise private schools.

6. On what school district does Goldberg mostly base his argument?

_____

7. Goldberg states a study that revealed two-thirds of U.S. high school seniors could not identify the significance of a photo of a theater with a sign reading "Colored Entrance." What point is he making by quoting this study?

_____

_____

8. T/F Goldberg does not blame or find fault with the school administrators but feels the real problem is the lack of funding for schools.

9. T/F Goldberg uses a metaphor in the last sentence of paragraph 9.

10. Goldberg believes that the government should mandate that every child has to go to school and then _____

_____

Vocabulary Check

Directions: Define the following underlined words from the selection.

1. the problem with all these bromides...

_____

2. in a blistering series

_____

3. to get proficient scores

_____

4. private, parochial and charter schools

_____

5. application for <u>vouchers</u>

_____

6. home schooling has <u>exploded</u>

_____

7. <u>Jim Crow</u> and the civil rights

_____

_____

_____

8. included in <u>syllabi</u>

_____

9. intelligently discuss <u>Manifest Destiny</u>

_____

_____

_____

10. this means <u>replicating</u> the public schools

_____

Record the results of the comprehension and vocabulary checks on the Student Record Chart in the Appendix. Each correct answer is worth 10 points, for a total of 100 points possible for comprehension and 100 points for vocabulary.

Class discussion questions:

1. Should we do away with public school education and let the government provide vouchers or subsidies to send children to private schools?

2. Discuss group attitudes toward their own education. Who went to public schools? Who went to private schools? How does each person value the education they received?

Application 1: Finding Figurative Language in Other Materials

In magazines, newspapers, or textbooks, find at least two examples of metaphors or similes and underline them. Write a sentence about how the figurative language shows the author's tone and attitude.

C. Comparing Biased Points of View

A writer's attitude toward a subject may not be ours. However, as critical readers, it is important not to let either the author's **bias** or our own interfere with critical comprehension. Being biased means being prejudiced about or having a special leaning toward something. For instance, you may be biased about the type of music you listen to. Maybe you have no patience with classical music and prefer hard rock. That is a bias. Perhaps you are biased when it comes to food and would rather eat vegetables than meat. Everyone is biased about something, whether it's music, food, religion, politics, or people. Many of our biases are unconsciously learned from parents, friends, people we admire, or teachers. Reading critically can help us examine our own biases for their value.

While we are free to make up our own minds about a subject, we must still examine carefully the arguments and reasons of an author with opinions different from ours. We must recognize those biases of the author and not allow our own biases to interfere with or shut out those of the author. Once we critically examine what we read, we should reflect on its worth before accepting or rejecting it.

Most of us tend to accept readily the ideas of writers who have the same biases we do, and we tend to reject the views of those we have biases against. To do so is to be closed minded. As critical readers, we must be willing to make critical judgments based on reason rather than emotion.

As you learn to read critically, you need to recognize bias in writing. If you don't, you may become the victim of an author's propaganda. You may miss seeing how an author misrepresents facts. You may not see that an author is being more subjective (using personal opinions) than objective (using undistorted facts). Or you may be unaware of how one-sided some writing is.

Sometimes recognizing an author's bias is easy; at other times it isn't. Bias is likely to be present in advertisements, newspaper and magazine editorials, and religious and political pamphlets. You generally pay little attention to an author's bias when it matches your own. When you don't agree with an author, the reverse is true. To read critically requires real involvement in the text and in thinking through what is being read. In effect, critical reading *is* thinking.

The following passage appeared in *Consumer Reports*, a publication of Consumers Union, a nonprofit organization. Read it and then answer the questions that follow.

> The letter, marked "confidential," was from the R. I. Research Special Human Being Laboratory in New York City and was signed by one Dr. Roger Grimstone. It informed the recipient that, based on the date and hour of her birth, she was an extraordinary individual, "apart from the rest of humanity," a "Beyonder."
>
> "Owing to some cosmic quirk," the letter went on, "your destiny operates independently of any stars....Why have you suffered so much? *Why has true happiness, true love, wealth, a happy home always been out of your reach? Why have the things you've yearned for most been snatched away?*"
>
> Simple. According to the good Dr. Grimstone, it's because the recipient has yet to send him 20 bucks for something entitled "The Guide."
>
> The reader who sent us Dr. Grimstone's solicitation has a different theory, however. He believes that his daughter, the recipient of the letter, has yet to find happiness, companionship, and financial security because she is only four months old. (From "Selling It," copyright © 1987 by Consumers Union of U.S., Inc., Yonkers, NY 10703-1057, a nonprofit organization. Reprinted with permission from the September 1987 issue of Consumer Reports © for educational purposes only. No commercial use or photocopying permitted. Log onto: *www.ConsumerReports.org.*)

1. What is the intent of the "confidential" letter sent by the R. I. Research Special Human Being Laboratory? *to sell the guide for twenty dollars.*

2. What is the intent of the article from *Consumer Reports*? *r be intent is expose the lab.*

3. What attitude toward the recipient is implied by the originators of the letter? *Phony*

4. What is *Consumer Reports*'s attitude toward the Laboratory?

5. What is the tone of the letter sent by Dr. Grimstone? *Promising*

6. What is the tone of the passage from *Consumer Reports*? *Sarcastic*

Your answers to the questions may be worded differently from the following, but see if they match up. The answer to the first question is to sell "The Guide" for twenty dollars by appealing to the recipient's "uniqueness" and desire for more wealth, happiness, and health, things most all of us want more of. The intent of *Consumer Reports*, the second question, is to expose the "Laboratory" as a fraud.

The third question can be answered by looking at such phrases as "apart from the rest of humanity," "owing to some cosmic quirk," and "Beyonder." The Laboratory believes there are enough people (suckers?) who believe in astrology and who are dissatisfied enough with their lives (or curious enough) that they are willing to spend twenty dollars to find "the answer." *Consumer Reports*'s attitude is that the whole thing is phony.

The tone of the letter is tied in with attitude. The letter's tone, based on what quotes are given, seems serious about wanting to help. Even the "doctor's" name is serious sounding—Grimstone (or is it a subtle touch of humor on the sender's part?). *Consumer Reports*'s tone is humorous. Waiting until the end of the passage to let us know that the "confidential" letter was sent to a four-month-old makes us chuckle. We realize that phrases such as "the good Dr. Grimstone" and "20 bucks" provide a light, playful tone.

Critical reading requires identifying an author's point of view and motives. Nearly all controversial subjects are written from a particular point of view or bias.

By their very nature, such controversial subjects cannot be written about with complete objectivity. For instance, if a Catholic priest were to write about abortion, chances are his point of view would reflect opposition by the very nature of his training and religious beliefs. On the other hand, a social worker who has seen many teenage lives destroyed because of unwanted pregnancies might very well speak in favor of abortion. Even though the priest and the social worker have different points of view, their motives are the same—to convince us that their particular viewpoint is the correct one. As critical readers—and thinkers—we need to be alert to as many points of view as possible before making up our own minds on controversial issues. Then we need to examine the reasoning used to support those viewpoints.

Here are a few guidelines to follow so that you don't fall victim to poor reasoning. Watch out for:

1. Statements that oversimplify or distort the issue being discussed.
2. Irrelevant or unsupported evidence.
3. Left-out or suppressed information or evidence.
4. Appeals to the emotions rather than reasonable evidence.
5. Mudslinging, or attacks on people or groups rather than the issue itself.
6. References to or quotations from the Bible or historical figures even though there is no connection to the issue.

These are the most frequent, although not all, of the devices used to sway people to accept a particular point of view. They appear in advertisements, political campaigns, newspaper and magazine columns, editorials, and television commentaries.

PRACTICE C-1: Recognizing Opinions

The next reading is a syndicated column from the *Boston Globe* that appeared in hundreds of newspapers around the country. The subject has to do with the censorship of movies, videocassettes, television programs, and rock music. Before you read it, answer the following questions about your own biases regarding censorship.

1. Do you believe in censorship of any kind? _yes_ Explain. _____
   yes, I do believe in censorship
   because it helps kids

2. Do you believe that the electronic media (TV, VHS and DVD recordings, music CDs, radio) are generally responsible for the rise in drug addiction, adolescent suicides, and a decline in SAT scores? _____ Explain. _____
   I do believe

politics
movies
brands,
sex
violence
profanity
nudity
Religion
privicy

Now read the following essay, using the six previously listed guidelines that outlined what you should watch for when reading about controversial issues.

SHIELD OUR YOUTH WITH CENSORSHIP

WILLIAM SHANNON

1   The United States today has a popular culture at war against the nation's children and youth. Movies, video cassettes, television programs, and rock music have produced what the late Harvard sociologist Pitirim Sorokin called a "sensate culture." The message of this popular culture is "Feel good." What one thinks hardly matters.

2   These media bombard young people with sounds and images for several hours each day. The two dominant themes are sexual pleasure and sadistic violence. The indescribable "highs" and mysterious charms of using drugs also lurk as subsidiary themes.

3   The effect of this non-stop sensual assault is anti-intellectual and anti-academic. It is difficult for any classroom teacher to compete with the exciting images projected by television and films. Serious use of the mind requires patience, self-discipline, and the ability to defer present gratification in favor of future achievement. Very little in our culture supports these serious values. On the contrary, the fast pace and pounding rhythms of rock music and violent films tell impressionable youngsters "Go, go, go . . . now, now, now."

4   Parents are engaged in an uneven battle against this popular culture. There are still young persons who read for pleasure and who do well in school, but their number dwindles. The middle range of children muddles through high school and some go through college, but the general level of their academic achievement is significantly below what it was 30 years ago. The number of vulnerable youngsters cruelly damaged or destroyed by this culture grows. Victims are at every level of intelligence and family income. Their vulnerability is a matter of temperament, family history, and perhaps genetic endowment.

5   The casualty figures in this uneven battle between conscientious parents and the popular culture appear in the form of a rising number of adolescent suicides and drug addicts and in the Scholastic Aptitude Test scores, which have fallen significantly from their levels of 20 years ago. Parents try various expedients. Wealthy families send their children to private boarding schools in the hope that tight scheduling of time and close supervision by teachers will reduce the risks.

6   Other families—some of them non-Catholic—turn to the Catholic schools, in the hope that the schools' traditionally stricter discipline and the greater respect for authority that they inculcate will save their children.

7   No place in this society is a sanctuary, however, from the brutal and corrupting pressures of our popular culture. Schools of every kind, public and private, secular and religious, struggle valiantly to instill good work habits and encourage intellectual values, but the opposing cultural pressures are too pervasive.

8   The film industry makes much of ratings such as "R" for restricted to adults, and "PG" for parental guidance suggested, but these ratings are close to useless.

9   The only solution is to restore prior censorship over the electronic media. Everyone older than 50 grew up in a time when Hollywood films were strictly censored by

the industry itself to exclude explicit sexual scenes, gruesome violence, and vulgar language. The Supreme Court in the 1950s struck down movie censorship. It extended to film makers the First Amendment protection traditionally enjoyed by newspapers and book publishers. The court also redefined the anti-pornography and anti-obscenity statutes into meaninglessness.

10   Those decisions were praised as liberal advances, but their consequences were unforeseen and disastrous. It would require a constitutional amendment to reverse those decisions. Unless they are reversed, the coarsening and corrupting of the nation's youth will continue.

Now answer the following questions.

1. What is the author's point of view toward censorship? _His point of view is blaming the electronic media corrupting our children_

2. What is his attitude toward movies, videocassettes, and rock music? _It's negative attitude._

3. What is his intent in writing this essay? _to push censorship_

4. The statements made in paragraph 3 are factual.

   a. True, because_____

   b. False, because_____

5. The statements made in paragraph 3 are supported with evidence.

   a. True, because_____

   b. False, because_____

6. Statements such as "The only solution is to restore prior censorship over the electronic media" oversimplify the issue being discussed.

   a. True, because_____

   b. False, because_____

7. By blaming today's problems on the Supreme Court of the 1950s, the author is mudslinging rather than dealing rationally with the issue.

   a. True, because_____

   b. False, because_____

8. Circle any of the following that you feel the author does:

   a. Makes irrelevant or unsupported statements_____

   b. Oversimplifies the problem and solution_____

   c. Refers to the Bible for support_____

   d. Appeals to the emotions rather than providing reasonable evidence_____

9. For each of the items you circled in question 8, find a passage in the essay that serves as an example.

   _____

   _____

It's not too difficult to answer the first question. The title of the essay provides us with our first clue: "Shield Our Youth with Censorship." As we read through the essay, the author makes it clear that he blames the electronic media as the corrupting pressure on today's youth. Thus, his attitude is negative. His intent seems to be to push for censorship of some kind, to bring a constitutional amendment that would reverse the Supreme Court's earlier decision. Otherwise, he says in the last paragraph, "the coarsening and corrupting of the nation's youth will continue."

The statements in questions 4 and 5 are both false. The author makes three statements in paragraph 3, each one an opinion as stated. Though he may be correct, he needs facts to support his opinions. But instead of providing facts, he moves on to "the effects of this non-stop sensual assault."

The statements in questions 6 and 7 are both true. The issue is too complex for such a simple solution. When he blames the Supreme Court of the 1950s for today's problems, he not only simplifies the issue again but also enters into what is called "mudslinging," attacking the Court rather than the problem he claims the electronic media are causing.

As to questions 8 and 9, he uses all but (c). We've already seen that paragraph 3 is full of unsupported statements. Another example is the last sentence in paragraph 3. The last three sentences in paragraph 4 are also unsupported. Then in paragraph 5, he links adolescent suicides, drug addiction, and a decline in SAT scores together as though all of these are related to the electronic media. Admittedly, he could be correct, but his argument is not very convincing. His tone is frequently emotional. Wording and phrases such as "vulnerable youngsters cruelly damaged," "no place is a sanctuary," and "a popular culture at war against the nation's children" all appeal to our emotions. Censorship of any type is a serious matter. To accept the author's premise and solution as written is to do so without solid facts or rational reasoning.

It's important to remember that Shannon may be right. What we as critical readers must do is recognize his point of view or bias, then see what facts he provides to support his thesis. If his facts or supporting arguments are valid, then we should consider his point of view before making up our minds, especially if we disagree with him. If we already agree with him, but have no more facts or reasons to support our point of view than he has, then we need to critically evaluate our own reasons for having the views we do. One of the primary reasons for reading a wide range of viewpoints is to acquire, broaden, and strengthen intelligent views of our own.

Too often we tend to accept the views of others we trust or admire without examining the logic or reasoning behind them. Many people practice the religion they do not because they have truly examined the creeds but because parents or friends are members of that religion. Many politicians have been elected to office not because they are the best qualified but because they make a good impression in public. Many countries have gone to war not because it was the right thing to do but because people were led to believe it was the only solution to a problem.

The next set of practices will help you develop your critical reading skills in these areas.

PRACTICE C-2: A Controversy: Should the Bible Be Taught in Schools?

Directions: Before reading the following selection, answer the questions that follow:

1. I believe that teaching the Bible in schools is

    a. important, because _____

_____

    b. unimportant, because _____

2. I believe in separation of church and state.

    a. Yes, because _____

    b. No, because _____

3. We should not talk about politics and religion in public.

    a. True, because _____

    b. False, because _____

Now read the following essay.

TEACH, DON'T PREACH, THE BIBLE

BRUCE FEILER

1   Yesterday's ruling by a federal judge that "intelligent design" cannot be taught in biology classes in a Pennsylvania public school district has the potential to put the teaching of the Bible back where it belongs in our schools: not in the science laboratory, but in its proper historical and literary context. An elective, nonsectarian high school Bible class would allow students to explore one of the most influential books of all time and would do so in a manner that clearly falls within Supreme Court rulings.

2   In the landmark 1963 Abington case (which also involved Pennsylvania public schools), the Supreme Court outlawed reading the Bible as part of morning prayers but left the door open for studying the Bible. Writing for the 8–1 majority, Justice Thomas Clark stated that the Bible is "worthy of study for its literary and historic qualities," and added, "Nothing we have said here indicates that such study of the Bible or of religion, when presented objectively as part of a secular program of education, may not be effected consistent with the First Amendment."

3   Though the far right may complain that this academic approach to teaching the Bible locks God out of the classroom, and the far left may complain that it sneaks God in, the vast majority of Americans would embrace it. But the devil, as some might say, is in the details. School board officials in Odessa, Tex., for example, have been embroiled in a running controversy over their choice of a curriculum for an elective high school Bible class. While the board's choice is now between two competing curriculums, pressure from civil liberties groups has prompted changes in even the more conservative alternative.

4   By helping to design an academic course in the Bible, moderates can show that the Bible is not composed entirely of talking points for the religious right. In fact, on a wide range of topics, including respecting the value of other faiths, shielding religion from politics, serving the poor and protecting the environment, the Bible offers powerful arguments in support of moderate and liberal causes.

5   In the story of David, the ruthless Israelite king who unites the tribes of Israel around 1000 B.C.E. but is rebuked by God when he wants to build a temple, the Bible makes a stirring argument in favor of separating religion and politics, or church and state to use contemporary terms.

6   In the Book of Isaiah, God embraces the Persian king Cyrus and his respect for different religions, even though Cyrus does not know God's name and does not

practice Judaism. By calling Cyrus "the anointed one," or messiah, God signals his tolerance for people who share his moral vision, no matter their nationality or faith.

7   In the Book of Jonah, God offers a message of forgiveness and tolerance when he denounces his own prophet and spares his former enemies, the Ninevehites, when they repent and turn toward him.

8   In recent decades, the debate over religion has been characterized as a struggle between two groups that Noah Feldman calls "values evangelicals," like Roy Moore, who placed the Ten Commandments in the Alabama Supreme Court, and "legal secularists," like Michael Newdow, who attacked the use of "under God" in the Pledge of Allegiance. This debate does not represent reality.

9   The Fourth National Survey of Religion and Politics, completed in 2004 by the University of Akron, shows that only 12.6 percent of Americans consider themselves "traditionalist evangelical Protestants," which the survey equates with the term "religious right." A mere 10.7 percent of Americans define themselves as "secular" or "atheist, agnostic." The vast majority of Americans are what survey-takers term centrist or modernist in their religious views.

10   These mainstream believers represent to their religiously liberal and conservative neighbors what independents do to Republicans and Democrats in the political arena. They are the under-discussed "swing voters" in the values debate who, the survey shows, are slightly pro-choice, believe in the death penalty, support stem-cell research and favor gay rights but oppose gay marriage.

11   Above all, they welcome religion in public life but are turned off by efforts to claim exclusive access to God.

12   At a time when religion dominates the headlines—from Iraq to terrorism to stem cells—finding a way to educate young people about faith should become a national imperative. Achieving this goal in a legal, nonsectarian manner requires Americans to get over the kitchen-table bromide, "Don't talk about politics and religion in public."

13   The extremists talk about religion—and spew messages of hate. Religious moderates must denounce this bigotry and reclaim Scripture as the shared document of all. When flamethrowers hold up Scripture and say, "It says this," moderates must hold up the same text and say, "Yes, but it also says this." The Bible is simply too important to the history of Western civilization—and too vital to its future—to be ceded to one side in the debate over values.

"Now answer the following questions." with the following head and text:

Comprehension Check

Answer the following questions.

1. Circle the best statement of the main point or thesis of Feiler's essay.

   a. The Bible should be taught in schools.

   b. The Bible should not be taught in schools.

   c. The Bible should be taught in schools as a historical and literary work.

   d. The Bible offers powerful arguments in support of moderate and liberal causes.

2. The author's basic intent is

   a. to persuade school boards to develop a Bible studies curriculum.

   b. to show that teaching religious faith in our schools should become a national imperative.

      c. to persuade religious moderates to denounce the bigotry of extremists' religious views and reclaim Scripture as the document of all.

      d. to show religious extremists and moderates that the Bible is too important to the history of Western civilization to leave out of a school curriculum.

3. The author's attitude is

    a. sarcastic.   **c.** sincere.

    b. condescending.   **d.** humorous.

4. The author's tone is one of

    a. anger.   **c.** concern.

    b. sadness.   **d.** sympathy.

5. The essay is mostly factual.

    a. True

    b. False, because_____

6. The author is biased toward the value of the Bible and its place in the school curriculum.

    a. True

    b. False, because_____

7. The author believes the Bible offers powerful arguments in support of both moderate and liberal causes.

    a. True

    b. False, because_____

8. What is the author's attitude toward publicly discussing politics and religion?

    _____

9. Is the essay mostly objective or subjective? Explain.

    _____

10. Explain how your own bias toward the subject may affect your reaction to the essay.

    _____

    _____

    _____

Vocabulary Check

Directions: Define the following words from the selection. The number in the parentheses is the paragraph in which the word appears.

1. nonsectarian (1) _____

2. landmark (2) _____

3. embroiled (3) _____

4. rebuked (5) _____

5. anointed (6) _____

6. evangelicals (8) _____

   _____

7. secularists (8) _____

8. agnostic (9) _____

9. imperative (12) _____

10. ceded (13) _____

Record the results of the comprehension and vocabulary checks on the Student Record Chart in the Appendix. Each correct answer is worth 10 points for a total of 100 points possible for comprehension and 100 points for vocabulary. Make certain you understand any reading or comprehension problems you may have had before going on.

PRACTICE C-3: A Controversy: Should Religion Be Separate from Government?

Directions: As you read the following selection, look for the author's thesis, supporting points, opinions, intent, attitude, and tone. How does this author's opinion of the Bible differ from the previous selection, "Teach, Don't Preach the Bible"?

GODS ARE CREATED IN OUR OWN IMAGE

RANDY ALCORN

1   Because religion has been an essential part of man's psychology, priests historically have wielded tremendous influence in affairs of state. The principle of keeping religion separate from government is a rather recent development in human history, and some folks haven't quite caught up yet.

2   There is growing pressure from some Americans to involve religion more deeply and directly into secular policy. Recently, we have seen Catholic bishops threatening to excommunicate Catholic politicians who, when conducting governmental duties, do not adhere to the tenets of their faith. We have seen an Alabama Supreme Court justice lose his job over his insistence on keeping the Biblical Ten Commandments displayed in stone in the lobby of that state's courthouse. We have seen the previous president of the United States exercising executive fiat to draw the church and government closer together to affect public policy.

3   Perhaps this atavistic behavior is to be expected. As soon as human creatures developed self-awareness they developed religions. Religion is man's way of explaining the mystery of his own existence, and reflects his own hopes and fears. The prehistoric talismans of plumply pregnant women represented the importance of female fertility and mirrored the overwhelming concern prehistoric man had for survival of

his species. The gods of ancient Egypt ruled over the annual cycle of Nile flooding so vital to food production. Matters of life and death have long been considered the province of the divine, so why shouldn't the divine be dictating the affairs of men on earth?

4   There are those who staunchly believe this should be so, and while it is the right of every human to believe in the religion of his or her choice, it's not the right of any human to dictate religious beliefs to, or interfere with the harmless behavior of, others. The consequences of governing with or through religion include such horrors as human sacrifice, mass murder, torture, and a variety of state-sanctioned persecutions and confiscations.

5   One of the vexing problems with religion is there are so many of them, and the followers of all these mythical explanations of existence unquestionably believe in the absolute truth of their particular explanation. Even within a particular religion, like Islam or Christianity, there can be a multitude of denominations and sects all devoted to a unique version of the "truth" that makes all others "infidels."

6   Christianity and Islam are founded on remarkably malleable, if not inconsistent, ancient documents. The Christian Bible has a curious capacity for contradiction frequently condoning and condemning the same behavior. Its variety of interpretations has not only provided the genesis of a multitude of sects and denominations, but has also proved useful in supporting conflicting positions on many issues. Quoting the Bible to support one's position becomes a form of verbal fencing that can even be amusing, except when it enters the arena of public policy: then it can become oppressive, even deadly.

Reprinted by permission of Don Addis

Don Addis. Reprinted by permission of the St. Petersburg Times.

7   The debate on marriage rights for homosexuals now swirls in the swill cooked up when religion becomes a primary ingredient in public policy. Christians in politics assert that their Bible clearly labels homosexuality as sin and an affront to God. Therefore government should not recognize or even permit legal matrimony between same-sex couples. Some good Christians don't want same-sex couples adopting and raising children for fear that the "unholy perversion" of homosexuality will be propagated among the innocent young. Have children been any safer in the care of Catholic clerics?

8   When religion infects government a nation can suffer some weirdly irresponsible public policy. Recall James Watt, interior secretary under President Reagan, who when questioned about the alarming depletion of natural resources, including clean water, forests, and topsoil, cavalierly responded that it didn't matter because Jesus is coming back soon anyway. Coming back to what?

9   Perverse notions of morality based on religion certainly are not peculiar to Christianity. Muslim terrorists interpret their religion's doctrine in a way that justifies mass murder and suicide, even of children. Nations ruled by theocracies or "holy" laws, such as Iran and Saudi Arabia, can in good conscience punish, persecute, even murder in the name of God. In nations brainwashed by religious dogma, what greater claim to legitimacy can those in power have than to be enforcing the will of God?

10   Why would the omnipotent creator of the universe require that fallible mortals record and enforce Its will? Why wouldn't God just come grab us by the lapels and say, "Listen buddy, this is what I want you to understand"? That would quickly silence the cacophony of religious opinions and eliminate the interpreters.

11   At the least, Christianity ought to retire the Bible as its doctrinal document and replace it with a primer, "The Essential Jesus Christ," containing only the profound fundamentals of moral behavior as Christ taught them. Then, there might be fewer opportunities for conveniently idiosyncratic interpretations of God's will.

12   Too many Christians are better at preaching what Christ practiced, than practicing what he preached. Christian doctrine affords an excuse for this failure—Christ, after all, was not mortal; he was a god divinely capable of perfect moral behavior. Mere mortals can never be. What an accommodating abrogation of responsibility.

13   But then, the Christian god has a divine plan that allows Its flawed human creatures to freely decide which myth is the correct one. Guess wrong and the loving Christian god condemns Its creatures to eternal torment. The notion that the creator of the vast infinite universe, with all its miraculous interconnectivity and perfect balance, now amuses Itself by playing a deadly game of cosmic Jeopardy with sentient creatures on some speck of a planet is accepted as reality by many folks, including some who hold power in our government.

14   The human capacity for mass delusion can never be underestimated. Five centuries ago, most people, following the dictates of religion, believed the Earth was the center of the universe. What nonsense passes as divine truth these days?

15   Gods are created in man's own image, not the other way around. Responsibility for determining morality is ultimately our own, not derived from or deflected to mythical deities. Religious beliefs are personal, and all the conversions to faith, forced or voluntary, do not make a myth a fact. In a free, rational nation with impartial justice for all, religious myths should not determine public policy.

Comprehension Check

Directions: Answer the following questions without looking back. Try to answer using complete sentences.

1. What is Alcorn's thesis or main point? _____

_____

_____

2. The author's attitude toward those who wish to inject religious beliefs into governmental policy can best be described as

   a. tolerant.

   b. bitter.

   c. angry.

   d. cautionary.

   e. negative.

3. T/F Alcorn's intent is to show how religion is humankind's way of explaining the mystery of its own existence.

4. Alcorn asks, "Matters of life and death have long been considered the province of the divine, so why shouldn't the divine be dictating the affairs of men on earth?" How would he answer his own question? _____

_____

_____

5. Which of the following reasons does Alcorn offer as a way of showing the growing pressure from some Americans to involve religion more deeply into civil policy?

   a. Catholic bishops threatening to excommunicate Catholic politicians who do not conduct their governmental duties according to Catholic beliefs

   b. An Alabama Supreme Court justice losing his job because he insisted on keeping the biblical Ten Commandments displayed in stone in the lobby of the state's courthouse

   c. The president of the United States using executive powers to pull the church and government closer together to affect public policy

   d. All of the above

   e. None of the above

6. What is Alcorn's opinion of the Christian Bible? On what does he base his opinion?

_____

_____

7. Reread paragraph 9. What is the intent of this paragraph? _____

_____

_____

8. Reread paragraph 14. What is the intent of this paragraph? _____

_____

_____

9. According to Alcorn, what are some of the consequences of governing with or through religion? _____

_____

_____

10. Alcorn says, "Gods are created in our own image, not the other way around." Explain what he means. _____

_____

_____

Vocabulary Check

Directions: Define the following underlined words from the selection.

1.   priests historically have <u>wielded</u> tremendous influence

_____

2.   <u>secular policy</u>

_____

3.   this <u>atavistic</u> behavior is to be expected

_____

4.   founded on remarkably <u>malleable</u>...ancient documents

_____

5.   a form of <u>verbal fencing</u>

_____

6.   will be <u>propagated</u> among the innocent

_____

7.   silence the <u>cacophony</u> of religious opinions

_____

8.   might be fewer...<u>idiosyncratic</u> interpretations

_____

9.   <u>abrogation</u> of responsibility

_____

10.   playing cosmic Jeopardy with <u>sentient</u> creatures

_____

Record the results of the comprehension and vocabulary checks on the Student Record Chart in the Appendix. Each correct answer is worth 10 points for a total of 100 points possible for comprehension and 100 points for vocabulary. Make certain you understand any reading or comprehension problems you may have had before going on.

Put It in Writing

Directions: Pick one of the following questions, write a response, and turn it in to your instructor.

1.   Of the two reading selections, "Shield Our Youth with Censorship" (page 231) and "Teach, Don't Preach, the Bible" (page 234), which author best supports his thesis? Support your answer with evidence from the reading selection.

2. How, if at all, have your opinions about the teaching of the Bible in public schools changed? What has either author said to change or support your opinion?

PRACTICE C-4: Timed Readings Comparing Two Authors

The next two reading practices offer opinions on the fate of newspapers. Editor and journalist Neil Morton argues that most people now get their news on the Internet and that newspapers are losing audience and influence. Arguing against this idea is Mark Briggs, an editor for the *Everett Herald*, a newspaper serving the northwest region of the state of Washington. Briggs believes that newspapers will continue to be indispensable. Time your reading on both practices.

An Argument against the Survival of Newspapers

Begin Timing: _____

ALL THE NEWS THAT'S FIT TO POST

NEIL MORTON

1   Growing up in Peterborough, Ontario (pop: 70,000), my parents, voracious readers, always had three newspapers delivered to their front door: the *Toronto Star*, the *Globe and Mail* (at the time, Canada's only national newspaper), and our local paper, the *Peterborough Examiner*.

2   This being the late '80s, meaning pre-web, the *Star* and *Globe* were my gateway to the outside world—to nearby Toronto, to Ontario, to Canada, to North America, to the rest of Planet Earth. My parents encouraged me to read them from cover to cover—"Not just the sports, Neil!"—and I did, including the Op-Ed pages on occasion.

3   As for the *Examiner* (for which, incidentally, novelist Robertson Davies served as editor and publisher in the 1940s, 1950s and 1960s), it was my resource for local politics (the heated planning board sessions were always exhaustively covered), entertainment (anything from local theater to bar fights that escalated into assault causing bodily harm charges) and sports, including the Ontario Hockey League's Peterborough Petes (and hey, once in a blue moon, me scoring 12 points to lead my Adam Scott Lions' b-ball senior team to victory).

4   Fast forward to 2002: My folks still turn to the papers as their primary source for news and analysis (they do go online, but it's primarily for email). Although I'll still buy a paper occasionally or grab one that's lying around the office (for Canadian news or a Canadian perspective on an international event), I don't turn to the papers much these days. For the most part, I rely on the Internet to let me know what's happening out there.

5   The *New York Times* on the Web, Slashdot, USAToday.com, Google News Headlines, NewScientist.com, Technology Review, Salon, CNN.com, Wired News, BBC.co.uk, Guardian Unlimited, Slate, LATimes.com, The Smoking Gun, PopBitch, Feed and Suck (when they were still alive and updating), the *Onion*, Modern Humorist and

an assortment of weblogs (Metafilter, Fark, Plastic, Shift.com's Filter section)—that's where I get my daily dose of news, analysis and humor.

6   I know many many others in their twenties, thirties and even forties who are in exactly the same boat.

7   So what does this all mean? Well, quite simply, it points to a significant shift—one that has many newspaper publishers squirming—away from papers as we know them. I fall in between the old and new vanguard of media in that I was raised on newspapers and am now weaning myself on the web, so I'm loyal to both. But a new generation is growing up on the net and for many of them, the print papers aren't even an option; even if they do read the papers, they tend to end up on the online version—adn.com, say, rather than the *Anchorage Daily News*—through a referral.

8   Newspapers have always been in the business of reporting news, breaking news, analyzing news, but now that job is done adequately, and with much more immediacy, on the Internet. For example, people flocked to the web in droves on 9/11 to learn everything they could about the disaster and to connect with others. Most of the print papers were light-years behind in their coverage of the biggest event of our generation—though some did put out special second editions that day, and of course their online versions were all over it.

9   Many 12- to 35-year-olds now view Salon and Slashdot as seminal news sources, news sources their parents likely haven't even heard of. With the net, now we go and find the news; editors and writers don't select the news for us. We go out and discuss various viewpoints on political events in threads and discussion boards rather than having them dictated to us by op-ed pages with their own agenda.

10   While many mainstream media outlets were feeding us their pro-U.S. version of the war in Afghanistan and American foreign policy, we could find blogs like Metafilter and Plastic discussing the flip-side of the coin and linking to superb articles at places like the *Guardian* that were giving us the Bigger Picture (for example, that the number of civilian casualties in Afghanistan has now overtaken the lives lost on 9/11).

11   There are countless other examples of what the web offers us that the print papers don't:

12   If you just couldn't get enough of the manslaughter trial of Boston hockey dad Thomas Junta, you could go to *Boston Globe* Online for expanded coverage. Similarly, for those that wanted more on the Gary Condit/Chandra Levy case last year, sites like WashingtonPost.com were the place to go. When Orlando Magic star Grant Hill went down with yet another season-ending injury late last year, hardcore basketball fans were able go online to get in-depth coverage of team—and community—reaction at OrlandoSentinel.com or ESPN.com. If you want to see celebrity divorce petitions for the likes of Pamela Lee, Janet Jackson and Michael Jordan, you can go to Smoking Gun.com.

13   The *Peterborough Examiner* has a tiny section called the Odd Spot on their cover page, which points to a ludicrous news story. Many other papers have similar sections. On the net, however, there's a gigantic and wonderful 24/7 Odd Spot at Fark. (For more info, take a look at Shift.com's recent profile of the blog.) Newspapers do a horrible job of covering videogames, now a mainstream phenomenon. On the Internet, there are plenty of webzines like GameCritics.com, Joystick101.org, RobotStreet Gang.com and Womengamers.com that are covering their cultural impact.

14   As a kid, I didn't have the option to turn to other sources for other viewpoints or peripheral information. I pretty much took as gospel what our national newspaper was saying. I thought the *Globe* was giving me 99 percent of the "news," but in truth, as I've discovered via the web, it's more like five to 10 percent of what's really going on. If I had had the choice to go online, I would likely have gravitated toward the Internet and away from the coffee table, like so many teens and young adults are doing now.

15   As cliché as it sounds, the world is your oyster on the net in the way it can never be in newspapers, which, by no fault of their own, have been overtaken by technology in the way radio was by TV.

16   Over the next 10 to 20 years—and this is a conservative estimate—newspapers will have to substantially re-invent themselves or they will perish. In some cases, maybe only the online version will exist; I already know many people—and this has to be considered a major concern among newspaper publishers—who used to buy or subscribe to a daily that now just check out the (free) online version. If the print version does survive, it will look much different—perhaps it will primarily be service-oriented, like a gigantic Life section or something.

17   Newspaper bigwigs are doing their strategizing behind closed doors, but they'll have to really have their thinking caps on. Soon, new wireless technologies will enable us to access the net whenever, wherever: in the kitchen, on the subway, on the toilet, at the cottage, in the car (an in-car web browser with text-to-speech synthesis can't be that far off), in the pool, at the Laundromat, at the hairdresser, on the treadmill. If I have the choice between reading a big clunky paper that leaves my hands stained with black ink and a portable Internet that offers insane amounts of legible news content and clean design, guess who's going to win out?

18   The web—still very much in its infancy but maturing rapidly as a new mass medium—is fast becoming the number one resource for news. It can disseminate information the way no other medium can. And that's where the next generation of Moms and Dads will be going with their morning cup of coffee.

Finish Timing: Record time here _____ and use the Timed Reading Conversion Chart in the Appendix to figure your rate: _____ wpm.

Comprehension Check

Directions: Answer the following questions without looking back.

1. Which of the following were Morton's sources of information in his youth?

    a. three newspapers

    b. television

    c. radio

    d. his hometown newspaper

2. T/F The author believes that people in their twenties, thirties, and forties get their news through the Internet rather than the newspaper brought to their doors.

3. T/F Morton's parents are gradually turning from the newspaper to the Internet.

4. T/F According to Morton, even if young people read newspapers, they do it on the Web.

5. T/F Most of the print papers are unable to keep up with the immediacy of current events as quickly as many sites on the Internet.

6. Which of the following are Internet sites Morton frequents?

    a. Salon

    b. Slashdot

   c. Metafilter

   d. Plastic

   e. BiggerPicture

7. T/F Many online newspapers, such as the *Washington Post* and the *New York Times*, offer expanded coverage on the Internet beyond what the print version offers.

8. T/F Morton admits that it will be a long time before the Internet offers what print papers do.

9. Morton bases his thesis mostly on

   a. facts.

   b. opinion.

10. What is the intent of the essay? _____

    _____

Vocabulary Check

Directions: Define the following underlined words from the selection.

1. fights that <u>escalated</u> into assaults

   _____

2. a Canadian <u>perspective</u> on an international event

   _____

3. an assortment of <u>weblogs</u>

   _____

4. Between the old and the new <u>vanguard</u> of media

   _____

5. as <u>seminal</u> news sources

   _____

6. which points to a <u>ludicrous</u> news story

   _____

7. there are plenty of <u>webzines</u>

   _____

8. would likely have <u>gravitated</u> toward

   _____

9. as <u>cliché</u> as it sounds

   _____

10. it can <u>disseminate</u> information

    _____

    _____

Record your rate and the results of the comprehension and vocabulary checks on the Student Record Chart in the Appendix. Each correct answer is worth 10 points, for a total of 100 points possible for comprehension and 100 points for vocabulary. Make certain you understand any reading or comprehension problems you may have had before going on.

An Argument for the Survival of Newspapers

Begin Timing: _____

VOX HUMANA

MARK BRIGGS

1   Television was supposed to kill the radio and the Internet was supposed to kill newspapers, so what happened? Most people today get some news from all four media, proving that Americans have an apparently insatiable appetite for news. More than 50 million newspapers will be delivered in the United States daily in 2001.

2   The past 100 years have seen great advancement at *The Herald*, and in newspapering in the United States. As we take time on *The Herald's* 100th anniversary to look back, it's also worth a glance forward. We may not be able to accurately predict how (some would say if) newspapers will progress to the year 2101, but we do know *The Herald* and other newspapers will be around for many years to come.

A NEWSPAPER'S CORE MISSION

3   Technology will obviously be the greatest influence of change in newspapering in the future. But no technological advancement will change *The Herald's* core mission: delivering timely, relevant, interesting and important news and advertising to Snohomish and Island counties. It will be the delivery of that news and advertising, however, that is likely to change the most through new technology.

4   Here's a look at where *The Herald* and the business of newspapering will travel during the next 100 years.

5   In five years: Currently, most newspapers publish a Web site that closely mirrors the printed newspaper. In 2006, there will be more reliance among readers on electronically delivered news content than today [2001].

6   The good news for readers is that news publishers will respond to this need, publishing their news for all kinds of wireless, digital and portable devices. The bad news is that the day of free content on the Web—or anywhere else in the wireless world—will have ended.

PAYING FOR CONTENT

7   News consumers will pay for content they receive—on the Web, on a cellular phone, on a handheld computer—but that content will be specifically tailored to their needs and tastes. The number of copies printed by news publishers will diminish, but the number of people who read the news and advertising will continue to grow.

8   Newspapers, TV stations and radio stations will have jettisoned their single-purpose identities and transformed into broad-reaching news companies. Internet and satellite radio will be common in new cars, forever changing the radio broadcast game in the same manner the World Wide Web altered the content publishing world in the late 1990s.

9   For newspapers, this will mean a new opportunity: to reach people in their cars. Newspaper reporters will routinely file audio reports of the stories they write for the paper. Around here, people will listen to *The Herald* in their cars and at work. We'll bring the newspaper to life.

10   In 10 years: The profession of news reporting became much more efficient with telephones, tape recorders and computers over the years. In the year 2011, the tools for news gathering will make the advent of the Internet look like the Stone Age.

11   Instead of a steno notebook and a pen, reporters will use a handheld, digital, wireless computer that will record interviews, shoot photographs, work as a cellular phone and connect to the Internet. This will be part of a 24-hour publishing cycle that will connect news consumers to the news.

12   With reporters wirelessly connected, readers won't have to wait for the morning paper to find out who won a high school football game or how the jury decided a big case. The morning newspaper will continue to be a valued product, however, since the immediacy of news consumption will not usurp the desire for great depth in news coverage.

CHANGING NEWSPRINT

13   In 20 years: Newsprint will evolve, finally, into a synthetically enhanced product that will look and feel just like the paper of the previous century. The Herald will install a new printing press that prints more efficiently on this new material.

14   The printing of newspapers will take only 20 percent of actual paper from trees. The rest will be manufactured out of a new-age plastic that is completely recyclable. To ensure the rate of recycling, *The Herald* will pick up old newspapers from subscribers' homes once a week, bringing the material back to the printing plant where the newspapers will be wiped clean and folded for reuse.

15   By cutting out the waste management companies in the recycling process, *The Herald* will dramatically increase the efficiency of the entire process. After years of electronic reader experiments that were supposed to doom the daily newspaper, subscriptions will increase dramatically with the introduction of this new synthetic "news-plastic."

A CENTURY FROM NOW

16   In 100 years: Will newspapers still exist in the year 2101? Yes, although you wouldn't recognize them today. Newsprint—and "news-plastic"—will be replaced by a reusable yet durable form of e-paper that will allow readers to "download" the new version of *The Herald* each morning as soon as they want it.

17   This e-paper will likely resemble today's newsprint: It will be flexible, foldable and very portable. Newspaper carriers will no longer go door-to-door each morning. Instead, they will deliver and service the electronic port machines that will receive and "print" the paper each morning. A subscription to *The Herald* will include this service.

18   The news will be gathered in fundamentally the same fashion, with professional reporters following leads, interviewing, researching and writing. It was essentially the same process in 1801, 1901 and today, in 2001, so there's no reason to think people won't desire well-reported, well-written and well-edited stories in 2101. The narrative story was with us long before newsprint, and it will remain with us long after.

19   Despite the challenges that newspapers have faced in recent years, including skyrocketing newsprint costs and massive mergers across the country, the newspaper is still the most respected source of news and information in the United States.

20   Will that ring true 100 years from now? Yes, but the process of printing the newspaper will change dramatically, and the ritual of walking out on the doorstep with a cup of coffee to pick up the morning paper will seem as antiquated as milk delivery on your doorstep seems today.

21   The year 2101 will be an even more wired world than the one we live in today, but *The Herald* will still be producing a product indispensable to those in and around Snohomish and Island counties.

Finish Timing: Record time here _____ and use the Timed Reading Conversion Chart in the Appendix to figure your rate: _____ wpm.

Comprehension Check

Directions: Answer the following questions.

1. T/F Most people today get their news from television, radio, newspapers, and the Internet.

2. T/F The core mission of a newspaper is to deliver timely, relevant, interesting, and important news and advertising.

3. T/F Only a few newspapers currently publish a Web site that closely mirrors the printed newspaper.

4. Which of the following does the author predict for the future?

   a. More people will rely on electronically delivered news.

   b. Free news content on the Web will end.

   c. The number of printed copies of newspapers will diminish, but the number of people who read news and advertising will continue to grow.

   d. Internet and satellite radio will be common in new cars.

   e. Newsprint will evolve into a synthetically enhanced recyclable product that will look and feel just like the present paper.

5. Briggs believes that in the year 2011, the tools for news gathering will make the advent of the Internet look like the _____

   _____

6. Instead of a steno pad and a pen, reporters of the future will use a

   _____

7. T/F In twenty years, newspaper companies will pick up old newspapers from homes once a week and recycle them, reducing the number of trees used for newsprint.

8. T/F Subscriptions to newspapers will increase in the next twenty years because of the introduction of a new synthetic "news plastic."

9. The "news plastic" will become outmoded in 100 years and be replaced by a durable but reusable form of _____ that will allow subscribers to download and print their paper each morning.

10. T/F In 100 years, newspapers will still be in demand because people have always wanted and always will want well-written and well-edited stories.

Vocabulary Check

Directions: Define the following underlined words from the selection.

1. have an <u>insatiable</u> appetite for news

   _____

2. a newspaper's <u>core</u> mission

   _____

3. more <u>reliance</u> among readers on electronically delivered news

   _____

4. will have <u>jettisoned</u> their identities

   _____

5. the <u>advent</u> of the Internet

   _____

6. will not <u>usurp</u> the desire for

   _____

7. reusable but <u>durable</u> form

   _____

8. the <u>narrative</u> story was with us long before newsprint

   _____

9. a product <u>indispensable</u> to readers

   _____

10. *vox humana*

   _____

Record your rate and the results of the comprehension and vocabulary checks on the Student Record Chart in the Appendix. Each correct answer is worth 10 points, for a total of 100 points possible for comprehension and 100 points for vocabulary. Make certain you understand any reading or comprehension problems you may have had before going on.

Practice C-5: Put It in Writing

Directions: Pick one of the following to write about and turn in your paper to your instructor.

1. Summarize the two essays you read in Practice C-4: "All the News That's Fit to Post" (page 242) and "*Vox Humana*" (page 246). Then explain which essay best expresses what you think is the future of newspapers.

2. Discuss your newspaper reading habits. Do you read a newspaper regularly? Do you read newsprint or online news? What information are you most interested in reading? What value do you find in the newspaper? Do you care about the future of the newspaper?

Questions for Group Discussion

1. Discuss Briggs's predictions regarding the technological changes he thinks will be made ten, twenty, and a hundred years from now.

2. As a group, discuss your various newspaper reading habits. How many of you read the newspapers regularly? How many of you don't read the newspaper? How many of you use the Internet as your source for news?

On Your Own

If you have access to a computer, do one of the following:

1. Go to http://www.onlinenewspapers.com.

2. Type "newspapers" into a search engine and explore the list of results.

3. Type the name of your local newspaper in a search engine and see if it has an online version.

D.   Putting It All Together

The next two reading selections provide practice in using what you have learned in this and previous chapters.

PRACTICE D-1 – TIMED READING

Directions: Read the following newspaper commentary. Because this selection appeared in a newspaper, you will notice many one- and two-sentence paragraphs. Apply what you have learned about reading, looking for the author's thesis, intent, attitude, tone, facts, and opinions. This is a timed reading. Try to read faster than your last timed reading rate without a loss in comprehension. Record your starting time and your finishing time.

Begin Timing: _____

TALK, NOT TORTURE GETS THE INFORMATION

MATTHEW ALEXANDER (written under a pseudonym for security reasons)

1   He was only 12 years old, but he knew how to sling invective.

2   "You Americans are infidels, and you deserve to die." A skinny kid with a black head of hair and soft brown eyes, Naji had been brought to the Iraqi prison where I

worked as an interrogator after his parents were killed. They died when the suicide bombers they'd been hosting blew themselves up to avoid being arrested. But Naji didn't yet know that he was an orphan, and he was furious at having been captured by the Americans.

3   Steve, one of a team of interrogators who worked for me, responded to the boy's tirade politely.

4   "Don't you think we're all just people and we need to get along?" Steve asked, speaking through our interpreter, Biggie. Naji, who's name I have changed to protect his identity, shook his head violently.

5   "No," Biggie translated. "You're all infidel pigs! I can't wait until I'm old enough to cut your heads off!"

6   There is more than one approach to extracting information from a captive. Interrogators are often encouraged to use threats and intimidation—and even harsher methods. But my small group of Air Force investigators, along with several military and civilian interrogators on my team, were committed to a different way. We believed that interrogation methods based on building a relationship and on intellectual engagement were far more effective than intimidation and coercion.

7   As I watched the interrogation from the monitoring room, Naji's invective seemed almost funny coming from such a scrawny kid. But it was a sign of how thoroughly he had embraced the Al Qaeda propaganda he had heard at home. We had to hope he was not the face of Iraq's future.

8   "Do you know who this is?" Steve asked, showing Naji a photo of Abu Musab Zarqawi, the leader of Al Qaeda in Iraq.

9   "Of course, that is Abu Musab Zarqawi. He is our hero."

10   "Your hero?"

11   "Of course! When we play, the tallest, biggest kid gets to be Zarqawi."

12   In response to Steve's probing questions, Naji proudly explained that his father was grooming him to be a mujahedin and a future leader of Al Qaeda. He also said that his father took him to important meetings.

13   A veteran interrogator the night before had told us we "should show the little punk who's in charge." This was the attitude of many of the old guard, the interrogators who had been at Guantanamo Bay and in Afghanistan and Iraq early in the war, when the "gloves were off." They mocked those of us who didn't imitate their methods of interrogation, which were based on fear and control. There was tremendous peer pressure to follow in their footsteps and not appear soft on our enemies.

14   We ignored the pressure. We believed that, particularly with a child, interviewing rather than interrogation got better results. Steve had been trained in interviewing children, and he used those skills with Naji, gently stroking the child's ego and noting that he must have been a very important boy to have attended meetings. Soon, Naji started rattling off places where meetings had taken place. He detailed who was at the gatherings, how many guns were stored at the houses, what was discussed and what plans were made. Naji talked because Steve was sympathetic and made him feel good.

15   From the information he provided, it was clear that Naji's father had been a mid- to high-level Al Qaeda leader with connections throughout Yousifiya and Al Anbar province. By the time the interview ended after an hour, Steve had filled up pages in his notebook with detailed information about Naji's father's network.

16   Back in our office, Steve and I marveled at all the intelligence Naji had provided—the names, the locations. He'd pinpointed the better part of Al Qaeda's operations around Yousifiya. In the two weeks that followed, our soldiers put this information to good use and took out a significant portion of Al Qaeda's suicide-bombing network in the area. For two weeks, violence dropped and many lives were saved.

17   During my time in Iraq, I personally conducted 300 interrogations and supervised more than 1,000. Naji was the most committed Al Qaeda member I met during that time. He and his father, who had clearly joined the group because they bought into the ideology, represented a very small percentage of the Sunni Iraqis. The overwhelming majority of Sunni Iraqis I interviewed joined for other reasons—economic need, to meet tribal obligations or, most common of all, to get protection from Shiite militias.

18   I interviewed Naji twice during the week after his first interview. By the end of his stay with us, after we had coddled him, ensured his comfort and treated him with affection despite his contempt for us, he started to warm up. By the day before he left, his vituperative speech had disappeared completely.

19   Good interrogation is not an exercise in domination or control. It's an opportunity for negotiation and compromise. It's a common ground where the two sides in this war meet, and it's a grand stage where words become giants, tears flow like rivers and emotions rage like wildfires. It is a forum in which we should always display America's strengths—cultural understanding, tolerance, compassion and intellect. But that's not how all interrogators see their role.

20   According to a recent report from the bipartisan Senate Armed Services Committee, "The abuse of detainees in U.S. custody cannot be attributed to the actions of a 'few bad apples' acting on their own." The effects of the policy that allowed torture to happen at Guantanamo Bay, the report concluded, spread to Iraq through the interrogators who had first been at Guantanamo. The preference for harsh interrogation techniques was extremely counterproductive and harmed our ability to obtain cooperation from Al Qaeda detainees. Even after the old guard interrogators were forced to play by the rules of the Geneva Convention, there was still plenty of leeway for interrogation methods based on fear and control. I believe their continued reliance on such techniques has severely hampered our ability to stop terrorist attacks against U.S. forces and Iraqi civilians.

21   We will win this war by being smarter, not harsher. For those who would accuse me of being too nice to our enemies, I encourage you to examine our success in hunting down Zarqawi and his network. The drop in suicide bombings in Iraq at two points in the spring and summer of 2006 was a direct result of our smarter interrogation methods.

22   I used to tell my team in Iraq: "The things that make you a good American are the things that will make you a good interrogator." We must outlaw torture across every agency of our government, restore our adherence to the American principles passed down to us and, in doing so, better protect Americans from future terrorist attacks.

Finish Timing: Record time here _____ and use the Timed Reading Conversion Chart in the Appendix to figure your rate: _____ wpm.

Comprehension Check

Directions: Answer the following questions without looking back.

1. Which best states the author's subject?

    a. Al Qaeda propaganda

    b. Zarqawi, leader of Al Qaeda in Iraq

    c. the abuse of detainees in U.S. custody

    d. proper interrogation techniques

2. What is the author's thesis?

_____

_____

3. T/F The author's thesis is based mostly on facts.

4. What is the author's attitude toward his subject?

   a. angry

   b. outraged

   c. annoyed

   d. troubled

   e. serious

5. Which of the following best states the overall tone of the selection?

   a. frustration

   b. apathetic

   c. morbid

   d. concerned

   e. sarcastic

6. Who is Naji? _____

_____

7. Which of the following are examples of figurative language?

   a. a grand stage where words become giants

   b. tears flow like rivers

   c. emotions rage like wildfires

   d. made him feel good

   e. gently stroking the child's ego

8. T/F The author personally conducted 300 interrogations and supervised more than a thousand.

9. T/F The author and his group of Air Force interrogators were pressured by those who had conducted interrogations in Guantanamo Bay and Iraq prisons to go more gently in their interviewing techniques.

10. What evidence does the author point to as support for his team's methods of interrogation? _____

Vocabulary Check

Directions: Define the following underlined words from the selection.

   1. knew how to sling <u>invective</u>

_____

   2. you Americans are <u>infidels</u>

_____

3. the boy's <u>tirade</u>

_____

4. his father was <u>grooming</u> him to be

_____

5. after we had <u>coddled</u> him

_____

6. his <u>vituperative</u> speech

_____

7. was extremely <u>counterproductive</u>

_____

8. bought into the <u>ideology</u>

_____

9. plenty of <u>leeway</u> for interrogation

_____

10. restore our <u>adherence</u> to principles

_____

PRACTICE D-2: Timed Reading

Directions: Read the following newspaper editorial. Apply what you have learned about reading, looking for the author's thesis, intent, attitude, tone, facts, and opinions. This is a timed reading. Try to read faster than your last timed reading rate without a loss in comprehension. Record your starting time and your finishing time.

Begin Timing: _____

WHAT'S ON TV TONIGHT? HUMILIATION TO THE POINT OF SUICIDE

ADAM COHEN

1   In November 2006, a camera crew from "Dateline NBC" and a police SWAT team descended on the Texas home of Louis William Conradt Jr., a 56-year-old assistant district attorney. The series' "To Catch a Predator" team had allegedly caught Mr. Conradt making online advances to a decoy who pretended to be a 13-year-old boy. When the police and TV crew stormed Mr. Conradt's home, he took out a handgun and shot himself to death.

2   "That'll make good TV," one of the police officers on the scene reportedly told an NBC producer. Deeply cynical, perhaps, but prescient. "Dateline" aired a segment

based on the grim encounter. After telling the ghoulish tale, it ended with Mr. Conradt's sister decrying the "reckless actions of a self-appointed group acting as judge, jury and executioner, that was encouraged by an out-of-control reality show."

3   Mr. Conradt's sister sued NBC for more than $100 million. Last month, Judge Denny Chin of Federal District Court in New York ruled that her suit could go forward. Judge Chin's thoughtful ruling sends an important message at a time when humiliation television is ubiquitous, and plumbing ever lower depths of depravity in search of ratings.

4   NBC's "To Catch a Predator" franchise is based on an ugly premise. The show lures people into engaging in loathsome activities. It then teams up with the police to stage a humiliating, televised arrest, while the accused still has the presumption of innocence.

5   Each party to the bargain compromises its professional standards. Rather than hold police accountable, "Dateline" becomes their partners—and may well prod them to more invasive and outrageous actions than they had planned. When Mr. Conradt did not show up at the "sting house"—the usual "To Catch a Predator" format — producers allegedly asked police as a "favor" to storm his home. Ms. Conradt contends that the show encourages police "to give a special intensity to any arrests, so as to enhance the camera effect."

6   The police make their own corrupt bargain, ceding law enforcement to TV producers. Could Mr. Conradt have been taken alive if he had been arrested in more conventional fashion, without SWAT agents, cameras and television producers swarming his home? Judge Chin said a jury could plausibly find that it was the television circus, in which the police acted as the ringleader, that led to his suicide.

7   "To Catch a Predator" is part of an ever-growing lineup of shows that calculatingly appeal to their audience's worst instincts. The common theme is indulging the audience's voyeuristic pleasure at someone else's humiliation, and the nastiness of the put-down has become the whole point of the shows.

8   Humiliation TV has been around for some time. "The Weakest Link" updated the conventional quiz show by installing a viciously insulting host, and putting the focus on the contestants' decision about which of their competitors is the most worthless. "The Apprentice" purported to be about young people getting a start in business, but the whole hour built up to a single moment: when Donald Trump barked "You're fired."

9   But to hold viewers' interest, the levels of shame have inevitably kept growing. A new Fox show, "Moment of Truth," in a coveted time slot after "American Idol," dispenses cash prizes for truthfully (based on a lie-detector test) answering intensely private questions. Sample: "Since you've been married, have you ever had sexual relations with someone other than your husband?" If the show is as true as it says it is, questions in two recent episodes seemed carefully designed to break up contestants' marriages.

10   There are First Amendment concerns, of course, when courts consider suits over TV shows. But when the media act more as police than as journalists, and actually push the police into more extreme violations of rights than the police would come up with themselves, the free speech defense begins to weaken.

11   Ms. Conradt's suit contains several legal claims, including "intentional infliction of emotional distress," for which the bar is very high: conduct "so outrageous in character, and so extreme in degree, as to go beyond all possible bounds of decency, and to be regarded as atrocious, and utterly intolerable in a civilized community."

12   Reprehensible as "Moment of Truth" is, it doubtless falls into the venerable category of verbal grotesquery protected by the First Amendment. The producers of "To Catch a Predator," however, appear to be on the verge—if not over it—of becoming brown shirts with television cameras. If you are going into the business of storming

people's homes and humiliating them to the point of suicide, you should be sure to have some good lawyers on retainer.

Finish Timing: Record time here _____ and use the Timed Reading Conversion Chart in the Appendix to figure your rate: _____ wpm.

Comprehension Check

Directions: Answer the following questions without looking back.

1. Which best states the author's subject?
   a. A televised arrest ending in suicide
   b. NBC's television program *Dateline*
   c. The First Amendment versus television censorship
   d. Television freedom
   e. Out-of-control reality television shows

2. Which best states the author's thesis or main idea about his topic?
   a. Some television shows intentionally go beyond the bounds of decency.
   b. The arrest of a suspect on the television series *To Catch a Predator* caused the suspect to commit suicide.
   c. The police often aid television producers in pursuing televised arrests.
   d. There is an ever-growing lineup of reality shows that appeal to an audience's worst instincts at seeing someone humiliated.

3. What is the author's attitude toward many reality television programs?
   a. favorable
   b. unfavorable

4. Which best describes the author's tone?
   a. humorous
   b. sarcastic
   c. serious
   d. playful
   e. angry

5. T/F The article is based mostly on supporting facts.

6. What is the author's opinion of the claims being made in Patricia Conradt's lawsuit?
   a. agrees
   b. disagrees

7. Which of the following are mentioned in the article?
   a. *The Apprentice*
   b. *The Weakest Link*

      c. *Moment of Truth*

      d. *To Catch a Predator*

      e. All of the above

  8. To whom is the author referring when he says "The producers…appear to be on the verge—if not over it—of becoming brown shirts with television cameras…storming people's homes…"? _____

  9. Why does the author believe the program *Moment of Truth* is deserving of censure?

      _____

      _____

  10. T/F The author believes that the police should not take part in reality television shows.

Vocabulary Check

Directions: Define the following underlined words from the selection.

  1. <u>allegedly</u> caught him

      _____

  2. cynical perhaps, but <u>prescient</u>

      _____

  3. humiliation television is <u>ubiquitous</u>

      _____

  4. depths of <u>depravity</u> in search of ratings

      _____

  5. prod them to more <u>invasive</u> actions

      _____

  6. the audience's <u>voyeuristic</u> pleasure

      _____

  7. a <u>coveted</u> time slot

      _____

  8. <u>First Amendment</u> concerns

      _____

  9. regarded as <u>atrocious</u>

      _____

  10. it doubtless falls into the <u>venerable</u> category

      _____

Be sure to record your rate and the results of the comprehension and vocabulary checks on the Student Record Sheet in the Appendix. Each correct answer is worth

10 points, for a total of 100 points possible for comprehension and 100 points for vocabulary. Understand any errors before you go on. Make certain you understand any reading or comprehension problems you may have had before going on.

Questions for Group Discussion

1. Discuss William Shannon's opinions about popular culture and its effects on youth (pp. 231–232). With what opinions do you as a group agree and disagree?

2. Discuss as a group your opinions about censorship. Is there a case for censorship? If so, under what circumstances?

3. Discuss Randy Alcorn's essay (pp. 237–239). On what issues does your group agree or disagree with Alcorn? Argue the pros and cons of Alcorn's last sentence.

4. As a group, see how many of you can use the following words in a sentence. Make certain you learn the ones you still may not be able to use or recognize by writing the definition in the blank space.

   a. escalated _____

   b. vanguard _____

   c. seminal _____

   d. ludicrous _____

   e. webzines _____

   f. disseminate _____

   g. insatiable _____

   h. usurp _____

   i. secular _____

   j. malleable _____

On Your Own

Pick ten new words you learned in this chapter, not necessarily those listed in question 4, and on a separate sheet of paper write a sentence for each word, using it correctly in context. Turn in the paper to your instructor.

ABOUT THIS READING

The web site *RateMyProfessors.com* has been online since 1999. It offers students from some 6,000 schools in the United States and elsewhere the chance to rate their teachers. The web site has generated a mix of reviews from students and teachers, yet it continues to expand in terms of the number of ratings it posts. Eric Strand was a graduate student in English at the University of California at Irvine when this article was published in the July 28, 2006, issue of *The Chronicle of Higher Education*.

Let's Sue

By ERIC STRAND

Class action: Professors, adjuncts, and graduate students of America vs. RateMyProfessors.com.

"Plaintiffs bring this action on behalf of themselves and others similarly situated, and allege upon personal knowledge and belief as to their own acts, that yellow smiley faces, green nonplussed faces, and blue frowning faces are not an accurate indicator of teaching ability, and that, moreover, defendant RateMyProfessors.com (hereafter RMP) has made a thankless task thoroughly unbearable."

A little extreme? Perhaps, but sometimes I really do feel like suing.

Make no mistake, my hands are not clean: I admit that every morning I go online to read the New York Post's Page Six gossip column, and then click over to the new evaluations on RateMyProfessors.com (the sites are basically equivalent). I'm still finishing my dissertation in English so I'm not yet on the job market. But I've decided that the site is a potential career liability, and even more important, largely detrimental to one's professional role as a teacher.

The obvious appeal of RateMyProfessors is its leveling quality—the way it gives a public voice to the student in the back row who has noticed that his Nobel-laureate professor wears mismatched

socks. One student claims, for example, that the once-innovative lectures of a certain luminary in the humanities are now like watching reruns of Leave It to Beaver.

There's something breathtaking about the way an entire oeuvre can be reduced to a flippant one-sentence dismissal, capped by a reference to a TV show that the student has probably only read about in a media-studies class.

At the same time that RateMyProfessors sends us all into the trough of the gossip column, the site also functions as the eggheads' substitute for Facebook or better yet, MySpace. I suspect that for academics who are slightly too old to have all their ex-classmates on those sites, RateMyProfessors is a way to "stay in touch," as it were, with old friends and enemies.

It's here that an aspect of my personality that I don't like very much is brought out—as per Thomas H. Benton's recent "The Seven Deadly Sins of Professors." My sin here is most definitely pride, and perhaps sloth as well. And now that I think of it, envy, greed, and lust—the whole shebang, basically, with some schadenfreude thrown into the mix.

My teaching career began well, or so I thought. I gave myself credit for being a direct, no-b.s. instructor, and tried to maintain a stress-free classroom. I gloried in the incandescent smiley faces that lit up on my RateMyProfessors profile: Not only am I enlightening America's youth, I thought, but for the first time in my life, I'm popular!

Over the next few months, however, a disturbing trend started to emerge. Students on the site began to remark on how easy I was as a grader. "It is easy to obtain an A; just follow the steps." Not good. In addition, I began to think that the frequent laughter in my class was not with me, but at me. "He's a bit strange with an awkward sense of humor."

I reached the nadir on a recent night when, tired of dissertating, I went online. Using the helpful "Last Rated" button, I trolled RateMyProfessors: Goodie, there were new evaluations, including a negative one of a teacher from another university who had turned me down for a date years ago. A student reviewer claimed that she was too demanding, chastised her for taking points off his perfectly decent essays, and concluded in gentlemanly fashion that she had a stick up her butt. I'll reserve comment here, except to say that my reaction fell under the heading of the eighth deadly sin named above.

I clicked over to my university's "Last Rated" page and received a shock: My own name was there. And, glancing at the "Overall Quality" column, I saw that my rating had dropped from 3.8 to 3.7—perilously close to "green face" territory. The review would not be a good one.

Steeling myself, I clicked over to the new evaluation: I was a "confusing" teacher, but made up for it by being such a pushover. "Grades really easy." And most glaring of all was the student's three-word assessment of my personality, put up on a Web site where anyone—adviser, gloating ex-friends, Oprah Winfrey—could see it: "Strange and awkward."

How effective am I as a teacher if my students can't think of any new words with which to slam me? What about "eccentric," or "clumsy and a bit daft"? Haven't they ever heard of a thesaurus?

For the next few minutes I paced my apartment, picking up my roommate's derelict box of Raisin Bran and smacking it back down on the counter, kicking the pillows on the couch and then guiltily fluffing them back up.

So that was it. I hadn't achieved after-the-fact popularity at all. No, I had replaced my role as class nerd with a creepier one: the guy who hung out at the edge of the parking lot who could get you stuff, opening his coat to reveal cheap B+'s. I was just a pushover—a weird pushover.

In short, my faith in the smiley faces had been shattered. One might argue that the way to deal with the scourge of RateMyProfessors is simply to overcome the deadliest sin, that of pride. After all, if the site is basically a popularity contest, then it involves a certain narcissism to pay so much attention to it.

But RateMyProfessors is viewed seriously or semi-seriously by important people and institutions. Our campus newspaper occasionally dismisses the site's importance but says that students should consult it when selecting courses. Last year a columnist on this site, Ivan Tribble, revealed that his department evaluates job candidates' blogs, and one wonders if clicking over to RateMyProfessors is also a convenient way to assess the "real person" behind jobseekers' facades.

Most stunningly, some instructors I know have been told that their ratings are read in order to track their performance.

If that's how it is, I thought, I better pay attention to this thing.

But I'm not sure evaluators and hiring committees should take the site seriously. To be sure, there are conscientious students who will note that a given teacher has done a good job of imparting knowledge. But more often the site seems to foster—and even enforce—a consumerist mentality, whose central maxims are that professors should:

• Entertain me.
• Grade more easily.

RateMyProfessors serves as a tool for students to punish teachers who resist that model of education. Of course, the same remarks might be made in the standard course evaluation forms that professors collect at the end of a semester. But with its frowning bloated-blue faces attached to comments, and a list of the funniest smackdowns that students have given to supposedly unbearable teachers, RateMyProfessors hypes that aspect of its service.

I suspect the main value of the site for students is how it makes dorm-room gossip about "easy" and "hard" classes public. Generally the magic number hovers around 2.8 on the site's 1-to-5 easiness scale (1 being extremely hard, 5 being very lax). A 2.4 grader is very likely to be judged a bad teacher, and conversely, teachers who are rated 3.0 or above tend to have chipper yellow smiles, despite their strange qualities and awkward moments.

Students can be quite brutal, especially to female instructors. But whether you're male or female, a bad rating can make you feel like hiding behind the podium, sometimes.

And I've now come to realize that those poor professors whom I chortled over were the brave ones. They weren't afraid to unsettle the students, and they weren't so concerned with whether the students liked them.

Meanwhile, I was a parasite: grading leniently and receiving smiling seals of approval, while tougher colleagues endured comments like "this arrogant hippie should not be teaching."

Henceforth, no more Mr. Nice Guy. Rate My Professors has created a teacher who is going to make sure his students sweat for their A's and B's. The hard-working students (and there are plenty of them) will not have a problem with that, but a few others will resent me and take revenge. And that's fine.

In fact, my new goal where RateMyProfessors is concerned is to have the sickly, sycophantic yellow smile beside my name change into a confident blue frown.

More fundamentally, it seems to me that as professionals, we should clarify just what our attitude toward the Web site should be. Given the way its anonymous brigands can exacerbate the problems of grade inflation and student consumerism, it seems that hiring committees, course supervisors, and fellow instructors should largely discount the site as a source of information. The other alternative, as far as I can see, is to adopt the angry-consumer model ourselves. Class action anyone?

ANALYZE THIS READING

1. The writer uses humor and sarcasm, directed both at himself and at students, throughout this article. In what ways is humor effective and in what ways does it detract from his concern with how students evaluate him on *RateMyProfessors.com*?

2. What is the chief complaint the writer discusses in his view of *RateMyProfessors.com*?

3. Who are the "brave" professors the writer refers to? Why does he admire them?

4. While the writer concludes on a humorous note, calling for a lawsuit against *RateMyPro-fessors.com*, and given the writer's position in life, what is the serious concern beneath this humor?

RESPOND TO THIS READING

1. What opportunities do you have to evaluate your teachers? What changes, if any, would you make to these opportunities?

2. Should *RateMyProfessors.com* be used by hiring committees when they evaluate job applicants for teaching positions? Explain.

3. The writer surmises that the appeal of *RateMy-Professors.com* is the leveling of power relations that occurs between student and teacher. To what extent is this leveling valuable? To what extent should a traditional student-teacher relationship be maintained?

ABOUT THIS READING

While this argument is aimed at teachers, the writer's ideas about grading will resonate with many students. These ideas look at teachers' grading policies through categories of accuracy, fairness, and effectiveness. Douglas B. Reeves is chairman of the Leadership and Learning Center, a consulting firm in Englewood, Colorado, and author of more than 20 books on leadership and education. This article appears in the September 18, 2009, issue of *The Chronicle of Higher Education*.

Remaking the Grade, from A to D

By DOUGLAS B. REEVES

TRY THE FOLLOWING EXPERIMENT at your next faculty meeting. First ask, "What is the difference between those *students* who earn A's and B's and those *students* who earn D's and F's?"

You will hear a litany of responses including work ethic, organization, high-school preparation, and class attendance.

Next ask your colleagues to calculate the final grade for a *student* whose 10 assignments during

Reprinted by permission of Douglas Reeves.

the semester had received the following marks: C, C, MA (missing assignment), D, C, B, MA, MA, B, A. Then calculate the distribution of the final grades.

I've done that experiment with more than 10,000 faculty members around the world and, every time, bar none, the results include final grades that include F, D, C, B, and A. It turns out that the difference between the *student* who earns A's and B's and the one who earns D's and F's is not necessarily a matter of work ethic, organization, high-school preparation, or class attendance. The difference is the professor's grading policy.

Now change the scene from the faculty meeting to a crisp fall day in the football stadium. As the afternoon shadows fall on the goal posts, a pass is thrown to a receiver who lunges for the ball and tumbles into the end zone. One official signals a touchdown, the second official signals an incomplete pass, and the third official scratches his head in bewilderment. Faculty members, *students*, alumni, and trustees rise as one, complaining bitterly of the unfairness and incompetence of athletics officials who seem unable to view the same *student* performance and make a consistent judgment.

Professorial prerogatives notwithstanding, we ought to have a standard for grading policies that at least rises to the basics we expect of officials on the athletics field: accuracy, *fairness*, and effectiveness. Professors are typically granted wide latitude to establish and enforce grading policies within certain boundaries. It is not acceptable for faculty members to make mathematical errors in grading or routinely award grades that reflect gender or racial bias. But many grading policies often fall short of the three basic standards:

Accuracy. The first great assault on accuracy is the use of the zero on a 100-point scale. If the grade of A represents a score of 90-100, B is 80-89, C is 70-79, and D is 60-69, then the interval between each letter grade, A to B to C to D, is 10 Points. But if a *student* fails to submit an assignment and receives a zero, then the interval

from D to zero is 60 points, a sixfold penalty compared with the other grading intervals.

Let us stipulate that work receiving a D is wretched, and that the failure of a *student* to submit work at all is abysmal. The use of the zero, however, requires us to defend the proposition that abysmal is six times as bad as wretched. *Students* who fail to turn in work deserve a punishment that fits the crime; perhaps they should be required to do the work, suffer constraints on their free time, or be denied Facebook and Frisbee privileges. But should they lose an entire semester of credit, which can be the ultimate impact of receiving zeros for missing assignments, because of an irrational and mathematically incorrect grading policy? Even Dante's worst offenders were consigned to the ninth—not the 54th—circle of hell. Poets, it seems, understand interval data better than professors in the hard sciences do.

The use of the arithmetic mean, or average, to calculate final grades—often the consequence of computerized grading technologies—is another offense against accuracy in grading. I have reviewed math standards in more than 100 countries and noticed that most *students* understand early that the average is not necessarily the best way to represent a data set. They understand alternative representations, including the mode, median, and weighted averages, to name a few. They learn that politicians and marketers, among others, will use averages in taxes, employment, and income to mislead voters and consumers. But a decade later, as 19- and 20-year-olds, they are sitting in college classes in which grading policies worship at the altar of mathematical accuracy—engineering, statistics, French literature, educational psychology (the similarities in grading policies can be eerie)—and the use of the average is pervasive.

I've taught graduate statistics courses in which mathematicians are seated next to nurses, teachers, marketers, and biologists. My task was not to evaluate where they started but where they finished. For some of them, multivariate analysis was a recent memory, while for others, high-school algebra was a distant and painful one. The mathematicians soared at the start of class but were challenged a month or two later; their colleagues struggled to remember the basics of algebra at first, but reached their "Now I get it" moments during the final days of the class. They argued quite persuasively that the professor should not use the average of their scores to calculate their final grade, but rather should consider their proficiency at the end of the term. I worried, however, that the same graduate *students* and instructors who argued against the average in that class would return to their own *students* and, within a few hours, casually apply the average to calculate final grades.

Fairness.   While I would not automatically extrapolate my research findings to other settings, the results are sufficiently alarming to invite introspection. I have found that faculty members sometimes conflate quiet compliance with proficiency. That sends the message to *students*— female *students* in particular—that the path to success is acquiescence rather than achievement.

My observation comes first from a simple analysis of the membership of the National Honor Society. In the high school where I volunteer, the gender balance of the *student* body is equal. Yet the ratio of women to men in the National Honor Society in this high school is eight to one. I have checked hundreds of coeducational institutions since that observation and found all of them to have a female-to-male advantage. A gender imbalance is also found in the college-matriculation rate of women to men: 58 percent to 42 percent, respectively. I've lost enough debates with women to stipulate that it may be true that they are smarter than men, but I doubt that they are eight times as smart. Some other factor is at work here, and it may be the societal value that elevates behavioral submission over academic performance.

I also analyzed the results of *students* who received A and B grades but failed external examinations in literacy and math. Those *students* were disproportionately female and self-identified as ethnic minorities. A cynic might label this the "bless her heart" effect, as in, "She really isn't very proficient, but bless her heart, she showed up every day, participated in class, and didn't give me any trouble."

That may not apply to your *student* body, but I would ask only that you find out if the dropout and failure rates of your *students* are equally distributed by gender and ethnicity. If not, it is at least possible that *students* were lured into the challenge of your institution based upon rewards for quiet compliance, and that then they were punished for not having the skills required for college-level work. Conversely, some minority male *students* may have never reached the front door of your institution because, as high-school *students*, they were not rewarded for academic proficiency but punished for abrasive behavior that was unrelated to academic performance.

The most perplexing part of unfair grading policies is that they are rarely intentional. I know of no college or school system that has an affirmative-action policy to secure more bigots and sexists on the faculty. On the contrary, the "bless her heart" effect (pronoun very deliberate) stems not from malice but from compassion.

Effectiveness.   Finally, we should consider whether the impact of grading policies has led to improved *student* performance. A basic question that faculty members must ask is, "Were my *students* last semester more engaged, responsive, and successful than *students* in previous years?" If the answer is "yes," then present grading policies are fine. I am astonished, however, at the number of professors who complain loudly that *students* are disrespectful, inattentive, disengaged, and unresponsive—and yet who wish to pursue the same grading policies they have used for a decade or more.

Fortunately, the solution to the quandary of effective grading practices is close at hand. On the athletics field, I've never seen a coach with a grade book and red pencil, yet I have witnessed many a coach who provides feedback designed to improve performance. Similarly, I've noticed, while watching the conductor of the collegiate orchestra or chorale lead a rehearsal, how infrequently quizzes and tests are administered and how rarely grades are awarded. Instead, the conductor frequently provides feedback for the singular purpose of improving *student* performance.

The Class of 2013 grew up playing video games and received feedback that was immediate, specific, and brutal-they won or else died at the end of each game. For them, the purpose of feedback is not to calculate an average or score a final exam, but to inform them about how they can improve on their next attempt to rule the universe.

Imagine a class in any other subject, from science to classics, conducted in the same way. The *students* wail, "Does it count?" and the professor responds, "I'm just giving you feedback to improve your performance—try to do better next time" I have never heard *students* thank their Nintendo machine for its insightful feedback, but I have observed many of them respond more attentively to those machines than to their professors.

Now is the time to make modest but important improvements in grading policy. Without leave of administrators or permission from grading-system programmers, professors can stop the use of the zero. They can suspend the use of the average. They can override the deterministic mentality that drives so many grading systems and provide regular feedback designed to help students actually learn. They can, in brief, be accurate, fair, and effective. It is no more than our *students* demand of athletics contests and video games. As teachers, we should do no less.

ANALYZE THIS READING

1. What point does the writer make when comparing teachers to athletic officials?
2. In the section on "Accuracy," why does the writer consider the grade of zero to be "irrational and mathematically incorrect"? Describe the problem with using the average of test scores to determine a final grade. With what should this average be replaced?
3. In the section on "Fairness," what concern does the writer have with "behavioral submission and academic performance"? What dangers are associated with this concern?
4. Describe the writer's position on feedback in the "Effectiveness" section.
5. Identify the writer's claim and warrant.

The Problem with Performance Pay

It can work—but only if performance is broadly defined and all parties agree to the plan.

By DONALD B. GRATZ

A new round of interest in performance *pay* has been growing for the past decade, as more states and districts have introduced mandates related to the push for ever-higher standards. This year [2009], President Obama and U.S. Secretary of Education Arne Duncan have included performance *pay* among their goals for education. At the 2009 National Education Association (NEA) convention, Secretary Duncan urged *teachers* to support performance *pay*, noting that although "test scores alone should never drive evaluation, compensation, or tenure decisions," not including student achievement in *teacher* evaluation is "illogical and indefensible" (ASCD Educator Advocates, e-mail communication, July 18, 2009).

Definitions of *teacher* performance *pay* take different forms. For example, many districts *pay* experienced *teachers* to mentor new *teachers*, serve as curriculum specialists or in similar posts, or teach in inner-city schools. The most common and controversial proposal is to *pay teachers* on the basis of their students' standardized test scores. It turns out, however, that test-based *pay* is more useful politically than it is effective educationally.

Reprinted by permission of the Association for Supervision and Curriculum Development and Donald Gratz dgratz@curry.edu.

Although few contemporary plans built on student test scores have lasted, this lack of success has not slowed proposals for more such plans. Given the growing prevalence of performance *pay*, it is worth exploring its history and assumptions.

A Not-So-Stellar Story

Education performance *pay* stretches back hundreds of years. In the mid-1800s, British schools and *teachers* were paid on the basis of the results of student examinations, for reasons much like today's. After more than 30 years, however, the testing bureaucracy had burgeoned, cheating and cramming flourished, and public opposition had grown dramatically. The practice was abandoned as a failure.

In 1907, Edmond Holmes, Great Britain's chief education inspector, described schooling in the era of test-based performance *pay* as the *teacher* engaged "in laying thin films of information on the surface of the child's mind, and then, after a brief interval, in skimming these off in order to satisfy himself that they have been duly laid" (Nelson, 2001, p. 386). Holmes referred to this kind of recall as being "the equivalent of food which its recipient has not been allowed to digest" (p. 386).

In 1918, 48 percent of U.S. public school districts described their payment systems as "*merit* based." But "*merit*" was subjective: White men were paid more than minorities and women, a disparity that eventually fueled a movement toward a uniform *pay* scale. Two years after women won the vote, the first uniform *pay* plans appeared in Denver, Colorado, and Des Moines, Iowa. By the 1950s, only 4 percent of U.S. school districts described themselves as *merit* based (Murnane & Cohen, 1986; Protsik, 1996).

There were brief attempts to implement performance-based *pay* in the early 1960s after Sputnik, and again when President Nixon launched an experiment with "performance contracting," which ended in cheating scandals and failure. In the early 1980s, when A Nation at Risk alarmed citizens with the prospect of "a rising tide of mediocrity" threatening to engulf U.S. schools, President Reagan reintroduced experiments with *merit pay*, with similarly negative results. Some school districts experimented through the 1980s with incentive programs based on *merit*, management by objectives, and career-ladder or differentiated staffing approaches. Few such experiments had any staying power. A new wave of experiments developed in the 1990s, most of which were also based on career ladders, *teacher* skills and knowledge, or differentiated staffing.

A New Approach Emerges

In 1999, the Denver, Colorado, school board and *teachers* association jointly sponsored a *pay* for performance pilot based largely on student achievement. As head of the outside research team for the first half of the pilot, I can attest to the energy and commitment with which the joint labor-management design team approached the task.

Although the pilot was successful and teachers in pilot schools supported it, designers saw that measures of student performance were still inadequate, that connections to *teacher* performance were hard to establish, and that standard measures of student learning were not applicable to more than half of the *teachers*—including gym, art, and music *teachers*; media specialists; special educators; and so forth. The model didn't address incentives for *teachers* to work in difficult situations and didn't include the contributions that many *teachers* make in support of their schools, younger colleagues, students, and their students' parents.

A much broader assessment of *teacher* performance was needed to capture the breadth of the *teacher's* role (Gratz, 2005). After four years and substantial effort, *teachers* and administrators collaborated to produce a new plan that the board, *teachers*, and voters ultimately approved. In the process, Denver expanded its definition of performance.

Denver's groundbreaking professional compensation plan replaces the traditional "steps and lanes" approach to compensation, in which *teachers* receive annual "step" increases as well as "lane" increases if they earn additional degrees. Only one of the new plan's four components directly addresses academic achievement goals—and that one is based significantly on *teacher*-set objectives, not just standardized test scores. In addition to student academic growth, the plan addresses *teacher* skill and knowledge, professional evaluation, and market incentives—compensating *teachers* who work in hard-to-serve schools or in hard-to-staff positions.

The Flawed Logic of Most Plans

Although today's performance *pay* plans take many forms, the most commonly proposed version—in which *teachers* are rewarded on the basis of their students' standardized test scores—flows from flawed logic and several troublesome assumptions.

Assumption 1: Teachers Lack Motivation

If we believe that additional *pay* will motivate *teachers* to work harder, we must also believe that *teachers* know what to do to improve student achievement—and that they aren't doing it because they aren't sufficiently motivated. The assumption is that they must value financial rewards more than student success.

Does anyone really think that large numbers of *teachers* know what their students need but are willfully withholding it? That they would help students learn more, if only someone offered them a bonus to do so? This is a highly cynical view of *teachers*, one that *teachers* understandably find demeaning, not motivational.

Most *teachers* care about their students and want them to succeed. Why else enter the profession? But although presenting information may be simple, successful teaching is more complex. Some *teachers* could certainly do a better job, but they mostly need mentoring, support, supervision, and training in new techniques—plus opportunities to learn, grow, and take on additional responsibilities—just like the rest of the workforce.

Assumption 2: Schools Are Failing

The broad call by state and national leaders for performance *pay* and other "reforms" is based on the widespread presumption that U.S. schools are failing. Schools have been labeled "in crisis" since the

1800s, but this designation has usually been more political than real. Schools were blamed for letting the I USSR's Sputnik "beat us into space" in the 1950s, for economic collapse in the 1980s, and for economic inequality in the early 2000s. U.S. students are accused of lagging behind their peers in other countries, and a wide range of reports over the past two decades has predicted economic disaster in the future because, the reports claim, today's students are unprepared for work and will not be productive.

In fact, the United States had a satellite nearly ready to launch in the 1950s, but kept it under wraps because of its anticipated use in spying. Explorer I was launched just four months after Sputnik. The downturn of the 1980s, for which schools were often blamed, was followed in the 1990s by the longest period of sustained growth in history, for which schools received little credit.

As for the failure of U.S. students to measure up to their foreign counterparts, this is largely not the case. Rather, as many researchers have shown, the test score gap often results from comparing older or more select students in other countries with a broader range of U.S. students and from confusing test scores with achievement (Bracey, 2005; Mathews, 2008; Rotberg, 2008).

In fact, although poor results on specific tests make headlines, U.S. students compare well with their international peers on many tests, and U.S. workers excel in measures of economic success, such as creativity and innovation. Further, test scores don't correlate with economic success. The countries whose students outscore their U.S. peers do not have stronger economies or more productive citizens. Worker productivity in the United States soared in the 1990s and has remained high.

Schools make an easy target, but school change moves too slowly to affect short-term economic cycles. It takes at least 12 years for a restructured K-12 curriculum to produce its first newly trained students. So, although an educated workforce is important, schools have little effect on economic cycles. Fortunately, schools have not yet been blamed for the current economic debacle.

It's true, of course, that we have some very troubled schools in the United States—mostly in large, bureaucratic districts and mostly serving poor children and children of color. By one estimate, the majority of failing schools in the United States are found in only 29 districts (T. W Slotnik, personal communication, July 10, 2008), suggesting that these districts need improvement at the school and district leadership levels, not just among *teachers*. Despite the existence of troubled schools and districts, however, most students achieve more academically now than in past decades, and most parents give their schools high marks and support them (Bradshaw & Gallup, 2008).

Assumption 3: Measuring Academic Achievement Is All That Counts

The third assumption—the most perilous for the United States—is that standardized test scores accurately measure student academic achievement and that academic achievement constitutes the full range of goals we have for students. However, beyond basic academic skills, corporate leaders have consistently cited the need for critical thinking, problem solving, teamwork and collaboration, communication skills, and a good work ethic as the keys to worker success. And because there is more to life than work, most citizens want children to learn about art, music, and other aspects of civilization; to explore and develop their own skills and talents; and to become good neighbors and active, productive citizens.

Look for the megacompanies that control standardized testing to produce new tests that claim to measure all these attributes—but don't believe them. If we want students to develop as well-rounded human beings who are empathetic, thoughtful, and creative, we will have to include these characteristics among our goals for schools and seek ways to gauge our success. A system that rewards schools, students, and *teachers* only for test scores will get mostly test scores. This is not what most of us want for our children.

The Upside

The most promising aspect of the current discussion is the surprising extent to which district leaders, corporate leaders, and *teachers* unions are recognizing that they have common interests—

interests that include accountability, expanded professional responsibility, and improvements in teaching conditions. Many parties are coming to see the value of higher and differentiated *pay*, and although we must carefully consider the specifics, the potential for change that benefits both *teachers* and students is real.

Denver's pilot has helped to demonstrate some of the possibilities. In an increasing number of districts, *teachers* who teach in hard-to-serve schools, such as those in inner cities, or in hard-to-fill positions, such as advanced physics, may earn additional *pay*. *Teachers* who mentor younger *teachers*, develop components of the curriculum, or take on other specialized duties may also earn more. Such *pay* doesn't insult *teachers*. Instead, it provides experienced *teachers* with the opportunity to learn, grow, and support their colleagues—critical opportunities in all professional fields to keep people refreshed and engaged.

Denver's plan also involves *teachers* in setting objectives for their own students, an approach that engages both their professional judgment and interest. Such opportunities have often been missing from teaching in the past.

Beyond Denver, it is also promising that some larger districts, often with outside technical assistance, are using performance *pay* as a catalyst for fundamentally changing how they do business—reorganizing their processes around their goals for their students and how best to reach them.

Defining Performance

Finally, it is crucial that the discussion of performance *pay*—which requires districts to develop a new definition of performance—leads states and districts, including Denver, to a new consideration of their true goals for their students. An exclusive focus on academic achievement is a relatively new idea in U.S. education. Thinkers like Thomas Jefferson and Ralph Waldo Emerson did not expect schools to teach all children the same facts over an extended 12-year period. Rather, they believed that schools should provide individual students with basic skills and tools for learning so these students could pursue their particular goals and find their own place in society.

This requires a national discussion. Do we want a world of critical thinkers or a world of test takers? Do we care about citizenship, civic engagement, and the ability to work with others? Do we value the arts and humanities? Do we want each child to develop his or her individual talents and abilities? If so, how do these goals fit into our definition of student and *teacher* performance? How do they align with No Child Left Behind?

Until we can answer these kinds of questions—until we determine the breadth, depth, and individual scope of student achievement that is worth pursuing—paying for performance will not produce the results we want for our children or our society.

Test-based *pay* is more useful politically than it is effective educationally.

The discussion of performance *pay* requires states and districts to develop a new definition of performance.

A system that rewards schools, students, and *teachers* only for test scores will get mostly test scores.

ANALYZE THIS READING

1. How does the Denver approach to performance pay differ from earlier approaches?

2. What is the major flaw in the assumption that teachers must be compensated monetarily because they lack motivation?

3. How does the writer counter the assumption that American schools are failing?

4. According to the writer, what is problematic about assuming that academic achievement is all that matters in terms of student performance? How does the Denver plan better accommodate expanding definitions of "performance"?

RESPOND TO THIS READING

1. While the issue of performance pay for teachers occurs in the context of our public schools, should performance pay plans be extended to public colleges and universities? Explain.

2. How were you evaluated as a student before entering college? What were the strengths and weaknesses of this kind of evaluation?

3. Do you agree with the writer's call for an expanded definition of "performance"? What would you add to or delete from the writer's recommendations for his revised definition?

References

Bracey, G. W. (2005, October). 15th Bracey Report on the condition of public education. *Phi Delta Kappan, 87*(28), 138–153.

Bradshaw, W. J., & Gallup, A. M. (2008, September). Americans speak out: Are educators and policy makers listening? *Phi Delta Kappan, 90*(10), 7–31.

Gratz, D. B. (2005). Lessons from Denver: The pay for performance pilot. *Phi Delta Kappan, 86*(8), 569–581.

CHAPTER THREE

Recognizing Inferences, Drawing Conclusions, and Evaluating Arguments

A.   Recognizing Inferences

All the skills you have been practicing in this unit are a basis for making critical judgments. You have been learning to recognize an author's attitude, intent, tone, and bias. Here's another important aspect of reading critically: recognizing **inferences**. An inference is a conclusion or an opinion drawn from reasoning based on known facts or events. For instance, when people smile we infer that they are happy. We base our inference on the fact that most smiles are from happiness or pleasure. A frown, we know from experience, generally means displeasure or pain. Thus, when someone frowns, we infer that the person is displeased. Our inferences are based on experience and/or knowledge. In his famous book *Language in Thought and Action*, S. I. Hayakawa defines an inference as "a statement about the unknown made on the basis of the known."

Drawing inferences is something we do every day. For instance, if you met a woman wearing a large diamond necklace and three platinum rings with rubies and pearls, you would no doubt infer that she is wealthy. You may not be right; the jewelry could belong to someone else or it could be fake. But because we know from experience that the type of jewelry she is wearing is expensive, it is natural to assume she is wealthy. It's a good educated guess based on experience and knowledge. Without experience or knowledge, however, any inferences we make are based on shaky ground.

Complete the following statements by drawing inferences from what is known in each case:

1. We may infer from a boy's crying and a melting ice cream cone on the ground that the boy ___ice cream fell._____

   _____

2. We may infer from a woman's grease-stained hands and fingernails that she probably has been __working with_____

   _____

3. We may infer from the many whitecaps on the ocean that sailing would be _____
   ___difficult_____

4. We may infer from the way a man threw his food on the floor and refused to pay the restaurant bill that he was ___outraged_____

   _____

5. We may infer from an F grade on a test that we ___didn't study._____

   _____

Let's look now at some of the possible inferences. In item 1, we can assume that the boy dropped his ice cream cone; however, we don't know for a fact that this is what happened. Someone may have knocked it out of his hands, or even thrown it at him. But based on the circumstances described, a good inference to draw is that he dropped it and is unhappy.

In item 2, we can infer that the woman has been working on something mechanical, such as an oily engine. Because we know that our hands and fingernails get greasy from such work, it's a good inference to make.

The circumstances in item 3 lead us to believe that sailing conditions might be rough, because whitecaps are caused by strong winds. However, a good sailor might like the conditions and think of it as a challenge. Of course, if you have never been around the sea, whitecaps might provide no information for drawing any kind of inference.

The man in item 4 might be angry, drunk, or "high" on something. We might further infer that he didn't like the food, didn't get what he ordered, or hated the service. Most of us don't make a habit of throwing our food on the floor and making a scene, so we can infer that something is greatly upsetting him to act this way.

In item 5, we probably infer that we failed. But is that technically an inference? The F grade is a symbol for failure. No inference need be drawn. But *why* did we fail? Maybe we didn't study hard enough, misunderstood the directions, or studied the wrong material; the test was a poor one; or the instructor made a mistake.

Drawing inferences while we read critically is no different from the kind of thinking done in the preceding examples. For example, read the following passage and then answer the questions that follow.

> If we compare college textbooks of just two decades ago with those of today, we see a dramatic decrease in the number of words, vocabulary level, and specificity of detail, but a sharp increase of graphics and, particularly, illustrations. Such textbook pictures can scarcely convey as well as words the subtle distinctions that emerge from scholarly or scientific work.

1. What is being compared in this paragraph? _____

_____

2. What inference can be drawn about the author's attitude toward college textbooks today? _____

_____

3. What inference can be drawn about today's college students? _____

_____

Notice that the first question has nothing to do with inference, but it reminds you that in order to read critically you also have to use literal comprehension skills. The paragraph contrasts college textbooks of today with those published twenty years ago. In order to draw inferences, you have to understand that first. The answer to question 2 is that the author's attitude is negative. We can infer that because of the last sentence of the paragraph. The answer to question 3 is that today's college students' reading levels are probably lower than they were twenty years ago. Because of the decrease in words, lower vocabulary level, and more pictures, we can infer that today's students don't read as well. However, we could also infer that publishers are merely changing their way of publishing, but chances are that's not the author's intent here.

Here's a passage taken from a short story. Read it and answer the questions that follow.

> In walks these three girls in nothing but bathing suits. I'm in the third checkout slot, with my back to the door, so I don't see them until they're over by the bread. The one that caught my eye first was the one in the plaid green two-piece. She was a chunky kid, with a good tan and a sweet broad soft-looking

can with those two crescents of white just under it, where the sun never seems to hit, at the top of the back of her legs. I stood there with my hand on a box of HiHo crackers trying to remember if I rang it up or not. I ring it up again and the customer starts giving me hell. She's one of those cash-register-watchers, a witch about fifty with rouge on her cheekbones and no eyebrows, and I know it made her day to trip me up. She'd been watching cash registers for fifty years and probably never seen a mistake before. (From John Updike, "A & P" from Pigeon Feathers and Other Stories, Knopf, 1962. Reprinted by permission of the author and Alfred A. Knopf, a Division of Random House, Inc., Copyright © 1962.)

Based on the information provided, answer the following questions by drawing inferences:

1. How old and what sex is the narrator or person telling the story? What makes you think so? _____ He is a Male, _____

   _____

2. Where is the story taking place? _____

   _____

3. People in bathing suits coming into the place where the narrator is working is not an everyday occurrence.

   a. True, because _____

   _____

   b. False, because _____

   _____

4. The narrator is not distracted by the girls.

   a. True, because _____

   _____

   b. False, because _____

   _____

5. The narrator is very observant.

   a. True, because _____

   _____

   b. False, because _____

   _____

As we find out later in the story, the answer to question 1 is "a nineteen-year-old male." But we can guess from the passage that the narrator is male because of his reaction to the girls, because of the language he uses, and because of his comments about the "witch about fifty" who catches his mistake. The tone has a youthful, informal quality about it.

In question 2, it's not too difficult to infer that the story is taking place in a supermarket of some type, probably a grocery store. He is working at a checkout slot ringing up HiHo crackers, and he comments that the girls were "over by the bread" before he saw them. These are clues to us.

The statement in question 3 is probably true, making the statement in question 4 false. He is distracted by the girls. No doubt girls come into the store all the time, but in this case they are wearing "nothing but bathing suits," making this an unusual event. It causes him to forget whether he has already rung up the crackers.

The statement in question 5 is true; he is very observant. His description of the one girl and the "cash-register-watcher" are full of details, reflecting an observant person.

The word *critical* often connotes finding fault with something. But making valid critical judgments, in its strictest sense, implies an attempt at objective judging so as to determine both merits and faults. Critical reading is thoughtful reading because it requires that the reader not only recognize what is being said at the literal level but also distinguish facts from opinions; recognize an author's intent, attitude, and biases; and draw inferences. A reader who is not actively involved is not reading critically.

PRACTICE A-1: Drawing Inferences

Part A

Directions: An inference, remember, is "a statement about the unknown made on the basis of the known." Complete the following statements, drawing inferences from what is known.

1. We may infer from the smile on the professor's face as he passed back the exams that ___everybody did well on the test.___

2. We may infer from the large turnout at our college orientation session that _class_
   ___of freshmen___

3. We may infer from the fact that a student in a college English class is consistently late for class that ___He dosen't know his time management skills___

4. We may infer from the number of Academy Awards a movie won that _____
   ___it has good acting or plot.___

5. We may infer from the extreme thinness of some current models and actresses that
   ___they have to keep up a public image.___

Part B

Directions: Read the following passages and answer the questions that follow.

1.   The word *concerto* originally meant a group of performers playing or singing together, as "in concert" or making a "concerted effort" of entertaining. The Gabrielis of sixteenth-century Venice called their motets, scored for choir and organ,

concerti ecclesiastici. Heinrich Schultz, a seventeenth-century German composer, titled his similar works *Kleine geistliche Konzerte.*

a. What is the intent of this paragraph? _____

_____

b. T/F The German word *Konzerte* probably means "concerto."

c. T/F We can infer that the author probably knows some history of music.

2.   He had a direct and unassuming manner and a candid way of speaking in a soft Minnesota voice. The interviewer rushed right in with questions, but he turned all the questions around and wanted first to know some things about the interviewer. She had a hard time getting the conversation centered on him until he was ready. He was a bright, insightful man who seemed oblivious to his genius.

a. What words best describe the man in the preceding passage? _____

_____

b. T/F The man is important or famous.

c. T/F The interviewer was impressed with this man.

d. T/F We can infer that the man is talkative and open.

3.   Infer as much as you can from each of the following statements:

a. The evening has proved to be most entertaining. I extend my deepest appreciation. _____

_____

b. Tonight's been a real blast! Thanks a bunch. _____

_____

c. Like, I mean, funwise, this night has blown me away, babe. _____

4.   There are all kinds of rumors about Ed Cantrell. Some say he can ride a horse for days without eating and still bring down a man at a thousand yards with a rifle. Some say he is almost deaf from practicing every day with a .38. Others say he can quote long passages from Hemingway's novels. And still others claim he has the eyes of a rattlesnake and faster hands. Most all who know him claim he is the last of the hired guns.

a. What is Ed Cantrell's occupation?

_____

b. T/F Based on the rumors, most people seem to admire him.

c. T/F Cantrell probably lives somewhere in the Western states.

d. What can we infer about Cantrell if it is true that he can quote long passages from Hemingway's works? _____

_____

e. Why would a man such as Cantrell be interested in Hemingway's works?

5.   During the Middle Ages, many scholars regarded printed books with apprehension. They felt that books would destroy the monopoly on knowledge. Books

would permit the masses to learn to improve their lives and to realize that no man is better than another. And not too long ago, slaves were strictly forbidden to learn to read and had to pretend that they were illiterate if they had learned how. Societies based on ignorance or repression cannot tolerate general education.

a. T/F The first sentence is fact.

b. What is the author's attitude toward education? _____

_____

c. What is the intent of the statement? _____

_____

PRACTICE A-2: Recognizing Inferences

Directions: Read the following passages and answer the questions that follow.

1. "Social science" in cold print gives rise to images of some robot in a statistics laboratory reducing human activity to bloodless digits and simplified formulas. Research reports filled with mechanical sounding words like "empirical," "quantitative," "operational," "inverse," and "correlative" aren't very poetic. Yet the stereotypes of social science created by these images are, I will try to show, wrong.

    Like any other mode of knowing, social science can be used for perverse ends; however, it can also be used for humane personal understanding. By testing thoughts against reality, science helps liberate inquiry from bias, prejudice, and just plain muddleheadedness. So it is unwise to be put off by simple stereotypes—too many people accept these stereotypes and deny themselves the power of social scientific understanding. (From Rodney Stark, *Sociology*, 2nd edition, Wadsworth, 1987, p. 28.)

    a. The author's intent in this passage is to _____

    _____

    b. T/F We can infer that the author feels that some of his readers have a negative attitude toward social science.

    c. T/F The author believes strongly in the scientific method of inquiry.

    d. T/F The author is probably a social science teacher.

2. On July 10, 1985, the following events worth reporting occurred around the world:

    — An Israeli court convicted fifteen Jewish terrorists of murder and violence against the Arabs.
    — Bishop Desmond Tutu, Nobel laureate, pushed himself through an angry mob to save an alleged police informer from being burned alive.
    — An Iraqi missile struck and heavily damaged a Turkish supertanker.
    — A ship photographer was killed when a Greenpeace protest ship was blown up in New Zealand.
    — The Nuclear Regulatory Commission (NRC) was accused of not properly considering earthquake hazards at the Diablo Canyon, California, atomic energy plant.
    — Numerous major fires in Northern California burned more than 300,000 acres of forests and destroyed many homes.

Yet the lead story of the day on two of the three major American television news broadcasts that evening had to do with the Coca-Cola Company's decision to return to its original formula after experimenting with a new taste that few seemed to like. Even the country's major newspapers featured the Coke story on their front pages at the expense of more newsworthy events. The headline of the *Denver Post*, for example, stated, "'The Real Thing' Is Back." In addition, a six-square-inch picture of a can of Coke in two colors appeared next to the column.

a. The intent of the passage is to _____

_____

_____

b. T/F The passage is mostly opinion.

c. T/F The author feels that the type of news reporting described reflects an erosion of values in our society.

d. T/F The author of the passage would probably agree with this statement: Coca-Cola has become a national institution of sorts and what it does is of interest to almost all Americans.

e. State the author's attitude toward the reporting he describes. _____

_____

3.   The United States Atomic Energy Commission, created by Congress in 1946, grew into a uniquely powerful, mission-oriented bureaucracy. One of its main goals, which it pursued with exceptional zeal, was the creation of a flourishing commercial nuclear power program.

By the late 1950s, the AEC began to acquire frightening data about the potential hazards of nuclear technology. It decided, nevertheless, to push ahead with ambitious plans to make nuclear energy the dominant source of the nation's electric power by the end of the century. The AEC proceeded to authorize the construction of larger and larger nuclear reactors all around the country, the dangers notwithstanding.

The AEC gambled that its scientists would, in time, find deft solutions to all the complex safety difficulties. The answers were slow in coming, however. According to the AEC secret files [obtained through the Freedom of Information Act], government experts continued to find additional problems rather than the safety assurances the agency wanted. There were potential flaws in the plants being built, AEC experts said, that could lead to "catastrophic" nuclear-radiation accidents—peacetime disasters that could dwarf any the nation had ever experienced.

Senior officials at the AEC responded to the warnings from their own scientists by suppressing the alarming reports and pressuring the authors to keep quiet. Meanwhile, the agency continued to license mammoth nuclear power stations and to offer the public soothing reassurances about safety. (From Daniel Ford, *The Cult of the Atom: The Secret Papers of the Atomic Energy Commission*. New York: Simon & Schuster, 1982). Copyright © 1982, 1984 by Daniel Ford. Reprinted by permission of Simon & Schuster, Inc.)

a. The intent of the passage is to _____

_____

b. Describe the author's attitude toward the AEC. _____

_____

c. T/F The passage is mostly opinion rather than factual.

d. T/F We can infer from the passage that the author is probably not worried about the number of atomic energy plants that have been built and are being built.

e. T/F The author implies that the AEC placed its own commercial desires over the safety of the American people.

f. What is your reaction to this passage and why? _____

_____

4.　　Futurists generally assume that twenty-first-century medicine will include new and more powerful drugs and technologies to fight diseases. They tend to forget, however, the serious problems presently arising from conventional medication prescribed by the average doctor. According to 1987 statistics, the average American receives 7.5 prescriptions per year. This is even more frightening when we realize that many people have not been prescribed any medication at all. This means that someone else is getting *their* 7.5 medications.

Most drugs have serious side effects, some quite serious. Since the sick person is often prescribed several drugs at the same time, there is often unfavorable reaction or illness from the drugs themselves. Studies also show that 25 to 90 percent of the time, patients make errors when taking their prescribed drug dosage. Despite the respect that people generally have for present-day doctors, there doesn't seem to be equal confidence in the treatments they prescribe because 50 percent of the time people do not even get their prescriptions filled.

Homeopathic medicine (using natural means to help the body build immune systems) offers an alternative. Instead of giving a person one medicine for headache, one for constipation, one for irritability, and so on, the homeopathic physician prescribes one medicine at a time to stimulate the person's immune system and defense capacity to bring about overall improvement in health. The procedure by which the homeopath finds the precise substance is the very science and art of homeopathy. (From Dana Ullman, "Royal Medicine," *New Age Journal*, September/October 1987, p. 46.)

a. The intent of the passage is to ___inform you that___ ___homeopathic is better than prescription medicine.___

b. T/(F) The author's attitude toward conventional doctors and homeopathic doctors is equal.

c. (T)/F The passage is mostly opinion.

d. (T/F) We can infer from the passage that the author is biased against homeopathic medicine.

e. T/(F) The author implies that many patients do not trust or want to take the medications prescribed by their doctors.

f. Would you be willing to go to a homeopathic doctor rather than a conventionally trained physician? _____ Explain. ___I would because there usualy are___ ___

_____

_____

_____

B.   Recognizing Inferences and Facts

When inferences are based on facts, much useful information can be obtained. Scientists and historians, to name a few, have been able to infer from facts and observation most of the knowledge we have today. The following passage is based on fact, with many inferences that are probably true. As you read, note the inferences and the facts.

1   Nine hundred years ago, in what is now north-central Arizona, a volcano erupted and spewed fine cinders and ash over an area of about 800 square miles. The porous cinder layer formed a moisture-retaining agent that transformed the marginal farmland into a country of rich farmland.

2   Word of this new oasis spread among the Indians of the Southwest, setting off a prehistoric land rush that brought together the Pueblo dry farmers from the east and north, the Hohokam irrigation farmers from the south, and probably Mogollon groups from the south and east and Cohonino groups from the west. Focal points of the immigrants were the stretches of land lying some 15 miles northeast and southeast of the volcano, bordering territory already occupied by the Sinagua Indians.

3   Nudged out of their now-crowded corner by the newcomers, some of the Sinagua moved to the south of the volcano to a canyon that offered building sites and a means of livelihood. Here they made their homes.

4   Remains of the Sinagua's new homes, built in the early 1100s, are now preserved in Walnut Canyon National Monument; the cone of the benevolent volcano, in Sunset Crater National Monument; and part of the focal points of the immigrants, in Wupatki National Monument. (From the brochure *Walnut Canyon*, 1968-306-122/97, revised 1982, Superintendent of Documents, Washington, D.C.)

Now answer these questions.

1. T/F Paragraph 1 is mainly fact rather than inference.
2. T/F The first sentence of paragraph 2 is inference.
3. T/F The information in the last sentence of paragraph 2 is based on inference.
4. T/F Paragraph 3 is mostly inference.
5. T/F Paragraph 4 is mostly inference.
6. T/F Chances are that someday this information will prove to be in error.

The answer to question 1 is false; it's mainly inference based on facts or evidence that when put together leads scientists to believe that the events described happened eight hundred years ago. We have no way to prove that the eruption occurred as stated, yet scientists basically agree that this is what did happen.

The statements in questions 2 and 3 are true. Again, no one was around to verify these statements, but the inference that it happened can be made from present-day evidence.

While the statement in question 4 is basically true, at least the first part, the last part is fact because the remains are still there to see. The statement in question 5 is false, because all statements can be verified by visiting the places mentioned.

The statement in question 6 is false; it's possible, but highly unlikely because of present-day facts and remains. However, in the future, this might be a "slippery fact," like the atom's being thought of as the smallest particle at one time. But based on all the known facts we have at present, the best answer is false.

You can see that much of what we call "fact" today is based on inferences. When scientists agree on inferences that are drawn from what is known, we tend to accept as fact their conclusions until more evidence shows that the inferences drawn were wrong.

The following practices will help you recognize the difference between facts and inferences.

PRACTICE B-1: Drawing Inferences from Facts

Directions: Read the following passages and answer the questions that follow.

1. The unit that is used to measure the absorption of energy from radiation in biological materials is the rem, usually abbreviated R. It stands for "roentgen equivalent in man." There is a unit called the rad, which corresponds to an amount of radiation that deposits 100 ergs of energy in one gram of material. The rem is defined as the radiation dose to biological tissue that will cause the same amount of energy to be deposited as would one rad of X-rays.

   A millirem (abbreviated mrem) is one thousandth of a rem. To give some idea of the size of the things we are discussing, you get about 1 mrem of radiation from a dental X-ray, about 25 mrem of radiation from a chest X-ray. Since the average dose of radiation to the average American is about 360 mrem, it is not hard to see that it would be very easy to absorb in medical and dental X-rays more radiation than one absorbs from natural causes.

   The "average" dose of radiation, of course, varies as much as 150 or so mrem per year depending on where one lives. For example, in Colorado and Wyoming the average mrem dose is about 250 per year, while in Texas the average dose is 100 mrem. It is higher in the mountains because there is less air to shield us from cosmic rays and because there are more radioactive elements in the soil.

   According to federal requirements in effect, the radiation dose at the fence of a nuclear plant can be no more than 5 mrem per year. We can see that based on the average dose most of us receive, living near a nuclear plant offers relatively little dosage risk.

   a. The intent of this passage is to _____

   _____

   _____

   b. T/F The first paragraph is mostly factual.

   c. T/F Living in higher altitudes is safer from radiation doses than living at sea level, based on the information in the passage.

   d. T/F We can infer that the author is opposed to nuclear power plants.

   e. T/F The last sentence in the passage is factual.

2. In the 1980s, in an ebullient bid to curtail drunk driving by teenagers, the government imposed a nationwide minimum drinking age of 21. It was a kind of second Prohibition, albeit for young adults only. The law's goal, of course, was to make young people happier, healthier, and safer.

   By now it is obvious that the law has not succeeded in preventing the under-21 group from drinking. The popular press and higher-education media are filled with reports of high-visibility, alcohol-related troubles on our campuses. Serious riots by students who want to do their boozing unhindered have broken out at many institutions. Some of the melees, such as those at Ohio University, the University of Colorado, and Pennsylvania State University, have involved significant injuries and many arrests.

Reports of binge drinking come from all types of campuses across the country. In 1992, researchers reported that more college students were drinking to get drunk than their counterparts a decade earlier, and one recent study reported an increase, just since 1994, in the number of students who drink deliberately to get drunk. Of particular pertinence, in another national study, Ruth Engs and Beth Diebold of Indiana University and David Hanson of the State University of New York at Potsdam reported in 1996 in the *Journal of Alcohol and Drug Education* that, compared with those of legal age, a significantly higher percentage of students under age 21 were heavy drinkers.

Worst of all are the reports of drinking-related deaths. In 1997, at least two fraternity pledges died of alcohol poisoning, and in 1995 a third choked to death on his own vomit, all after initiation-night parties. One informal survey of alcohol-related deaths among college students during 1997 turned up 11 more fatalities: Three students fell from dormitory windows, one darted into the path of a motorcycle, one fell through a greenhouse roof, another was asphyxiated, and five died in highway crashes. At Frostburg State University, seven students were charged with manslaughter in 1997 in connection with the death of a freshman who guzzled beer and 12 to 14 shots of vodka in two hours at a fraternity party.

American's second experiment with Prohibition seems to have been no more effective than the first one. (From Document X3010 2152230, Opposing Viewpoints Resource Center, Gale Group, 2003. http://www.galenet.com/servlet/OVRC.)

a. The intent of this passage is to _____

_____

b. T/F The passage is mostly factual.

c. T/F We can infer that the author believes the legal drinking age should be lowered from 21.

d. T/F We can infer that the author believes the drinking age of 21 has driven college students to partying less in public and into more dangerous places.

3.   To understand the debate over global warming, it is important to understand the scientific concept known as the greenhouse effect. The greenhouse effect is a natural phenomenon involving the interaction of the sun's energy with atmospheric gases. After the sun's energy, or solar radiation, enters the atmosphere, the earth absorbs most of it while the rest is reflected back into space. Atmospheric gases, known as greenhouse gases, absorb a portion of this reflected energy. The energy trapped by these gases warms the planet's surface, creating the greenhouse effect. This natural process keeps Earth's atmosphere warm enough to support life. However, as the amount of greenhouse gases in the atmosphere increases, so too does the amount of heat they absorb: Global warming is the result.

The atmospheric concentrations of greenhouse gases have increased dramatically in the past century. Concentrations of carbon dioxide (CO_2), the primary greenhouse gas, have increased 30 percent, according to the Intergovernmental Panel on Climate Change (IPCC), a group of about 2,000 scientists from

116 countries assembled to address the problem of climate change. Concentrations of the other main culprits, methane and nitrous oxide, have risen 145 percent and 15 percent, respectively. At the same time, the average atmospheric temperature has also risen between 0.3 and 0.6 degrees Celsius. Most scientists agree that human activity is the cause of the rise in greenhouse gases, which are in turn responsible for global warming. Thus, in its definitive 1995 report, the IPCC concluded, "The balance of evidence suggests that there is a discernible human influence on global climate." (From Document X3010101223, Opposing Viewpoints Resource Center, Gale Group, 2003. http://www.galenet.com/servlet/OVRC.)

a. The intent of this passage is to _____

_____

b. T/F The passage is mostly factual.

c. T/F We can infer that the author is concerned with the increase of greenhouse gases in the atmosphere.

d. T/F We can infer that the author agrees with scientists who claim that human activity is the cause for the increase of global warming.

4. From the seller's viewpoint advertising is persuasion; from the buyer's viewpoint it is education. No single group of people spends as much time or money per lesson to educate the masses as do the creators of ads.

Ads participate in a feedback loop. They reflect a society they have helped to educate, and part of the advertising reflection is the effect of the advertising itself. Every ad that exploits a personality hole educates the audience toward using a particular product to fill that hole. Just as drug ads teach a crude and sometimes dangerous form of self-medication, psychosell ads teach a form of self-analysis and cure for psychological problems.

An ad that stirs a hidden doubt, that causes a person to ask, "Why does no one love me?"; "Why don't I have more friends?"; "Why am I lonely?" invariably goes on to suggest a partial cure—use our product. If an announcer for Pepsi would appear on screen and say:

> Are you lonely? Do you feel left out? Do you sometimes feel that everybody else has all the fun in life? Are you bored and isolated? Well, if you are, drink Pepsi and find yourself instantly a part of all those energetic, joyful, young-at-heart people who also drink Pepsi.

Such an ad would be greeted as either laughable or insulting by the viewing audience. Yet the old "Pepsi generation" campaign used pictures and a jingle to make exactly such a point.

The danger in psychosell techniques is not that people might switch from Coke to Pepsi in soft-drink loyalties or abandon Scope for Listerine. The danger is that millions learn (especially if the message is repeated often enough, as ads are) that problems in self-acceptance and boredom can be alleviated by corporate products. Which brand to buy is secondary to ads as education; the primary lesson is that the product itself satisfies psychological needs. (From Jeffrey Schrank, *Snap, Crackle and Popular Taste: The Illusion of Free Choice in America*, Delacorte, 1977.)

   a. What is the intent of the author? _____

_____

   b. Is the passage primarily fact or opinion? _____

Explain. _____

_____

   c. T/F The author thinks ads may be silly and repetitive, but basically harmless.

Explain. _____

_____

   d. T/F The author believes that some advertising is a dangerous form of education because it brainwashes us into thinking we can solve many of our personal problems by buying corporate products.

Explain. _____

_____

   e. T/F The author's bias is easy to identify.

Explain. _____

_____

PRACTICE B-2: Drawing Inferences from Descriptive Passages

Directions: Read the following passages and answer the questions that follow.

1.   Daddy's genial voice sometimes traveled slowly through sentences, shaping each syllable correctly. He was polishing the skin of a second language. He would come to speak it much more eloquently than most people who grew up speaking only English. Sometimes he slipped Arabic words into our days like secret gift coins into a pocket, but we didn't learn his first language because we were too busy learning our own. I regret that now.

    When someone else who spoke Arabic came to visit us, their language ignited the air of our living room, dancing, dipping and whirling. I would realize: all those sounds had been waiting inside our father! He carried a whole different world of sounds—only now did they get to come out! (From Naomi Shihab Nye, "Wealthy with Words," *The Most Wonderful Books*, Milkweed Editions, 1997, p. 193.)

   a. T/F We can infer that the author's father's first language was Arabic.

   b. T/F We can infer that her father learned to speak English well.

   c. T/F We can infer that the author did not like the sound of Arabic being spoken.

   d. T/F The author is bilingual.

   e. What do you infer about the author's view of language? _____

2.   My van (and the passage of nearly 200 years) had made my journey both faster and easier than theirs. For much of their journey west—as they fought the Missouri's relentless current for its entire 2,400-mile length, then trudged through the snowy Bitterroot Range—Lewis and Clark would have defined substantial progress as making 12 miles a day. Shooting down the Snake and Columbia Rivers in their dugout canoes for the final stretch must have seemed like hyperdrive, although in fact it only increased their speed to 30 or 40 miles per day. No wonder it took them a year and a half to reach Cape Disappointment. Allowing plenty of time for unhurried stops and side trips, my camper covered the same distance in 60 days.

Needless to say, I also hadn't suffered the hardships the Corps of Discovery routinely faced: backbreaking toil, loss of a comrade to illness, encounters with enraged grizzlies, near-starvation in the ordeal across the Bitterroots, demoralizing coastal rains that rotted the clothes on their backs, and so much more. They had been making history; I was merely retracing it. (From Dayton Duncan, "American Odyssey," *Land's End Catalog,* July/August 2003.)

a. T/F We can infer that the author followed the same route as the Lewis and Clark expedition in the early 1800s.

b. T/F We can infer that the author admires what the Corps of Discovery went through.

c. T/F The author feels proud of himself for having retraced the Corps of Discovery's route in only sixty days.

d. What do you infer about the author, based on this passage? _____

_____

3.   With that thought in mind, I raised my head, squared my shoulders, and set off in the direction of my dorm, glancing twice (and then ever so discreetly) at the campus map clutched in my hand. It took everything I had not to stare when I caught my first glimpse of a real live football player. What confidence, what reserve, what muscles! I only hoped his attention was drawn to my air of assurance rather than to my shaking knees. I spent the afternoon seeking out each of my classrooms so that I could make a perfectly timed entrance before each lecture without having to ask dumb questions about its whereabouts.

The next morning I found my first class and marched in. Once I was in the room, however, another problem awaited me. Where to sit?...After much deliberation I chose a seat in the first row and to the side. I was in the foreground (as advised), but out of the professor's direct line of vision.

I cracked my anthology of American literature and scribbled the date on the top of the crisp ruled page. "Welcome to Biology 101," the professor began. A cold sweat broke out at the back of my neck. (From Evelyn Herald, "Fresh Start," *Nutshell* magazine, 1989.)

a. Where can we infer that the event described in the passage is taking place?

_____

How can you tell? _____

_____

b. T/F The narrator telling the story is female. Explain. _____

_____

c. T/F We can infer from the author's tone that the author has a sense of humor. Explain. _____

_____

d. Why did the author break out in a cold sweat when the professor greeted the class? _____

_____

e. T/F We can infer that the author is not trying to conceal her true feelings. Explain. _____

_____

C.   Drawing Conclusions Using Induction and Deduction

A big part of critical reading is being able to draw conclusions based on the information authors provide. Once you understand the thesis or main idea of a reading selection, recognize fact from opinion, and understand intent, attitude, and inference, you almost automatically draw conclusions of your own. In fact, some of the questions you have been answering in the preceding practices require drawing conclusions based on the evidence provided.

Drawing conclusions is based on making **reasoned judgments**. Reasoned judgments usually come from two basic methods of reasoning: **deductive reasoning** and **inductive reasoning**. Deductive reasoning occurs when you begin with a general statement of truth and infer a conclusion about a particular specific. For instance, the old standby definition of deductive reasoning is shown through a **syllogism**, a three-step statement that begins with a general statement recognized as a truth and moves to a specific statement:

> All humans are mortal.
> Britney Spears is a human.
> Therefore, Britney Spears is mortal.

Deductive reasoning is the subject of formal logic courses and involves a process of stating a series of carefully worded statements, such as the example just given, each related to the other statements. Deductive reasoning begins with a generalization:

> All dogs are animals.   *or*   Athletes are physically strong.

The next statement identifies something as belonging (or not belonging) to that class:

> _____ is a dog.

What would be a second statement for the athlete generalization?

_____

For the first example, you should have given the name of a dog you know or a famous dog. For example, Lassie is a dog. For the second statement, you should have named an athlete. "Lance Armstrong is an athlete" would be one example.

The third statement of deductive reasoning is the inference you arrive at if the first two statements are true:

All dogs are animals.	Athletes are physically strong.
Lassie is a dog.	Lance Armstrong is an athlete.
Lassie is an animal.	Lance Armstrong is physically strong.

Fully understanding deductive reasoning takes a lot of study but, for the purpose of this introduction, you should be aware that you start with a generalization and use a careful reasoning process to arrive at a conclusion.

You can make errors with deductive reasoning if you start with faulty generalizations or premises. If you started with the generalization that "all college students have high IQs," you would be starting with a false premise. Some college students have high IQs; others may be conscientious workers with average IQs.

Inductive reasoning works in the opposite way of deductive reasoning. With inductive reasoning, you begin with observing specifics and draw a general conclusion. You might move to a new town and notice that every time you see police officers they are wearing bright green uniforms. After seeing no police officer wearing anything other than this color, you might inductively reason that in this particular town the official police uniform is bright green.

Inductive reasoning is often used when you can't examine all the data but need to come to conclusions based on what you know. Political polls do this when they look at some voters and base conclusions on what "the people" want by that sample. You may come to inductive conclusions based on sensory observations (what you see or hear), lists or groups, cause-effect thinking, or pattern recognition.

Sensory observation: Using your eyes, ears, taste, touch, or smell involves sensory observation. The police uniform example in the previous paragraph is an example of sensory observation.

Lists or enumeration: Often we look at lists of items and come to conclusions based on those lists. You may look at lists of what prevents heart problems and conclude that you will not smoke and will exercise every day.

Cause-effect: When two events happen, we may decide that the first one was the cause of the second one (effect). Historians use this kind of reasoning. Cause-effect thinking means you notice that every time you run a red light, you are almost in an accident. The cause (running the red light) has a certain effect (near accident).

Pattern recognition: Pattern recognition involves looking at parts and drawing conclusions. A professor may notice one student who is rarely in class, doesn't turn in work, and flunks the midterm. That professor is likely to conclude that the student is a poor college student.

The conclusion you draw in inductive reasoning is usually called a hypothesis. Scientists use this method all the time.

As with deductive reasoning, you can make many errors with inductive reasoning. Some of these are listed in Practice C-3 of this chapter and include such obvious errors as oversimplification and using the wrong facts to come to your conclusion.

Perhaps the best way to explain these two types of reasoning is to quote Robert M. Pirsig in a passage from his book *Zen and the Art of Motorcycle Maintenance*:

> If the cycle goes over a bump and the engine misfires, and then goes over another bump and the engine misfires, and then goes over another bump and the engine misfires, and then goes over a long smooth stretch of road and there is no misfiring, and then goes over a fourth bump and the engine misfires again, one can logically conclude that the misfiring is caused by the bumps. That is induction: reasoning from particular experiences to general truths.

Deductive inferences do the reverse. They start with general knowledge and predict a specific observation. For example if, from reading the hierarchy of facts about the machine, the mechanic knows the horn on the cycle is powered exclusively by electricity from the battery, then he can logically infer that if the battery is dead the horn will not work. That is deduction. (From Robert M. Pirsig, *Zen and the Art of Motorcycle Maintenance,* Morrow, 1974, p. 107.)

We use these two types of reasoning every day, often without even knowing it.

To look more closely at how we draw conclusions, read the following passage and then answer the questions that follow.

In 1832, a twenty-four-old Englishman named Charles Darwin, aboard the HMS Beagle on a surveying expedition around the world, was collecting beetles in a rain forest near Rio de Janeiro. In one day, in one small area, he found over sixty-eight different species of small beetles. That there could be such a variety of species of one kind of creature astounded him. In his journal he wrote that such a find "... is sufficient to disturb the composure of an entomologist's mind...." The conventional view of his day was that all species were unchangeable and that each had been individually and separately created by God. Far from being an atheist, Darwin had taken a degree in divinity in Cambridge. But he was deeply puzzled by his find. (Adapted from James Burke, *The Day the Universe Changed,* Little, Brown, 1985, p. 267.)

1. T/F We can draw the conclusion that Darwin was not actually out searching for what he found.

2. T/F The evidence provided for our conclusion is based partly on Darwin's journal.

3. T/F What Darwin discovered was contrary to the beliefs of his day.

4. T/F Darwin's later "theory of evolution," that species were not fixed forever, probably began with his discovery about the beetle.

All of the answers to these questions are true. Based on his journal statement that the find was "sufficient to disturb" his composure, the statement that he was "deeply puzzled," and the fact that what he found was contrary to what he had been taught to believe all provide evidence to support our conclusions that he was not looking for what he found.

Even though no one living today was with Darwin in 1832, his journal notes leave evidence to help answer question 2 as true. As to question 3, if Darwin had a degree in divinity from Cambridge, he would have been taught to believe what was accepted as "fact" in his day: that God individually and separately created all species. The fact that he found sixty-eight different species is contrary to such a belief.

The statement in question 4 is true, but unless you know what Charles Darwin's "theory of evolution" is, you might have difficulty drawing such a conclusion. If you know that he continued to pursue the suspicion in his mind that all species were not fixed forever, and that he eventually wrote *On the Origin of Species by Means of Natural Selection,* then there's no problem in answering this question as true.

The following practices are designed to help you develop your ability to draw conclusions from what you read.

PRACTICE C-1: Drawing Conclusions from Paragraphs

Directions: Read the following paragraphs and answer the questions that follow.

1.   Look for a moment at the situation in those nations that most of us prefer to label with the euphemism "underdeveloped," but which might just as accurately be described as "hungry." In general, underdeveloped countries (UDCs) differ from developed countries (DCs) in a number of ways. UDCs are not industrialized. They tend to have inefficient, usually subsistence agricultural systems, extremely low gross national products and per capita incomes, high illiteracy rates, and incredibly high rates of population growth.... Most of these countries will never, under conceivable circumstance, be "developed" in the sense in which the United States is today. They could accurately be called "never-to-be-developed" countries. (From Paul Ehrlich and Anne Ehrlich, *Ecoscience: Population, Resources and Environment*, Freeman, 1977.)

a.   The intent of the passage is to _____

_____

b.   T/F The authors of the passage have drawn the conclusion that UDCs exist because they are not industrialized and have poor agricultural systems, high illiteracy rates, low incomes, and too much population growth.

c.   T/F If a UDC has a population growth that is too high for its agricultural system, we can draw the conclusion that it will never become a DC.

d.   T/F We can draw the conclusion from the information in the passage that the authors feel UDCs can eventually become DCs.

e.   Identify what kind of reasoning (inductive or deductive) is required to answer question 1 (d). _____

_____

2.   Science is sometimes confused with technology, which is the application of science to various tasks. Grade-school texts that caption pictures of rockets on the moon with the title, "Science Marches On!" aid such confusion. The technology that makes landing on the moon possible emerged from the use of scientific strategies in the study of propulsion, electronics, and numerous other fields. It is the mode of inquiry that is scientific; the rocket is a piece of technology.

Just as science is not technology, neither is it some specific body of knowledge. The popular phrase "Science tells us that smoking is bad for your health" really misleads. "Science" doesn't tell us anything; people tell us things, in this case people who have used scientific strategies to investigate the relationship of smoking to health. Science, as a way of thought and investigation, is best conceived of as existing not in books, or in machinery, or in reports containing numbers, but rather in that invisible world of the mind. Science has to do with the way questions are formulated and answered; it is a set of rules and forms for inquiry created by people who want reliable answers. (From Kenneth R. Hoover, *The Elements of Social Scientific Thinking*, 3rd edition, St. Martin's, 1984, pp. 4–5.)

a.   The intent of the passage is to _____

_____

b. T/F According to the author, some grade-school textbooks contribute to the confusion between science and technology.

c. T/F The author does not think there is much difference between the terms *science* and *technology.*

d. T/F The author does not believe that science is something that cannot be written down.

e. T/F The author would agree with the statement, "Science has proven that too much sun causes skin cancer."

f. T/F The author has respect for scientific thinking.

g. What kind of reasoning (inductive or deductive) did you use to answer question 2 (f)? _____

---

3.   Some years ago, I ran into an economist friend at the University of Michigan in Ann Arbor who told me, with concern bordering on shock, that assembly-line workers at the nearby Ford plant in Dearborn were making more money than an assistant professor at the University. It occurred to me that quite a few at Ford might prefer the more leisured life of a young professor: Certainly there seemed no need to fear any major movement of academic talent from Ann Arbor to the noisome shops in Dearborn. (From John Kenneth Galbraith, "When Work Isn't Work," *Parade*, February 10, 1985.)

a. T/F The author's economist friend believes that a university professor should be paid more than an assembly-line worker.

b. T/F The author agrees with his friend.

c. T/F The author feels that a university professor's work is easier than factory work.

d. T/F Because the pay is better for factory work, many professors will probably leave the university to seek factory jobs.

e. T/F The author probably believes that the usual definition of *work* can be misleading when comparing various types of jobs.

4.   Almost everyone in the middle class has a college degree, and most have an advanced degree of some kind. Those of us who can look back to the humble stations of our parents or grandparents, who never saw the inside of an institution of higher learning, can have cause for self-congratulation. But—inevitably but—the impression that our general populace is better educated depends on an ambiguity in the meaning of the word education, or fudging of the distinction between liberal and technical education. A highly trained computer specialist need not have any more learning about morals, politics or religion than the most ignorant of persons. . . . It is not evident to me that someone whose regular reading consists of *Time, Playboy* and *Scientific American* has any profounder wisdom about the world than the rural schoolboy of yore with his McGuffey's reader. (From Allan Bloom, *The Closing of the American Mind*, Simon and Schuster, 1987, p. 59.)

a. T/F The author believes that the general public today is better educated than before.

b. T/F The "McGuffey's reader" must have been a widely used textbook in schools at one time.

c. T/F The author believes that learning about morals, politics, and religion is not the function of institutions of higher learning.

   d. T/F The author favors a technical education over a liberal one.

   e. T/F The passage suggests that the author is pleased with the direction education is taking and thinks it is much better than it was in his grandparents' day.

   f. Identify the type of reasoning (*inductive* or *deductive*) the author uses to come to his conclusion. _____

PRACTICE C-2: Arguments and Responses

Directions: The legal drinking age in the United States is 21. Some people want to lower the age, in most cases to age 18. Presented here are some argumentative statements or claims as reasons for lowering the legal age to 21. Responses to those arguments follow. Read each argument and response, then answer the questions that follow.

Statement 1
Argument
Lowering the drinking age will reduce the allure of alcohol as a "forbidden fruit" for minors.

Response
Lowering the drinking age will make alcohol more available to an even younger population, replacing "forbidden fruit" with "low-hanging fruit."

The practices and behaviors of 18-year-olds are particularly influential on 15–17-year-olds. If 18-year-olds get the OK to drink, they will be modeling drinking for younger teens. Legal access to alcohol for 18-year-olds will provide more opportunities for younger teens to obtain it illegally from older peers.

Age-21 has resulted in decreases, not increases in youth drinking, an outcome inconsistent with an increased allure of alcohol. In 1983, one year before the National Minimum Purchase Age Act was passed, 88% of high school seniors reported any alcohol use in the past year and 41% reported binge drinking. By 1997, alcohol use by seniors had dropped to 75% and the percentage of binge drinkers had fallen to 31%. (From Opposing Viewpoints Resource Center, document X3010084223, http://www.galenet.galegroup.com/servlet/OVRC.)

   a. The argument for lowering the drinking age uses the term "forbidden fruit." Explain what is meant. _____

      _____

   b. T/F The argument is based mostly on fact.

   c. T/F The response to the argument is based mostly on facts.

   d. Draw your own reasoned conclusion on the argument. If you support the argument, what reasons do you have? _____

      _____

      _____

Statement 2
Argument
At 18, kids can vote, join the military, sign contracts, and even smoke. Why shouldn't they be able to drink?

Response

Ages of initiation vary—one may vote at 18, drink at 21, rent a car at 25, and run for president at 35. These ages may appear arbitrary, but they take into account the requirements, risks, and benefits of each act.

When age-21 was challenged in Louisiana's State Supreme Court, the Court upheld the law, ruling that "statutes establishing the minimum drinking age at a higher level than the age of majority are not arbitrary because they substantially further the appropriate governmental purpose of improving highway safety, and thus are constitutional."

Age-21 laws help keep kids healthy by postponing the onset of alcohol use. Deferred drinking reduces the risks of:

- developing alcohol dependence or abuse later in life.
- harming the developing brain.
- engaging in current and adult drug use.
- suffering alcohol-related problems, such as trouble at work, with friends, family, and police. (From Opposing Viewpoints Resource Center, document X3010084223, http://www.galenet.galegroup.com/servlet/OVRC.)

    a. T/F As stated, the argument is mostly opinion.

    b. Explain why you agree or disagree with the argument. _____

    _____

    c. T/F The response uses more facts than opinions.

    d. State your own conclusion regarding the argument and what reasoning you used. _____

    _____

Statement 3

Argument

Minors still drink, so age-21 laws clearly don't work.

Response

Age-21 laws work. Young people drink less in response. The laws have saved an estimated 17,000 lives since states began implementing them in 1975, and they've decreased the number of alcohol-related youth fatalities among drivers by 63% since 1982.

Stricter enforcement of age-21 laws against commercial sellers would make those laws even more effective at reducing youth access to alcohol. The ease with which young people acquire alcohol—three-quarters of 8th graders say that it is "fairly easy" or "very easy" to get—indicates that more must be done. Current laws against sales to minors need stiff penalties to deter violations. Better education and prevention-oriented laws are needed to reduce the commercial pressures on kids to drink. (From Opposing Viewpoints Resource Center, document X3010084223, http://www.galenet. galegroup.com/servlet/OVRC.)

    a. T/F As stated, the argument is mostly opinion, but true.

    b. Explain why you agree or disagree with the argument. _____

    _____

    c. T/F The response uses more facts than opinions.

    d. State your own conclusion regarding the argument and what reasoning you used.

Questions for Group Discussion

1. As a group, discuss your views on lowering the drinking age. Are your views and conclusions based on reasoned judgment? Review pages 274–276 on reasoning.

2. Of late, "binge drinking" on college campuses has received widespread coverage. Does this occur on your campus? Why does drinking seem to attract many students?

3. If your group has access to the online Opposing Viewpoints Research Center, go there and read the article "The Drinking Age Should Be Lowered" by Michael Clay Smith and compare it with what you just read. Is it mostly facts or opinions? Is the argument based on reasoned judgments?

Logical Fallacies

Of course, we can make mistakes in our reasoning. Sometimes we make statements that draw the wrong conclusions. These are called **logical fallacies**. Here are some of the more common fallacies that you should avoid making and that you should look for when you are reading:

1. *Either-or thinking* or *oversimplification* occurs when a simplistic answer is given to a large problem: "You want to get rid of abortion clinics? Let's blow them up." Either-or thinking is also oversimplifying issues: "Let's either get rid of all the nuclear weapons in the world, or learn to live with the bomb." Such thinking ignores or covers up other possible answers to a problem.

2. *Stereotyping* ignores individuality. There are stereotypes about political parties (Republicans are pro-rich people; Democrats are pro-poor people), stereotypes about Jews (they always look for bargains), stereotypes about blacks (they are better athletes), and so on. Stereotyping disallows looking at people, groups, or ideas on individual merit.

3. *Attacking a person's character* (the Latin term for this reasoning is *ad hominem*) to discredit someone's views is also a faulty way to reason: "Sure, Senator Nicely favors a bill to stop acid rain from being carried to Canada. Why shouldn't he? He owns a big farm in Canada and probably plans to retire there."

4. *Non sequiturs* (just a fancy Latin name for "it does not follow") occur when a logical reason is not provided for the argument being made. It's a contradiction when a person says, "Clint Eastwood would make a good president; his Dirty Harry movies show you how tough he'd be on crime." The two assertions don't logically follow, since one has nothing to do with the other.

5. *Arguments because of doubtful sources* occur when an unknown source or a source lacking authority is cited: "The government doesn't want us to know about UFOs, but the *National Enquirer* has been providing a lot of evidence that proves contrary." While it might be true that the government is hiding something, the *National Enquirer's* reputation for sensationalism does not make it a good source to use as a convincing argument. Also, be careful when you read that a story comes from an unnamed "high-level official."

6. *Begging the question* occurs when an argument uses circular reasoning. An argument is circular if its premise assumes that its central point is already proven and uses this in support of itself. Arguing that drunken drivers are a menace is begging the question since it's already been proven that they are.

7. *Irrational appeal* occurs when appeals to our emotions, to our religious faith, or to authority are made rather than appeals or reasons based on logic. "Of course you'll vote Republican; our family always has." "I'll get even. The Bible says 'an eye for an eye.'" "My country, right or wrong."

8. *Mistaking the reason for an occurrence* happens when we fail to see there may be other causes or we are misled. "John is a naturally brilliant student." (Is John brilliant, or does he do well in school because his parents make him study more than others? Maybe he's trying to impress a girl in his class.) "Karla is absent from class again. She must not be a serious student." (Maybe Karla has a health problem, or a small child to attend, or lacks transportation to campus on certain days.)

There are many kinds of faulty reasoning, but the ones described in this chapter are some of the more common ones you should begin to look for and avoid using when you draw conclusions or make inferences.

PRACTICE C-3: Identifying Logical Fallacies

Directions: Read the following dialogues and determine which of the following logical fallacies or errors in reasoning appear in the argument. There may be more than one type in a dialogue.

a.	either-or thinking (oversimplification)	**e.**	doubtful sources
b.	stereotyping	**f.**	begging the question
c.	attacking character	**g.**	irrational appeal
d.	non sequitur (contradiction)	**h.**	mistaking the reason

1. SAM: There's only one real aim of education—to learn all you can while going to school.

GEORGE: Nonsense. Today, the only real reason to go to college is to get the skills necessary for a good job.

Error in reasoning: _____

Explain: _____

2. PAULA: Let's go hear the Nicaraguan ambassador at Fraley Hall tonight. It should be interesting to hear his views.

SUE: There's nothing that little commie's got to say that I want to hear.

Error in reasoning: _____

Explain: _____

3. HARRY: George is forming an organization to protest the dumping of toxic waste near the bird wildlife sanctuary. He really seems concerned about this. Quite a few people I know are joining with him. I think I will, too.

SALLY: Don't be a sucker: George's just doing it to bring attention to himself. He plans to run for president of the student body next term and wants to look good. Anyway, I dated him once and he came on too strong for me.

Error in reasoning: _____

Explain: _____

4.   KIP: You going to vote for Sally? She'd make a good school representative on the board of education. She gets As in all her classes.

PIP: You kidding? What does she know about politics? Anyway, a female's place is in the home, not running for office.

Error in reasoning: _____

Explain: _____

5.   DALE: Did you hear that Sue is moving to the Midwest? She's convinced a major earthquake is going to hit us any day now.

FRED: She may be right. Have you been reading that series on natural disasters in the local newspaper? They predict an 8.8 earthquake will occur here in the next two years. The Midwest is a lot safer, that's for sure.

Error in reasoning: _____

Explain: _____

6.   RAUL: Did you read about the junior high kid who stabbed and killed his friend after they watched the movie *Friday the 13th* on TV?

PAM: Isn't that terrible? Maybe now they'll stop showing that worthless junk on television. Everybody knows what a big influence TV viewing has on kids.

RAUL: But how will this incident change anything?

PAM: Now there's proof of the harm.

Error in reasoning: _____

Explain: _____

PRACTICE C-4: Evaluating Pros and Cons of an Argument

Directions: Disagreements on what type of sex education should be provided in public schools continues. One camp believes that teenagers should be taught abstinence only. Another camp believes teaching abstinence only does not work alone and that teaching comprehensive safe sex and contraception methods should be part of a sex education program for teens. One of the following selections advocates abstinence-only programs, the other argues for comprehensive sex education programs. Apply all the reading skills you have learned as you read each one. How well is each opinion supported?

Pro Argument

At the time she wrote the following selection, Kathleen Tsubata was codirector of the Washington AIDS International Foundation and taught HIV/AIDS prevention.

ABSTINENCE-ONLY PROGRAMS BENEFIT YOUTHS

KATHLEEN TSUBATA

1   The current tug-of-war between "abstinence-only" and "comprehensive" sexual-education advocates is distracting us from the real issue. We are in a war against forces far more unforgiving than we ever have encountered. We must look at what works to save lives. My work brings me to deal with teens every day, in public schools, churches and community organizations, teaching HIV/AIDS prevention. I train teens to teach others about this genocidal plague that is sweeping nations around the world and depleting continents of their most-productive population. I can tell you that most teens have a very superficial understanding of HIV and that many are putting themselves at risk in a wide variety of ways.

2   While teen pregnancy is serious, it is still, in one sense, the lesser evil. It's a difficult thing to bear a child out of wedlock, with the accompanying loss of education, financial stability and freedom. However, compared to HIV, it's a walk in the park. Make no mistake about it: The choice of sexual activity is a life-and-death matter, as Third World nations are finding out in stark terms.

THE PROBLEM WITH CONDOMS

3   Having multiple sexual partners is the No. 1 risk factor for contracting HIV and 19 percent of teens have had four or more sexual partners.

4   "So teach them to use condoms!" we are told. Studies indicate that condoms, if used correctly and consistently, may lower the transmission rate to 15 to 25 percent. That's not a fail-safe guarantee, as any condom manufacturer under litigation quickly would point out.

5   But there are two additional problems with condoms being the central pillar of HIV prevention. First, correct usage of condoms is hard to achieve in the dimly lit, cramped back seat of a car. Second, and more importantly, kids simply make decisions differently than adults. Janet St. Lawrence, of the Centers for Disease Control and Prevention (CDC), related the results of one behavioral study to me in a phone conversation [in 2002]. In that study, teens reported using a condom for their first sexual contact with someone, and subsequent contacts, "until they felt the relationship was permanent," St. Lawrence said. Then they stopped using condoms. These teens were asked what defines a "permanent" relationship. "Lasting 21 days or longer," was their response. In other words, such a teen could start a relationship, initiate sex using a condom, decide ater three weeks that it is "safe" to stop using a condom, break up and replay the whole cycle, convinced that this was responsible sexual behavior.

6   Teens are not realistic because they are young and not fully developed in key mental and emotional areas. They tend to imbue love with magical properties, as if the emotion is a sanitizing force, and that their trust can be shown by the willingness to take risks. Kids process information differently than adults. Parents know this. Saying "It's best not to have sex, but if you do, use a condom" is translated in their minds to "It's okay to have sex if you use a condom." Then, if they feel "this is true love," they convince themselves that even that is unnecessary. That's why during four decades of sex education we witnessed steep increases in sexual activity and the consequential increases in teen pregnancy, sexually transmitted diseases and poverty.

From "Insight in the News." Used with permission.

THE BENEFITS OF ABSTINENCE EDUCATION

7   Only when abstinence education began in recent years did the numbers of sexually active teens go down a full 8 percentage points from 54 percent of teens to 46 percent, according to the 2001 *Youth Risk Behavior Surveillance*, published by the CDC. Simultaneously, teen pregnancies went down, abortions went down and condom use went up among those who were sexually active. Raising the bar to establish abstinence as the best method indirectly resulted in more-responsible behavior in general.

8   You would think such good news would have people dancing in the aisles. Instead, the safe-sex gurus grimly predict that increased abstinence education will result in teens giving in to natural urges without the benefit of latex. Or, the critics of abstinence-until-marriage education insisted that their programs (which pay lip service to abstinence) somehow reached teens more effectively than the programs that focused on abstinence. A third interpretation is that contraception, not abstinence, has lowered the numbers.

9   However, a study of lowered teen-pregnancy rates between 1991 and 1995 (published in *Adolescent and Family Health* by Mohn, Tingle et al., April 2003) showed that abstinence, not contraceptives, was the major cause of the lowered pregnancy rate. Another 1996 study, by John Vessey, of Northwestern University Medical School, followed up on 2,541 teens, ages 13 to 16, who completed an abstinence-education program. He reported that one year after completing the program, 54 percent of formerly sexually active teens no longer were sexually active. This puts to rest the idea that "once a teen has sex, they will continue to be sexually active."

10   It often is claimed that most parents want pro-contraceptive education for their kids. In fact, a nationwide Zogby International poll of 1,245 parents in February [2003] (see poll results at www.whatparentsthink.com) commissioned by the pro-abstinence Coalition for Adolescent Sexual Health found that when shown the actual content of both comprehensive and abstinence-only sex-education programs, 73 percent of parents supported abstinence education and 75 percent opposed the condom-based education, with 61 percent opposing the comprehensive sex-ed programs.

11   But what do teens themselves think? In a 2000 study by the National Campaign to Prevent Teen Pregnancy, 93 percent of the teens surveyed said there should be a strong message from society not to engage in sex at least until graduation from high school. Will abstinence education cause sexually active teens to be unable to find out about contraception? The small amount in abstinence-education funding requested by Congress ($135 million among three programs) is miniscule compared with the $379 million funding of only six of the 25 federal programs teaching contraceptive-based education. This is Goliath complaining that David is using up all the rocks.

12   But, in all good conscience, can we teach something that would put kids in danger of contracting HIV, even if at a somewhat-reduced risk? Can we glibly decide, "Oh, only 15 percent of users will die?" That's acceptable? The stakes simply are too high. Even one life is too important to lose. When we're talking about life and death, we can't settle for the soggy argument of "Kids are going to do it anyway." That's what used to be said about racial discrimination, drunk driving and cigarette smoking, but when people became serious about countering these behaviors, they receded. If we realize the necessity of saving every teen's life, we can't help but teach them that because sex is wonderful, powerful and life-changing, it must be treated with great care.

THE NEED TO LIMIT SEXUALITY

13   Sex is most pleasurable and joyful when there is no fear of disease, when both partners feel absolute trust in the other, when the possibility of a pregnancy is not a destructive

one and when each person truly wants the best for the other. This takes self-development, investment, emotional growth, responsibility and a whole host of other elements a typical teen doesn't possess, unless they are guided. In reality, every person already is aware of the need to limit sexuality to certain times and places, like many activities. Sexuality is far more complex than the physical mechanics of orgasm. That stuff is pretty much automatic. It's far more important to know that orgasm is the perfectly engineered system for creating life, and for experiencing the fulfillment of love.

14   Abstinence isn't a vague ideal but a practical, feasible life skill. Studies show that kids who are able to say no to sex also can say no to drugs, alcohol and tobacco. The skills in one area automatically transfer to other areas of health. Learning to delay gratification can have positive impacts on academic goals and athletic accomplishments.

15   Without the soap-opera distractions of sex, kids feel more confident and free to enjoy the process of making friends, developing their own individuality and working on their dreams. That's why virtually no one looks back on the decision to be sexually abstinent and says "I wish I had never done that," But 63 percent of teen respondents who have had sex regretted it and said they wish they had waited, according to an International Communications Research of Media survey in June 2000 commissioned by the National Campaign to Prevent Teen Pregnancy. Further, 78 percent of the 12- to 17-year-old respondents said teens should not be sexually active, and only 21 percent thought sex for teens was okay if they used birth control.

YOUTHS WANT SUPPORT

16   Teens are telling us that they need support to resist the pressure to have sex. Even just making an abstinence pledge was found to delay sexual debut by 18 months on average, according to the National Longitudinal Study on Adolescent Health in 1997. And teens who know their parents have a strong belief and expectation of abstinence are far more likely to abstain, as shown in two 2002 studies released by the University of Minnesota Center for Adolescent Health and Development in which more than 80 percent of teens stayed abstinent when they knew their mothers strongly disapproved of premarital sex.

17   Even if it were only to end the spread of HIV/AIDS, that would be a valid reason to support abstinence education.

18   But teaching abstinence goes beyond preventing disease and unwanted pregnancy. It helps kids improve in the areas of self-esteem, academic attainments and future careers. It increases refusal skills toward drugs, alcohol and smoking. It equips teens with tools that they will use successfully through-out life, especially in their eventual marriage and family life. In other words, it has a positive ripple effect both in terms of their current and future life courses.

19   In my estimation, that definitely is worth funding.

Now answer the following questions. You may need to skim the selection for the answers.

1. What does Tsubata believe has helped lower teen pregnancy rates and can help protect youths from life-threatening diseases? _____

_____

2. What two reasons does the author see as a problem with teaching the use of condoms? _____

_____

3. What proof does the author provide for her statement that abstinence, not contraception, has lowered teen pregnancy rates? _____

_____

4. Besides health benefits, the author feels that by practicing sexual abstinence, teens improve in self-esteem and academic attainments; learn refusal toward drugs, alcohol and smoking; and acquire tools used successfully throughout life. What factual evidence does the author give to support the benefits? _____

_____

5. Why does Tsubata mention that she works with teens everyday in public schools, churches, and community organizations, teaching HIV prevention? _____

_____

6. Is the author's argument logical and balanced? _____

_____

Con Argument

The following essay was published by the American Civil Liberties Union (ACLU), a civil rights and individual liberties advocacy group.

As you read, look for the arguments used to counter the previous selection on sex education.

ABSTINENCE-ONLY PROGRAMS DO NOT WORK

American Civil Liberties Union

1
- Nearly two-thirds of all high school seniors in the U.S. have had sexual intercourse.
- Each year, approximately 9.1 million 15–24 year olds are infected with sexually transmitted diseases (STDs), accounting for almost one-half of the total new STDs occurring annually in the U.S.
- The Centers for Disease Control and Prevention estimate that one-half of all new HIV infections occur among people under age 25, with the majority contracted through sexual intercourse.
- An estimated 757,000 pregnancies occurred among 15–19 year olds in 2002.

2   These statistics demonstrate a high level of sexual activity and risk taking among U.S. teens. Indeed, the U.S. has one of the highest teen pregnancy rates in the developed world. The good news is that in recent years this rate dropped. From 1995–2002, the pregnancy rate among 15–19 years olds declined by nearly 24 percent. Researchers attribute 86 percent of this decline to improved contraceptive use and only 14 percent to teens choosing not to have sexual intercourse. Despite this reality, Congress has allocated more than a billion dollars since 1996 for programs that focus exclusively on abstinence until marriage and censor vital health care information about contraceptives.

3   The ACLU supports programs that give teens the information they need to make healthy and responsible decisions about sex. Evidence shows that stressing

American Civil Liberties Union, "Abstinence-Only-Until-Marriage Programs Censor Vital Health Care Information," August 2007, http://www.aclu.org/reproductiverights/sexed/12670res20070319.html.

the importance of waiting to have sex while providing accurate, age-appropriate, and complete information about how to use contraceptives can help teens delay sex and reduce sexual risk taking. In addition to censoring vital health care information, abstinence-only-until-marriage programs raise other serious civil liberties concerns: They create a hostile environment for gay and lesbian teens; reinforce gender stereotypes; and in some instances use taxpayer dollars to promote one religious perspective.

Abstinence-Only-Until-Marriage Programs Censor Vital Health Information

4   Currently, there are three federal programs dedicated to funding abstinence-only-until-marriage programs. Each requires eligible programs to censor critical information that teens need to make healthy and responsible life decisions.

5   To receive funds under any of the federal programs, grantees must offer curricula that have as their "exclusive purpose" teaching the benefits of abstinence. In addition, recipients of abstinence-only-until-marriage dollars may not advocate contraceptive use or teach contraceptive methods except to emphasize their failure rates.

6   Thus, recipients of federal abstinence-only-until-marriage funds operate under a gag order that censors vitally needed information. Grantees are forced either to omit any mention of topics such as contraception, abortion, homosexuality, and AIDS or to present these subjects in an incomplete and thus inaccurate fashion.

7   **Research Shows that Abstinence-Only-Until-Marriage Programs Don't Work** A rigorous, multi-year, scientific evaluation authorized by Congress and released in April 2007 presents clear evidence that abstinence-only-until-marriage programs don't work. The study by Mathematica Policy Research, Inc., which looked at four federally funded programs and studied more than 2,000 students, found that abstinence-only program participants were just as likely to have sex before marriage as teens who did not participate. Furthermore, program participants had first intercourse at the same mean age and the same number of sexual partners as teens who did not participate in the federally funded programs.

8   In addition, an academic study of virginity pledge programs—which encourage students to make a pledge to abstain from sex until marriage and are often a component of abstinence-only-until-marriage curricula—found that while in limited circumstances virginity-pledgers may delay first intercourse, they still have sex before marriage and are less likely than non-pledgers to use contraception at first intercourse and to get tested for STDs when they become sexually active.

9   On the other hand, there is ample evidence that programs that include information about both abstinence and how to use contraceptives effectively delay sex and reduce sexual risk taking among teens. Many of these programs have been shown to "delay the onset of sex, reduce the frequency of sex, reduce the number of sexual partners among teens, or increase the use of condoms and other forms of contraception" among sexually active teens. Research also shows that sex education curricula that discuss contraception—by presenting accurate information about contraceptive options, effectiveness, and use—do not increase sexual activity.

Abstinence-Only-Until-Marriage Programs Withhold Information Teens Need to Make Healthy and Responsible Life Decision

10   Abstinence-only-until-marriage programs are increasingly replacing other forms of sex education in high schools. Between 1995 and 2002, "[t]he proportion of adolescents who had received any formal instruction about methods of birth control declined significantly," and by 2002, one-third of adolescents had not received any instruction on contraception. At the same time, in 1999, 23 percent of secondary school sexuality

education teachers taught abstinence as the only way of avoiding STDs and pregnancy, up from 2 percent in 1988. When abstinence-only-until-marriage programs do present information about pregnancy prevention and testing and treatment of STDs, they do so incompletely and/or inaccurately. For example, a 2004 congressional report concluded that many federally funded abstinence-only-until-marriage curricula "misrepresent the effectiveness of condoms in preventing sexually transmitted diseases and pregnancy" by exaggerating their failure rates.

11   We need to help teenagers make healthy and responsible life decisions by giving them full and accurate information about the transmission and treatment of STDs, and how to use contraception effectively. Abstinence-only-until-marriage programs jeopardize the health of sexually active teens and leave those who become sexually active unprepared.

Abstinence-Only-Until-Marriage Programs Create a Hostile Environment for Lesbian and Gay Teens

12   Many abstinence-only-until-marriage programs use curricula that discriminate against gay and lesbian students and stigmatize homosexuality. The federal guidelines governing these programs state that they must teach that a "mutually faithful monogamous relationship in [the] context of marriage is the expected standard of human sexual activity." In a society that generally prohibits gays and lesbians from marrying, such a message rejects the idea of sexual intimacy for lesbians and gays and ignores their need for critical information about protecting themselves from STDs in same-sex relationships.

13   A review of the leading abstinence-only-until-marriage curricula found that most address same-sex sexual behavior only within the context of promiscuity and disease, and several are overtly hostile to lesbians and gay men. For example, materials from an abstinence-only-until-marriage program used recently in Alabama state, "[S]ame sex 'unions' cannot provide an adequate means of achieving a genuine physical relationship with another human being because this type of 'union' is contrary to the laws of nature."

14   By talking only about sex within marriage and teaching about STDs as a form of moral punishment for homosexuality, abstinence-only-until-marriage programs not only undermine efforts to educate teens about protecting their health, but create a hostile learning environment for lesbian and gay students and the children of lesbian and gay and/or single parents.

Many Abstinence-Only-Until-Marriage Programs Feature Harmful Gender Stereotypes

15   In addition to false and misleading information, many abstinence-only-until-marriage programs present stereotypes about men and women as scientific facts. In an attempt to demonstrate differences between men and women, one popular program, WAIT Training, instructs teachers to "[b]ring to class frozen waffles and a bowl of spaghetti noodles without sauce. Using these as visual aids, explain how research has found that men's brains are more like the waffle, in that their design enables them to more easily compartmentalize information. Women's minds, on the other hand, are interrelated due to increased brain connectors." Similarly, the teacher's manual for Why Know Abstinence Education Programs suggests that girls are responsible for boys' inability to control their sexual urges: "One subtle form of pressure can be the way in which a girl acts toward her boyfriend. If the girlfriend is constantly touching him and pressing against him, or wearing clothing which is tight or revealing of her body, this will cause the guy to think more about her body than her person, and he may be incited toward more sexual thoughts."

16   Many abstinence-only-until-marriage programs are riddled with similarly troubling discussions of gender. Such stereotypes and false information undermine women's equality and promote an outmoded and discredited view of women's and men's roles and abilities.

Some Abstinence-Only-Until-Marriage Programs Use Taxpayer Dollars to Promote One Religious Perspective

17   Although the U.S. Constitution guarantees that the government will neither promote nor interfere with religious belief, some abstinence-only-until-marriage grantees violate this core freedom by using public dollars to convey overt religious messages or to impose religious viewpoints. The ACLU has successfully challenged this misuse of taxpayer dollars:

- In May 2005, the ACLU filed a lawsuit challenging the federally funded promotion of religion by a nationwide abstinence-only-until-marriage program called the Silver Ring Thing. The program was rife with religion. In its own words, "The mission of Silver Ring is to saturate the United States with a generation of young people who have taken a vow of sexual abstinence until marriage.... This mission can only be achieved by offering a personal relationship with Jesus Christ as the best way to live a sexually pure life." The lawsuit, *ACLU of Massachusetts v. Leavitt*, brought swift results: In August 2005, the U.S. Department of Health and Human Services (HHS) suspended the Silver Ring Thing's funding, pending corrective or other action. And in February 2006, the parties reached a settlement in which HHS agreed that any future funding would be contingent on the Silver Ring Thing's compliance with federal law prohibiting the use of federal funds to support religious activities. Soon after, HHS released new guidelines for all abstinence-only-until-marriage grantees to ensure that government funds will not be used to promote religion. These guidelines were modeled after the settlement agreement in *ACLU of Massachusetts v. Leavitt*.

- In 2002, the ACLU challenged the use of taxpayer dollars to support religious activities in the Louisiana Governor's Program on Abstinence (GPA), a program run on federal and state funds. Over the course of several years, the GPA had funded programs that, among other things, presented "Christ-centered" theater skits, held a religious youth revival, and produced radio shows that "share abstinence as part of the gospel message." In violation of the Constitution, a federal district court found that GPA funds were being used to convey religious messages and advance religion. The court ordered Louisiana officials to stop this misuse of taxpayer dollars. The case was on appeal when the parties settled. The GPA agreed to closely monitor the activities of the programs it funds and to stop using GPA dollars to "convey religious messages or otherwise advance religion in any way."

Parents, Teachers, and Major Medical Groups Support Comprehensive Sexuality Education

18   The vast majority of U.S. parents, teachers, and leading medical groups believe that teens should receive complete and accurate information about abstinence and contraception.

- In a nationwide poll conducted in 2004 for the Kaiser Family Foundation, National Public Radio, and the Kennedy School of Government, researchers found that an overwhelming majority of parents want sex education curricula to cover topics such as abortion and sexual orientation, as well as how to use and where to get contraceptives, including condoms.

- A 1999 nationally representative survey of 7th-12th grade teachers in the five specialties most often responsible for sex education found that a strong majority believed that sexuality education courses should cover birth control methods (93.4%), factual information about abortion (89%), where to go for birth control (88.8%), the correct way to use a condom (82%), and sexual orientation (77.8%), among other topics.
- Similarly, major medical organizations have advocated for and/or endorsed comprehensive sexuality education, including the American Medical Association, the American Academy of Pediatrics, the American College of Obstetrics and Gynecology, and the Society for Adolescent Medicine.

Now answer the following questions.

1. What position does the ACLU take regarding abstinence-only education programs?

_____

_____

2. T/F The ACLU believes that federal funds should support comprehensive sex education in high school courses which includes teaching contraceptive methods.

3. On what sources does the ACLU base its information stating there is no link between abstinence-only education with a downward trend in teens reporting they have had sex? _____

_____

4. Does the ACLU provide sources for their statement that parents, teachers, and medical groups believe students should receive comprehensive sex education?

_____

5. Is the ACLU's argument well balanced and logical? _____

_____

_____

Considering the Pros and Cons of Both Arguments

1. Whether or not you are for or against comprehensive sex education, which argument is most persuasive? Why? _____

_____

2. Even if you agree with her, what might Tsubata have done to be more convincing?

_____

_____

3. Even if you agree with the ACLU, what might have made their argument more convincing? _____

_____

4. How much do your own attitudes and bias on the subject have to do with which argument you think is most convincing? _____

_____

_____

Application 1: Recognizing Attitude, Bias, and Inference in Other Materials

From a magazine, newspaper, or textbook, choose a selection and come up with your own questions about attitude, bias, and inference (at least one question about each). Bring the selection and questions to class and exchange with a classmate. Each of you should answer the other's questions. Discuss what you learned from each article by using critical reading skills.

D.   Putting It All Together

The word *critical* often connotes finding fault with something. But as you have seen in this unit, reading critically implies an attempt at objective judging so as to determine both merits and faults. Critical reading is thoughtful reading because it requires that the reader recognize not only what is being said at the literal level but also facts, opinions, attitudes, inferences, and bias. A reader who is not actively involved is not reading critically.

Knowingly or unknowingly, you make critical judgments all the time, from deciding on the type of toothpaste to buy to choosing a topic for an English theme. The trick is always to be aware of your critical judgments and to know the reasoning behind your decisions.

Making critical judgments is a two-way street. As a reader you must be aware of the judgments the author is making and you must also be aware of the judgments you make, based on evidence rather than bias. For instance, you may dislike the subject of history so much that you have a bias against anything you read before you even get started. Your mind is already partly closed to the author. On the other hand, you could be biased in favor of what you read and accept what is being said simply because you already agree with the author. True critical reading should leave you a little wiser, a little better informed, and less biased than before—about both the subject and yourself.

The following three reading selections can be used to practice increasing your reading speed of comprehension as well as developing your critical reading skills. You may want to look at your Student Record Chart to review your rate and comprehension scores from the last timed readings you did. You may want to just use these as reading comprehension practices and not time yourself. It's up to you and your instructor.

Each of the following reading practices contains comprehension and vocabulary checks that require using all the skills taught in this and the first unit of the book. Remember that you are competing against yourself. Try to learn from any mistakes you may make so that you can do better on each consecutive practice.

PRACTICE D-1: Timed Reading

Directions: Practice speed-reading strategies on the following 745-word selection. Start with a one-minute survey, making sure you look at the questions during the survey too. Push yourself to read faster than before.

Begin Timing: _____

SELF-ESTEEM IS EARNED, NOT LEARNED

MIKE SCHMOKER

1   The word *self-esteem* has become an educational incantation. Every educational discussion, every stated school district goal and mission takes a bow in its direction. Its influence on academic and behavioral standards in our schools cannot be overstated. There is even an official California Task Force to Promote Self-Esteem and Social Responsibility, and the University of California recently published a book linking low self-esteem to societal problems.

2   At first, the word seems innocent enough and something about which we should be concerned. But if the meaning of a word is its use, we must look to pop psychology, which gave us this word, in order to fully understand its importance. Before it reached education, it had already taken on the fatuous implication that what is precious can be gotten cheaply. Self-esteem, as it is now used, isn't something earned but given. It isn't wrought but spontaneously realized. Such thinking is inimical to what schools should be trying to accomplish.

3   What disturbs me is that self-esteem has been sentimentalized. The new self-esteem has less to do with forging a connection between it and achievement and more to do with simply creating good feelings.

4   This is an understandable reaction to a difficult problem. So many young people are burdened with negative, defeatist feelings. We want to help them, and the quicker the better. But as time has passed, it is mystifying that we have not seen this impulse for what it is. I've seen whole auditoriums full of students being told, indiscriminately, to feel good about themselves, being asked at random to stand up and give testimonials on how swell they are, and being reassured that by clinging to this confidence they will succeed mightily.

5   This is a flimsy notion, and no one believes it. Not for very long anyway. Like it or not, self-esteem is very much a function of such unyielding realities as what we can do, what we've done with what we have and what we've made of ourselves. And so the school—with every effort toward sensitivity, compassion and encouragement—should reinforce this, while cultivating ability, talent, decency and the capacity for sustained effort, the belief that you get what you pay for.

6   Shortcuts, such as routinely heaping inordinate praise on shoddy work, or lowering academic standards, do not work. Ask any teacher, in a moment of candor, if he or she can get average kids, the majority of students, to make a sufficient effort in school, make good use of class time or do fairly conscientious work on homework and assignments. An alarming number of teachers don't think so. Many complain of a malaise among students, adding that only about half of their students will even do homework. Despite this, there has never been more pressure for teachers to be enormously upbeat in dealing with students and student efforts. Promotion is nearly automatic, and grades are higher than ever.

7   What this tells students, at least tacitly, is that what they are doing is good enough and that our insistence on quality is a bluff.

8   It's ironic that the reason often cited for generous grading and reluctance to fail students centers on self-esteem. In the name of self-esteem, then, we are asked to give young people something they didn't earn in the mistaken hope that they can go on to master what is presumably harder than what they have already failed to learn.

9   What they do learn is to play the game, the essence of which is that standards are not based on what students should do, or are able to do, but on what they will do, no matter how low the common denominator. And that is, as we know, pretty low; among industrialized nations, we rank embarrassingly in every academic category.

10   But you'll seldom see these deficiencies reflected in American report cards. The plain, unpleasant truth is hidden behind the good grades, lost in the peculiarly positive climate that too often prevails in our schools. If you're not sure that's true, consider this: A recent international survey showed that South Korean students rank first in mathematics, American students near the bottom. When asked where they thought they ranked, the American students ranked themselves at the top and the Koreans at the bottom.

11   It is common knowledge that so much groundless praise can breed complacency. It can. And it has.

12   For our part, the best we can do is teach young people, in an atmosphere of compassion, that self-esteem is earned, often with considerable difficulty, and equip them to earn it.

Finish Timing: Record time here _____ and use the Timed Reading Conversion Chart in the Appendix to figure your rate: _____ wpm.

Comprehension Check

Directions: Answer the following questions without looking back.

1. The author's main idea or thesis is that

   a. self-esteem has been sentimentalized.

   b. self-esteem can be taught in the classroom.

   c. an official California Task Force to Promote Self-Esteem and Social Responsibility recently published a book linking low self-esteem to societal problems.

   d. we need to teach young people that self-respect is earned, often with difficulty.

2. What does the author mean when he says that "the word *self-esteem* has become an education incantation"? _____

   _____

   _____

   _____

3. The author states, "The new self-esteem has less to do with forging a connection between it and achievement and more to do with simply creating good feelings." Based on this, how do you think the author defines *self-esteem*? _____

   _____

   _____

   _____

4. T/F According to the author, self-esteem is a function of what we are capable of doing, what we've done with our ability, and what we've made of ourselves.

5. Explain why the author does not believe in automatic promotion. _____

   _____

   _____

   _____

6. What does the author mean when he says that students "learn to play the game"?

   _____

   _____

   _____

7. According to the author, where do American students rank academically among industrialized nations? To what does he attribute this? _____

   _____

   _____

8. According to a recent survey, where do American students academically rank themselves in mathematics in comparison to South Korean students? Where do they really rank? _____

   _____

   _____

   _____

9. According to the author, too much groundless praise can breed or cause _____

   _____

   _____

10. Explain what the title means. _____

    _____

    _____

    _____

Vocabulary Check

Part A

Directions: Define the following underlined words from the selection.

1. The word *self-esteem* has become an education <u>incantation</u>. _____

   _____

2. We must look to <u>pop psychology</u>, which gave us this word ["self-esteem"]. _____

   _____

3. So many young people are <u>burdened</u> with negative, defeatist feelings. _____

   _____

4. They stand up and give <u>testimonials</u> on how swell they are. _____

_____

5. It is common knowledge that so much <u>groundless</u> praise can breed complacency.

_____

Part B

Directions: Write each word from the following list in the appropriate blank.

> Candor   shoddy   conscientious   routinely   malaise

Shortcuts, such as **(6)** _____ heaping praise on **(7)** _____ work, or lowering academic standards, do not work. Ask any teacher, in a moment of **(8)** _____ if he or she can get average kids, the majority of students, to make a sufficient effort in school, make good use of class time or do fairly **(9)** _____ work on homework and assignments. An alarming number don't think so. Many complain of a **(10)** _____ among students. Despite this, there has never been more pressure for teachers to be enormously upbeat in dealing with students' efforts.

Record your rate and the results of the comprehension and vocabulary checks on the Student Record Chart in the Appendix. Each correct answer is worth 10 points, for a total of 100 points possible for comprehension and 100 points for vocabulary.

PRACTICE D-2: Timed Reading

Directions: Take about one minute to preview the following 465-word selection and questions. After your preview, time yourself on the reading.

Begin Timing: _____

PUSH FOR DE-EMPHASIS OF COLLEGE SPORTS

DAVID HOLAHAN*

1   How many exalted muck-a-mucks with advanced degrees to burn does it take to restate the obvious and then miss the whole point? Twenty-two in the case of the Knight Foundation Commission on Intercollegiate Athletics.

2   It took these wizards more than a year to determine that big-time college athletics are out of control, something high school equivalency degree holders have known for decades.

3   The Knight posse also recommended many wondrous things, including this startling caveat: Colleges should not admit athletes who are unlikely to graduate. Small wonder that news of this long-awaited report was buried on page 4 of my local sports section. Page 1 was devoted to pictures of "scholar-athletes" jumping about in short pants.

* David Holahan, a freelance writer, played football and baseball for Yale.

4   The principal advice of this pedantic treatise is that college presidents should take an active role in administering and overseeing their schools' athletic programs. Or, in plain language, let the big boss ride the tiger that big-time sports has become.

5   What a preposterous proposal. It presumes athletics are so important that the heads of universities should divert time and energy from overseeing education to monitoring the sideshow. The house is rotten to the core and the Knight panel recommends a fresh coat of paint.

6   What is wrong with big-time college sports is not who administers them or which department rakes in the booty or how many jocks can master majors like "family studies." What's wrong is the sports themselves, how perversely important they have become to the players, the coaches, the colleges, the alumni and the fans.

7   It would be tempting to say that money is the disease, the billions that TV networks pay schools to entertain us. But money is just the symptom. The root cause is that we simply value sports too highly. They have become the new opiate of the masses.

8   This is where the commission dropped the ball. Its 20 men and two women (men monitoring sports is a bit like foxes regulating chicken coops) should have insisted on de-emphasis. We are now in the midst of "March madness," CBS's term for the NCAA basketball tournament. Madness, indeed, with sanity nowhere in sight.

9   Even those athletes who do manage to pass their courses are doing so, by and large, so that they can continue their sporting careers. Education, if that is the right word for what these young men and women experience, is the means. Basketball, to cite the semi-pro sport du jour, is the end.

10   How sad that these teenagers head off to college thinking that being a star athlete is the most important, perhaps the only, goal to strive toward. Rarely does anything they encounter on sports-factory campuses disabuse them of this notion. They are there to run and jump and dribble. With a world of possibilities surrounding them, they limit themselves to the one thing they have already mastered. We all should be ashamed of ourselves.

Finish Timing: Record time here _____ and use the Timed Reading Conversion Chart in the Appendix to figure your rate: _____ wpm.

Comprehension Check

Directions: Answer the following questions without looking back.

1. The main idea or thesis of the article is that our society has placed too much value on college sports.

    a. True, because _____

    _____

    b. False, because _____

    _____

2. The intent of this article is to

    a. criticize the findings of the Knight Foundation Commission on Intercollegiate Athletics.

    b. advocate the findings of the Knight Foundation Commission.

    c. blame the overemphasis of the value of college sports on the presidents of the universities involved.

    d. show that many college athletes are more interested in sports than in getting an education.

3. The author's attitude toward his subject is

    a. playful.

    b. serious.

    c. angry with a touch of sarcasm.

    d. disinterest.

4. The author's question "How many exalted muck-a-mucks with advanced degrees to burn does it take to restate the obvious and then miss the whole point?" is an example of the way writers create tone.

    a. True, because _____

    _____

    b. False, because _____

    _____

5. We can infer from what the author says that he does not care for college sports.

    a. True, because _____

    _____

    b. False, because _____

    _____

6. Explain the statement that sports have "become the new opiate of the masses."

    _____

7. We can infer that the Knight Foundation Commission on Intercollegiate Athletics met for over a year to investigate college athletics.

    a. True, because _____

    b. False, because _____

8. What inference can we draw from paragraph 3 regarding the author's opinion of the Knight Foundation Commission? _____

    _____

9. What does the author mean when he says, "With a world of possibilities surrounding them, they [college athletes] limit themselves to the one thing they have already mastered"? _____

    _____

10. What inferences can we draw regarding *why* the author feels as he does about college athletics? _____

    _____

Vocabulary Check

Directions: Define the following underlined words from the selection.

1. many <u>exalted</u> muck-a-mucks with advanced degrees _____

    _____

2. recommended many wondrous things, including this startling <u>caveat</u> _____

_____

3. this pedantic <u>treatise</u> _____

_____

4. this <u>pedantic</u> treatise _____

_____

5. a <u>preposterous</u> proposal _____

_____

6. how <u>perversely</u> important _____

_____

7. to <u>cite</u> the semi-pro sport du jour _____

_____

8. to cite the semi-pro <u>sport du jour</u> _____

_____

9. <u>disabuse</u> them of this notion _____

_____

10. <u>intercollegiate</u> athletics _____

_____

Record your rate and the results of the comprehension and vocabulary checks on the Student Record Chart in the Appendix. Each correct answer is worth 10 points, for a total of 100 points possible for comprehension and 100 points for vocabulary. Discuss your results with your instructor.

PRACTICE **D-3**: Timed Reading

Directions: The author of the following essay, Macarena Hernández, is a writer for the *Dallas Morning News*. Time yourself as you read, looking for the author's arguments, opinions, biases and facts.

Begin Timing: _____

AMERICA, STAND UP FOR JUSTICE AND DECENCY

Macarena Hernández

1   On the last night of September, while they slept after a long day of work in the fields, six men were beaten to death with aluminum bats. One was shot in the head. Among the victims, a father and son killed in the same battered trailer.

2   The killers demanded money as they broke their bones.

Macarena Hernández, "America, Stand Up for Justice and Decency," *Dallas Morning News*, October 15, 2005. Reprinted with permission of the *Dallas Morning News*.

3   The victims were all Mexican farm workers living in rundown trailer parks spread across two counties in southern Georgia. They had earned the money the killers were after by sweating their days on cotton and peanut farms or building chicken coops—the kind of jobs you couldn't pay Americans enough to do.

4   In a few hours, the killers hit four trailers. In one, they raped a woman and shot her husband in the head, traumatizing their three small children, who were present. In others, they left at least a half-dozen men wounded. Some are still in the hospital with shattered bones, including broken wrists from trying to protect their faces from the bats.

5   The news of the killings in Georgia reverberated outside Tift and Colquitt counties, but it didn't cling to national headlines like you would expect with such a bloodbath. Two weeks later, residents are still afraid the attackers will come back, even though the Georgia Bureau of Investigation has arrested six suspects and charged them with the slayings.

6   Across the country, assaults on immigrants are common and happen at a much higher rate than reported. Two years ago in Grand Prairie, a pushcart ice cream vendor was shot to death and robbed. Seven months later, another one met the same fate in west Oak Cliff. In March, at a Far North Dallas apartment complex, two thieves raped and killed a 20-year-old woman. They slit her husband's throat.

7   In Dallas, attacks against immigrants are one reason individual robberies have gone up in the last five years. Authorities call undocumented immigrants "ready-made victims." Without proper documentation to open bank accounts, many resort to stashing their sweat-soaked earnings under mattresses, in kitchen cabinets, in their socks or boots. If they are robbed, many don't call police for fear of deportation or because, back home, cops aren't trusted, anyway.

8   Some solutions are simple and concrete, such as making it easier for immigrants to establish bank accounts. Wells Fargo and Bank of America are among the banks that require only a Mexican consulate-issued ID card to open an account; others require documentation many immigrants lack. If there was ever a reason for adopting the more lenient policy, this is it.

9   More globally, horrors like these demand that a nation descended from immigrants take a hard look at the ways we think and speak about these most recent arrivals.

10   When Paul Johnson, the mayor of Tifton, where three of the four attacks took place, responded by flying the Mexican flag at City Hall, some residents complained. "I did that as an expression of sorrow for the Hispanic community," he told reporters. "For those who were offended, I apologize, but I think it was the right thing to do."

11   Were the complainers angrier about the red, white and green Mexican flag fluttering in the Georgia air than they were about the horrific murders? Do they watch Fox's *The O'Reilly Factor*, where the anchor and the callers constantly point to the southern border as the birth of all America's ills? (Sample comment: "Each one of those people is a biological weapon.")

12   It is one thing to want to secure the borders and another to preach hate, to talk of human beings as ailments. Taken literally, such rhetoric gives criminals like those in southern Georgia license to kill; it gives others permission to look the other way. In this heightened anti-immigrant climate, what Mr. Johnson did was not only a welcome gesture, but a brave one, too.

13   There are those who will want to gloss over the deaths of these six men because they are "criminals" and "lawbreakers," in this country illegally. But regardless of where you stand on the immigration reform debate, you can't stand for the senseless death of the vulnerable.

14   We should all be outraged. We must demand justice. Or else the real criminals here will win.

Finish Timing: Record time here _____ and use the Timed Reading Conversion Chart in the Appendix to figure your rate: _____ wpm.

Comprehension Check

Directions: Answer the following questions without looking back.

1. Which of the following best states Hernández's thesis?

    a. Assaults on immigrants are common with little done about it.

    b. A nation descended from immigrants needs to take a hard look at the way we think and speak about recent arrivals.

    c. We need to establish more lenient policies to help provide documents many immigrants lack.

    d. We are living in a heightened anti-immigrant climate.

2. What events prompted Hernández to write this essay? _____

    _____

3. The author's attitude toward such banks as Wells Fargo and Bank of America is

    a. positive.

    b. negative.

    c. neutral.

    d. not able to tell.

4. Why did the mayor of Tifton, Georgia, fly the Mexican flag at City Hall?

    _____

5. Authorities call undocumented workers _____

    _____

6. What can we infer is Hernández's attitude toward *The O'Reilly Factor* television program and those who watch and agree with the anchors and commentators?

    a. favorable

    b. neutral

    c. delight

    d. disgust

7. What is the tone of Hernández's essay? _____

    _____

8. Is Hernández's essay based mostly on fact or opinion? _____

    _____

9. What inference can be drawn from Hernández's statement that the Georgia killings "didn't cling to national headlines like you would expect with such a bloodbath"? _____

    _____

    _____

10. Hernández says, "Regardless of where you stand on the immigration reform debate, you can't stand for the senseless death of the vulnerable." Explain whether or not this is a logical statement. _____

_____

_____

Vocabulary Check

Directions: Define the following underlined words from the selection.

1. <u>traumatizing</u> their three children

_____

2. <u>reverberated</u> outside Tift and Colquitt counties

_____

3. the more <u>lenient</u> policy

_____

4. for fear of <u>deportation</u>

_____

5. about the <u>horrific</u> murders

_____

6. human beings as <u>ailments</u>

_____

7. those who want to <u>gloss over</u>

_____

8. death of the <u>vulnerable</u>

_____

9. such <u>rhetoric</u> gives criminals permission

_____

10. where the <u>anchor</u> and the callers

_____

Record your rate and the results of the comprehension and vocabulary checks on the Student Record Chart in the Appendix. Each correct answer is worth 10 points, for a total of 100 points possible for comprehension and 100 points for vocabulary. Discuss your results with your instructor.

Questions for Group Discussion

1. As a group, pick any one of the reading selections in Practice C-4. After you agree on the author's thesis, take another side and disagree with the author. Support your views by showing errors in the author's support.

2. Pick any of the readings in this chapter and find examples of logical fallacies. Decide the effect of these fallacies on your understanding of the material.

3. As a group, discuss David Holahan's bias about college sports. Did he cause any of you to look at sports in a different light? Why do some of you agree or disagree with him? Are personal biases interfering with seeing his side? What arguments do you have for disagreeing with him?

4. As a group, concentrate on the immigration debate. Take pro and con sides and argue your positions.

5. As a group, see how many of you can use the following words in a sentence. Make certain you learn the ones you still may not be able to use or recognize by writing the definition in the blank space.

   a. preposterous _____

   b. lenient _____

   c. pedantic _____

   d. disabuse _____

   e. caveat _____

   f. treatise _____

   g. malaise _____

   h. shoddy _____

   i. candor _____

On Your Own

Pick ten new words you learned in this chapter, not necessarily those listed in question 5, and on a separate sheet of paper write a sentence for each word, using it correctly in context. Turn in the paper to your instructor.

If You Want

Go online and examine Web sites on one or more of the following subjects and share your findings in class:

a. Virginity pledges

b. Sex education

c. Illegal immigration

d. College sports: pro and con

A Final Check

At the beginning of this unit, you looked at a diagram that illustrated the three facets of comprehension. Now you have completed the unit that is represented by the left leg of the triangle.

For the diagram below, fill in the blank lines with information from this section. Working with a partner or small group is acceptable if your instructor sets up groups.

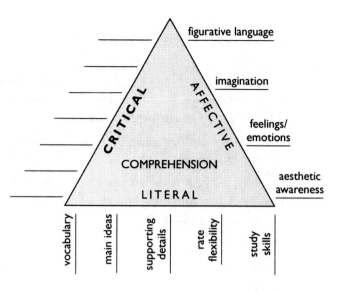

Hints: The first line has to do with information and judgments. The next four lines have to do with the author's worldview and how it influences our reading. The sixth line has to do with reading between the lines. The seventh line deals with what the reader does based on the information given.

When you have finished, check your answers with the triangle at the beginning of Unit Two, page 164.

ABOUT THIS READING

The U.S. Congress continues to struggle with comprehensive immigration reform legislation, especially with regard to border security and pathways to citizenship. In this reading, the writer highlights some of the costs of delaying this legislation. The writer is a coordinator for Interfaith Worker Justice, a national network based in Chicago that mobilizes faith communities to improve conditions for low-wage workers. This article appeared in the December 19, 2008, edition of *Commonweal*, an independent journal of opinion edited and managed by lay Catholics.

I'm Not Dangerous

By DANNY POSTEL

The past six months have seen three of the largest workplace immigration raids in U.S. history. In May, the rural Iowa town of Postville was convulsed when 900 Immigration and Customs Enforcement (ICE) agents stormed a kosher meatpacking plant and arrested 389 workers. In August, ICE agents descended on an electrical equipment factory near Laurel, Mississippi, detaining nearly 600 workers. And in October, the scene was repeated in Greenville, South Carolina, where 330 workers were swept up at a chicken-processing plant.

The humanitarian costs of the raids, according to a statement issued by the U.S. Conference of Catholic Bishops Committee on Migration, were "immeasurable and unacceptable in a civilized society." Children were separated from their parents for days. Those arrested were not immediately afforded the rights of due process. And local communities were, in the words of John C. Wester, bishop of Salt Lake City and chairman of the Committee on Migration, "disrupted and dislocated." These raids, he said, "strike immigrant communities unexpectedly, leaving the affected immigrant families to cope in the aftermath. Husbands are separated from their wives, and children are separated from their parents. Many families never recover; others never reunite."

The bishop called on the Department of Homeland Security, of which ICE is an agency, on President George W. Bush, and on then-candidates John McCain and Barack Obama to "reexamine the use of worksite enforcement raids" as an immigration-enforcement tool. He noted that immigrants "who are working to survive and support their families should not be treated like criminals."

Having visited Laurel after the ICE crackdown, I must report that is exactly how the workers there have been treated and made to feel. The majority of the immigrant workers caught up in the raid were taken immediately to a holding facility in Louisiana. ICE released a number of women, some of them pregnant, on "humanitarian" grounds. But many of them were shackled with ankle bands equipped with electronic monitoring devices. Several expressed their humiliation and shame—not to speak of their physical discomfort—at having been branded this way. For days, one of them told me, she avoided going out in public or to the grocery store. "It makes me look like a criminal, like a dangerous person," she lamented. "I'm not dangerous."

This woman told me she had come to the United States out of sheer desperation. She said she was unable to feed her children in her home village in Mexico. Now, with deportation imminent and no means to pay her bills, she and her coworkers were facing a further harrowing fate.

Immigration raids, even large, media-covered ones, are selective and symbolic in nature. They are orchestrated to send a political message that the government is willing and able to enforce the law. But why penalize the least among us—hardworking people who earn very little and endure some of the harshest conditions in the American workplace? The Postville and Laurel plants both have long histories of taking advantage of their workers. Iowa's attorney general recently filed charges against the Postville meatpacking plant for more than nine thousand labor violations. In July, religious and labor leaders joined more than a thousand marchers in the town to show solidarity with those seized in the ICE raid.

Indeed, religious communities have been playing a pivotal role in the aftermath of these raids. Catholic parishes have been safe havens for families scrambling to feed their children amid the turmoil. Immaculate Conception Church in Laurel and Sacred Heart Catholic Church in Hattiesburg worked virtually round-the-clock to feed and provide for the affected families.

To remedy what the U.S. bishops call "the failure of a seriously flawed immigration system," they "urge our elected and appointed officials to turn away from enforcement-only methods and direct their energy toward the adoption of comprehensive immigration reform legislation." That is now up to the new administration and to Congress.

ANALYZE THIS READING

1. In paragraphs two and four, the writer follows factual information about the largest immigration raids in U. S. history with emotional examples. Describe these examples and analyze them in terms of how they might affect readers of *Commonweal*.

2. On what grounds does the writer question the government's ability to enforce current immigration law?

3. The next-to-last paragraph honors religious communities for providing "safe havens" for families affected by ICE raids. Contrast the values of these communities with the values of the government agency ICE.

4. While the writer is not specific in the final paragraph as to the kind of reform legislation he favors, can you infer the kinds of changes he has in mind? Explain.

RESPOND TO THIS READING

1. Many immigrants travel to the United States for jobs and better living conditions. Indeed, numerous states are home to tens of thousands of working illegal immigrants. In the context of the immigration debate, what should the role be of those who employ illegal workers?

2. With special attention to employment and citizenship, describe the kinds of legislative reform you would argue for. What kind of claim would work best with your argument?

3. Should illegal immigrants and their children be allowed to enroll in publicly funded colleges and universities in the United States? Explain.

Concerned Citizen Community

ABOUT THIS READING

In this reading, the author argues that an open immigration system should replace a quota system and takes on the thorny issues of government infringing on individual rights, immigrants stealing jobs from native workers, and the role of immigrants in creating wealth for a country. This argument is authored by Harry Binswanger, professor of philosophy at the Ayn Rand Institute. It originally appeared in *Capitalism Magazine* in April 2006.

The United States Should Adopt Open Immigration

By HARRY BINSWANGER

This is a defense of phasing-in open immigration into the United States. Entry into the U.S. should ultimately be free for any foreigner, with the exception of criminals, would-be terrorists, and those carrying infectious diseases. (And note: I am defending freedom of entry and residency, not the automatic granting of U.S. citizenship.)

An end to immigration quotas is demanded by the principle of individual rights. Every individual has rights as an individual, not as a member of this or that nation. One has rights not by virtue of being an American, but by virtue of being human.

One doesn't have to be a resident of any particular country to have a moral entitlement to be secure from governmental coercion against one's life, liberty, and property. In the words of the Declaration of Independence, government is instituted "to

Binswanger, Harry. The United States Should Adopt Open Immigration. Captalism Magazine, April 2006. Reprinted by permission of TOF Publications.

secure these rights"—to protect them against their violation by force or fraud.

A foreigner has rights just as much as an American. To be a foreigner is not to be a criminal. Yet our government treats as criminals those foreigners not lucky enough to win the green-card lottery.

Quotas Treat Immigrants as Criminals

Seeking employment in this country is not a criminal act. It coerces no one and violates no one's rights (there is no "right" to be exempt from competition in the labor market, or in any other market).

It is not a criminal act to buy or rent a home here in which to reside. Paying for housing is not a coercive act—whether the buyer is an American or a foreigner. No one's rights are violated when a Mexican, or Canadian, or Senegalese rents an apartment from an American owner and moves into the housing he is paying for. And what about the rights of those American citizens who want to sell or rent their property to the highest bidders? Or the American businesses that want to hire the lowest cost workers? It is morally indefensible for our government to violate their right to do so, just because the person is a foreigner.

Immigration quotas forcibly exclude foreigners who want not to seize but to purchase housing here, who want not to rob Americans but to engage in productive work, raising our standard of living. To forcibly exclude those who seek peacefully to trade value for value with us is a violation of the rights of both parties to such a trade: the rights of the American seller or employer and the rights of the foreign buyer or employee.

Thus, immigration quotas treat both Americans and foreigners as if they were criminals, as if the peaceful exchange of values to mutual benefit were an act of destruction.

The Rights of the Individual Above All

To take an actual example, if I want to invite my Norwegian friend Klaus to live in my home, either as a guest or as a paying tenant, what right does our government have to stop Klaus and me? To be a Norwegian is not to be a criminal. And if some American business wants to hire Klaus, what right does our government have to interfere?

The implicit premise of barring foreigners is: "This is our country, we let in who we want." But who is "we"? The government does not own the country. Jurisdiction is not ownership. Only the owner of land or any item of property can decide the terms of its use or sale. Nor does the majority own the country. This is a country of private property, and housing is private property. So is a job.

American land is not the collective property of some entity called "the U.S. government." Nor is there such thing as collective, social ownership of the land. The claim, "We have the right to decide who is allowed in" means some individuals—those with the most votes—claim the right to prevent other citizens from exercising their rights. But there can be no right to violate the rights of others.

Our constitutional republic respects minority rights. 60% of the population cannot vote to enslave the other 40%. Nor can a majority dictate to the owners of private property. Nor can a majority dictate on whom private employers spend their money. Not morally, not in a free society. In a free society, the rights of the individual are held sacrosanct, above any claim of even an overwhelming majority.

The rights of one man end where the rights of his neighbor begin. Only within the limits of his rights is a man free to act on his own judgment. The criminal is the man who deliberately steps outside his rights-protected domain and invades the domain of another, depriving his victim of his exclusive control over his property, or liberty, or life. The criminal, by his own choice, has rejected rights in favor of brute violence. Thus, an immigration policy that excludes criminals is proper.

Likewise, a person with an infectious disease, such as smallpox, threatens with serious physical harm those with whom he comes into proximity. Unlike the criminal, he may not intend to do damage, but the threat of physical harm is clear, present, and objectively demonstrable. To protect the lives of Americans, he may be kept out or quarantined until he is no longer a threat.

But what about the millions of Mexicans, South Americans, Chinese, Canadians, etc. seeking entry who are not criminal and not bearing infectious diseases? By what moral principle can they be excluded? Not on the grounds of majority vote, not on the grounds of protecting any American's rights, not on the grounds of any legitimate authority of the state.

Understanding the Nature of Rights

That's the moral case for phasing out limits on immigration. But some ask: "Is it practical? Wouldn't unlimited immigration—even if phased in over a decade—be disastrous to our economic well-being and create overcrowding? Are we being told to just grit our teeth and surrender our interests in the name of morality?"

This question is invalid on its face. It shows a failure to understand the nature of rights, and of moral principles generally. Rational moral principles reflect a recognition of the basic nature of man, his nature as a specific kind of living organism, having a specific means of survival. Questions of what is practical, what is to one's self-interest, can be answered only in that context. It is neither practical nor to one's interest to attempt to live and act in defiance of one's nature as a human being.

Yet that is the meaning of the moral-practical dichotomy. When one claims, "It is immoral but practical," one is maintaining, "It cripples my nature as a human being, but it is beneficial to me"—which is a contradiction.

Rights, in particular, are not something pulled from the sky or decreed by societal whim. Rights are moral principles, established by reference to the needs inherent in man's nature qua man. "Rights are conditions of existence required by man's nature for his proper survival." ([philosopher and author] Ayn Rand)

Every organism has a basic means of survival; for man, that means is: reason. Man is the rational animal, *homo sapiens*. Rights are moral principles that spell out the terms of social interaction required for a rational being to survive and flourish. Since the reasoning mind cannot function under physical coercion, the basic social requirement of man's survival is: freedom. Rights prescribe freedom by proscribing coercion.

"If man is to live on earth, it is right for him to use his mind, it is right to act on his own free judgment, it is right to work for his values and to keep the product of his work." (Ayn Rand)

Rights reflect the fundamental alternative of voluntary consent or brute force. The reign of force is in no one's interest; the system of voluntary cooperation by mutual consent is the precondition of anyone achieving his actual interests. . . .

Work Is Limitless

One major fear of open immigration is economic: the fear of losing one's job to immigrants. It is asked: "Won't the immigrants take our jobs?" The answer is: "Yes, so we can go on to better, higher-paying jobs."

The fallacy in this protectionist objection lies in the idea that there is only a finite amount of work to be done. The unstated assumption is: "If Americans don't get to do that work, if foreigners do it instead, we Americans will have nothing to do."

But work is the creation of wealth. A job is a role in the production of goods and services—the production of food, of cars, computers, the providing of internet content—all the items that go to make up our standard of living. A country cannot have too much wealth. The need for wealth is limitless, and the work that is to be done is limitless. . . .

Unemployment is not caused by an absence of avenues for the creation of wealth. Unemployment is caused by government interference in the labor market. Even with that interference, the number of jobs goes relentlessly upward, decade after decade. This bears witness to the fact that there's no end to the creation of wealth and thus no end to the useful employment of human intelligence and the physical effort directed by that intelligence. There is always more productive work to be done. If you can give your job to an immigrant, you can get a more valuable job.

What is the effect of a bigger labor pool on wage rates? If the money supply is constant, nominal wage rates fall. But real wage rates rise because total output has gone up. Economists have demonstrated that real wages have to rise as long as the immigrants are self-supporting. If immigrants earn their keep, if they don't consume more than they produce, then they add to total output, which means that prices fall (if the money supply is constant).

And, in fact, rising real wages was the history of our country in the nineteenth century. Before the 1920s, there were no limits on immigration, yet our standard of living rocketed upward. Self-supporting immigrants were an economic benefit not an injury.

The protectionist objection that immigrants take away jobs and harm our standard of living is a solid economic fallacy.

Welfare and Overcrowding Concerns

A popular misconception is that immigrants come here to get welfare. To the extent that is true, immigrants do constitute a burden. But this issue is mooted by the passage, under the [Bill] Clinton Administration, of the Personal Responsibility and Work Opportunity and Reconciliation Act (PRWORA), which makes legal permanent residents ineligible for most forms of welfare for 5 years. I support this kind of legislation.

Further, if the fear is of non-working immigrants, why is the pending legislation aimed at employers of immigrants?

America is a vastly underpopulated country. Our population density is less than one-third of France's.

Take an extreme example. Suppose a tidal wave of immigrants came here. Suppose that half of the people on the planet moved here. That would mean an unthinkable eleven-fold increase in our population—from 300 million to 3.3 billion people. That would make America almost as "densely" populated as today's England (360 people/sq. km. vs. 384 people/sq. km.). In fact, it would make us less densely populated than the state of New Jersey (453 per sq. km.). And these calculations exclude Alaska and Hawaii, and count only land area.

Contrary to widespread beliefs, high population density is a value not a disvalue. High population density intensifies the division of labor, which makes possible a wider variety of jobs and specialized consumer products. For instance, in Manhattan, there is a "doll hospital"—a store specializing in the repair of children's dolls. Such a specialized, niche business requires a high population density in order to have a market. Try finding a doll hospital in Poughkeepsie. In Manhattan, one can find a job as a Pilates Method teacher or as a "Secret Shopper" (two jobs actually listed on Craig's List [www.craigslist.org]). Not in Paducah.

People want to live near other people, in cities. One-seventh of England's population lives in London. If population density is a bad thing, why are Manhattan real-estate prices so high?

The Value of Immigrants

Immigrants are the kind of people who refresh the American spirit. They are ambitious, courageous, and value freedom. They come here, often with no money and not even speaking the language, to seek a better life for themselves and their children.

The vision of American freedom, with its opportunity to prosper by hard work, serves as a magnet drawing the best of the world's people. Immigrants are self-selected for their virtues: their ambitiousness, daring, independence, and pride. They are willing to cast aside the tradition-bound roles assigned to them in their native lands and to redefine themselves as Americans. These are the people America needs in order to keep alive the individualist, hard-working attitude that made America.

Here is a short list of some great immigrants: Alexander Hamilton, Alexander Graham Bell, Andrew Carnegie, most of the top scientists of the Manhattan Project, Igor Sikorsky (the inventor of the helicopter), Ayn Rand.

Open immigration: the benefits are great. The right is unquestionable. So let them come.

ANALYZE THIS READING

1. What does the writer claim, and what qualifiers does he attach to his claim?

2. On what value or principle is the claim based?

3. On what grounds does the writer support his contention that quotas treat immigrants like criminals?

4. In paragraphs 9 through 15, the writer makes a moral case for phasing out limits on immigration. Describe this moral case.

5. What objections, or rebuttals, to his argument does the writer anticipate? How does he counter them?

6. This argument concludes with attention to the value of immigrants. How are immigrants valuable?

RESPOND TO THIS READING

1. Do you agree with the writer's position on open immigration? Explain.

2. Issues that fall under the topic of immigration are numerous. What immigration issues are current in your community? Describe a recent conversation you had about immigration.

3. What single immigration issue motivates you to argue? What would you claim, and what kinds of support would you bring to your argument?

4. The writer grounds his argument in values of rights, individuality, and property. What values would motivate you to argue on an immigration issue?

ABOUT THIS READING

Writer H. L. Mencken (1880–1956) was a journalist, editor, and literary critic for *The Baltimore Sun*. Mencken made frequent use of satire in his steady critique of American life. This reading appeared in Mencken's 1926 book, *Prejudices: Fifth Series*.

The Penalty of Death

By H. L. MENCKEN

Of the arguments against capital punishment that issue from uplifters, two are commonly heard most often, to wit:

1. That hanging a man (or frying him or gassing him) is a dreadful business, degrading to those who have to do it and revolting to those who have to witness it.

2. That it is useless, for it does not deter others from the same crime.

The first of these arguments, it seems to me, is plainly too weak to need serious <u>refutation</u>. All it says, in brief, is that the work of the hangman is unpleasant. Granted. But suppose it is? It may be quite necessary to society for all that. There are, indeed, many other jobs that are unpleasant, and yet no one thinks of abolishing them—that of the plumber, that of the soldier, that of the garbageman, that of the priest hearing confessions, that of the sand-hog, and so on. Moreover, what evidence is there that any actual hangman complains of his work? I have heard none. On the contrary, I have known many who delighted in their ancient art, and practiced it proudly.

In the second argument of the abolitionists there is rather more force, but even here, I believe, the ground under them is shaky. Their fundamental error consists in assuming that the whole aim of punishing criminals is to deter other (potential) criminals—that we hang or electrocute A simply in order to so alarm B that he will not kill C. This,

I believe, is an assumption which confuses a part with the whole. Deterrence, obviously, is one of the aims of punishment, but it is surely not the only one. On the contrary, there are at least half a dozen, and some are probably quite as important. At least one of them, practically considered, is *more* important. Commonly, it is described as revenge, but revenge is really not the word for it. I borrow a better term from the late Aristotle: *katharsis*. *Katharsis*, so used, means a salubrious discharge of emotions, a healthy letting off of steam. A school-boy, disliking his teacher, deposits a tack upon the pedagogical chair; the teacher jumps and the boy laughs. This is *katharsis*. What I contend is that one of the prime objects of all judicial punishments is to afford the same grateful relief (*a*) to the immediate victims of the criminal punished, and (*b*) to the general body of moral and timorous men.

These persons, and particularly the first group, are concerned only indirectly with deterring other criminals. The thing they crave primarily is the satisfaction of seeing the criminal actually before them suffer as he made them suffer. What they want is the peace of mind that goes with the feeling that accounts are squared. Until they get that satisfaction they are in a state of emotional tension, and hence unhappy. The instant they get it they are comfortable. I do not argue that this yearning is noble; I simply argue that it is almost universal among human beings. In the face of injuries that are unimportant and can be borne without damage it may yield to higher impulses; that is to say, it may yield to what is called Christian charity. But when the injury is serious Christianity is adjourned, and even saints reach for their sidearms. It is plainly asking too much of human nature to expect it to conquer so natural an impulse. A keeps a store and has a bookkeeper, B. B steals $700, employs it in playing at dice or bingo, and is cleaned out. What is A to do? Let B go? If he does so he will be unable to sleep at night. The sense of injury, of injustice, of frustration will haunt him like pruritus. So he turns B over to the police, and they hustle B to prison. Thereafter A can sleep. More, he has pleasant dreams. He pictures B chained to the wall of a dungeon a hundred feet underground, devoured by rats and scorpions. It is so agreeable that it makes him forget his $700. He has got his *katharsis.*

The same thing precisely takes place on a larger scale when there is a crime which destroys a whole community's sense of security. Every law-abiding citizen feels menaced and frustrated until the criminals have been struck down—until the communal capacity to get even with them, and more than even, has been dramatically demonstrated. Here, manifestly, the business of deterring others is no more than an afterthought. The main thing is to destroy the concrete scoundrels whose act has alarmed everyone, and thus made everyone unhappy. Until they are brought to book that unhappiness continues; when the law has been executed upon them there is a sigh of relief. In other words, there is *katharsis.*

I know of no public demand for the death penalty for ordinary crimes, even for ordinary homicides. Its infliction would shock all men of normal decency of feeling. But for crimes involving the deliberate and inexcusable taking of human life, by men openly defiant of all civilized order—for such crimes it seems, to nine men out of ten, a just and proper punishment. Any lesser penalty leaves them feeling that the criminal has got the better of society—that he is free to add insult to injury by laughing. That feeling can be dissipated only by a recourse to *katharsis,* the invention of the aforesaid Aristotle. It is more effectively and economically achieved, as human nature now is, by wafting the criminal to realms of bliss.

The real objection to capital punishment doesn't lie against the actual extermination of the condemned, but against our brutal American habit of putting it off so long. After all, every one of us must die soon or late, and a murderer, it must be assumed, is one who makes that sad fact the cornerstone of his metaphysic. But it is one thing to die, and quite another thing to lie for long months and even years under the shadow of death. No sane man would choose such a finish. All of us, despite the Prayer Book, long for a swift and unexpected end. Unhappily, a murderer, under the irrational American system, is tortured for

what, to him, must seem a whole series of eternities. For months on end he sits in prison while his lawyers carry on their idiotic buffoonery with writs, injunctions, mandamuses, and appeals. In order to get his money (or that of his friends) they have to feed him with hope. Now and then, by the imbecility of a judge or some trick of juridic science, they actually justify it. But let us say that, his money all gone, they finally throw up their hands. Their client is now ready for the rope or the chair. But he must still wait for months before it fetches him.

That wait, I believe, is horribly cruel. I have seen more than one man sitting in the death-house, and I don't want to see any more. Worse, it is wholly useless. Why should he wait at all? Why not hang him the day after the last court dissipates his last hope? Why torture him as not even cannibals would torture their victims? The common answer is that he must have time to make his peace with God. But how long does that take? It may be accomplished, I believe, in two hours quite as comfortably as in two years. There are, indeed, no temporal limitations upon God. He could forgive a whole herd of murderers in a millionth of a second. More, it has been done.

ANALYZE THIS READING

1. How does the writer evaluate the two most common attitudes toward capital punishment? What elements of humor does the writer use in his evaluations?

2. What use does the writer make of Aristotle's term *katharsis*? Is the writer sympathetic with those who demand it? Explain.

3. What does the writer claim regarding the death penalty? What kind of claim is it?

RESPOND TO THIS READING

1. Given the grave and serious nature of this issue, is the writer's extensive use of humor effective? Explain.

2. With reference to the four kinds of argument discussed in Chapter 8, what kind of argument is this? Explain why it is effective or ineffective.

CHAPTER FOUR

Developing Computer Reading Skills

A. Reading on the World Wide Web

In a relatively few years, the World Wide Web has become a major player in providing information on practically every subject. Daily, the number of homes and schools hooking up to the Internet grows. Many schools and colleges require students to buy computers and use the Internet as a matter of course, providing

Internet hookups in libraries and dormitories. Even hotels now provide rooms with Internet access. Many children in elementary schools are growing up learning how to read both print and electronic text. Some of us have to learn to read anew.

The fast-growing availability and use of computers and Web sites on the Internet have changed the way we read. As the sophistication of Web sites continues to grow, so must our skills in using them intelligently and correctly.

Right now you are reading traditional print, following along from the beginning of a passage to the end. You read in a single, familiar direction. Your eyes can glance over a whole page, noting titles, headings, and paragraph forms and lengths. You can quickly flip pages back and forth. You have been taught to read printed matter that conforms to an understood pattern.

Reading Web sites is different. You've probably already experienced reading on the Internet. If so, you know that data on many Web sites are not presented in a traditional way, varying widely in the way information is presented on the screen. The computer screen limits the amount of text you can see at one time, often surrounded by color, sounds, or animation. The information may not appear as a typical paragraph with topic sentence and supporting detail. Each sentence may itself be a topic needing further support provided on yet another screen page.

In most cases, reading on a computer screen is slower than reading printed text. Information is not presented in a linear fashion, but divided up into links. It becomes a matter of moving from link to link.

Web Site Links

Most Web sites lead you in many directions. You are offered choices, called links, which take you to other pages on the site. For instance, Figure 7.1 shows the home page (or first page) of a Web site for the University of California, Davis. Notice all the links above and below the photos, serving as a table of contents for the Web site. For information on any one of those topics, you click on it and wait while the site loads the page you want. How fast the page comes up depends on the computer's speed. Once you get to that page, you may have other link choices for more detailed information. Sometimes you will click on a subject link and discover it does not contain the information you want. You then have to go back to the home page and start over. Some Web sites, as in Figure 7.1, retain a list of the major links on one side of the screen so you can move from page to page.

An Example of Reading a Web Site

As an example of reading on the Internet, let's say you wanted to attend the University of California at Davis. You want to know their admissions requirements. On the home page in Figure 7.1, you click "Admissions." The page shown in Figure 7.2 loads on your screen. Notice the various links provided for admissions in Figure 7.2. As an undergraduate, you click "Undergraduate Admissions: All you need to know about UC Davis."

This brings up the UC Davis Undergraduate Admissions page shown in Figure 7.3. Now you have another batch of links to choose from. You want to learn when and how to apply to UC Davis and their requirements, so you click "Admissions" to get to the page shown in Figure 7.4. Once again, choices for various types of information in this section are provided. Notice more links are provided for selection depending on whether you're applying as a freshman, transfer student, or international student along with application basics.

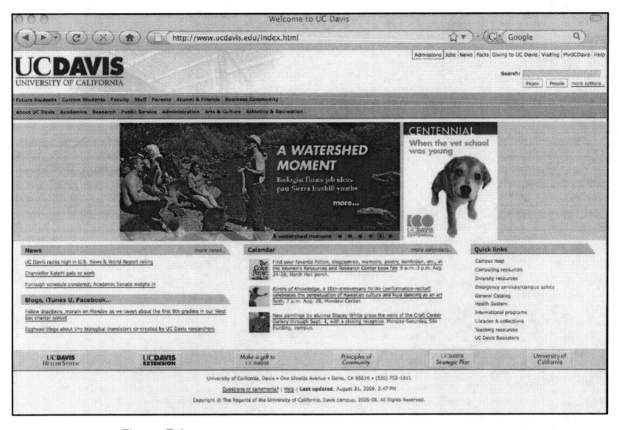

Figure 7.1

At this point you can see how different reading on the Web is compared with traditional printed text. While you may be clicking on one link, another user may be clicking on other links for different information. There is a skill in learning to follow multiple links or paths that contain what you want.

Many Web sites follow this UC Davis example: a home page with various links for you to follow. Clicking on the links provided serves as turning the pages in a book.

Web Reading Tips

Here are a few tips to help you get the most from reading on the Internet:

1. Be patient. Computers vary in speed, in screen size, and in the way they are linked to the Internet. Going from one link to another may take time, because the Web page may contain pictures, sound, or animation that can distract as well as aid. These all take time to load onto the computer screen. Sometimes a Web site may be "down" for some technical reason, and you may need to try loading the site later. It's also possible the site no longer exists. Many Web sites come and go.

2. Expect little of the information you are seeking on the first page of a Web site. Home pages are usually "grabbers." Sounds, movement, and flashing colors are often used to get your attention. Unlike when you read traditional print, you often must respond to these sights and sounds in order for any action to take place. Advertisements often pop up and intrude on your reading. This usually occurs only when a Web site has something to sell, but it's also a good way to question the legitimacy of the Web site.

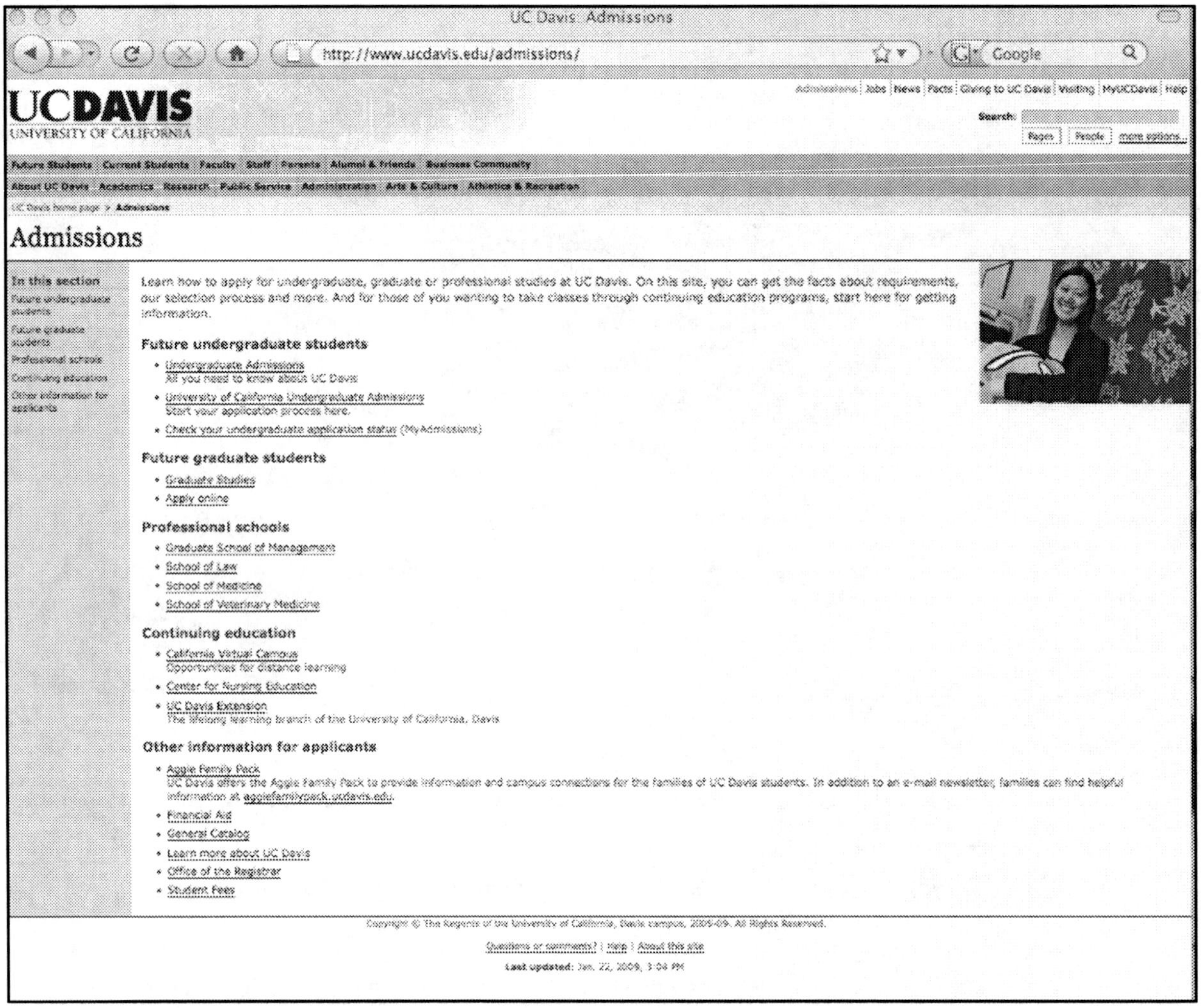

Figure 7.2

3. Read a Web site's home page carefully. Make certain the Web site contains the information you need. Notice the way the information is arranged on the screen. Look again at Figure 7.1. Notice that in the upper right-hand corner is a small box labeled "Search." This box may also be labeled "Find." If you don't see exactly what you want on the Web page itself, you can type in a keyword, such as "tuition costs," and click "Go." The Web site will bring up any pages with information it contains on tuition costs. Some Web sites, however, don't have this feature.

4. As you move from link to link, bookmark the beginning site's home page. At the top of your Internet browser, you'll see a function called Bookmarks or Favorites. You can save the Web site's location and open it up again later by clicking on the site's name.

5. Before you start clicking different links, determine which ones will lead you to what you want to know. You could spend a long time going from link to link without obtaining what you are looking for. The Web site may not be worth investigating, and you may need to select another Web site.

6. Print out any material you want to save to read later. It's advisable to take notes as you move from link to link, because some pages may not be printable, or you may need to return to that link at a later date.

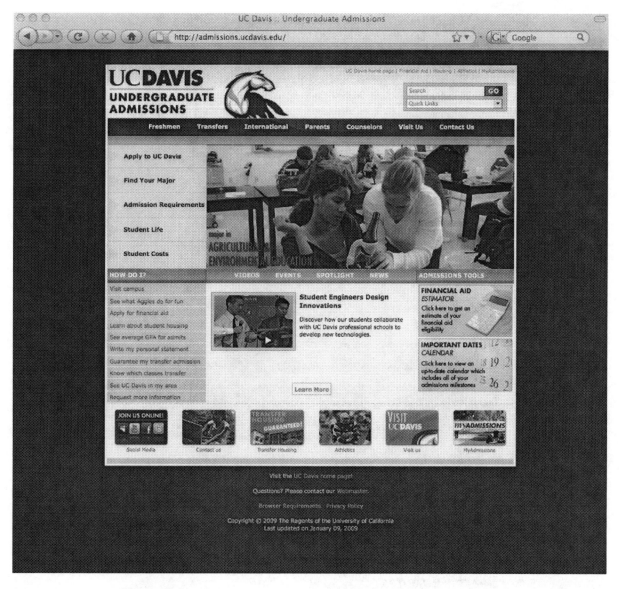

Figure 7.3

Copyright (c) 2005–09, The Regents of the University of California. Used by permission.

7. Don't trust everything you read on the Internet. Anyone can create a Web site. Check to see who provided the information. Is it a trustworthy source? Is the information dated? What is the purpose of the Web site: to sell something or to provide knowledgeable information? Don't accept what is presented just because it is on the Internet.

Internet Language

The Internet contains millions of Web sites. A Web site address is known as the URL, or uniform resource locator. The Web address for the University of California, Davis, for instance, is: http://www.ucdavis.edu. The "http" stands for hypertext transport protocol, the language of the Web. The "www" refers to the World Wide Web. The last part of the address is called the domain name and ends with ".com" for commercial sites, ".edu" for educational sites, ".gov" for government

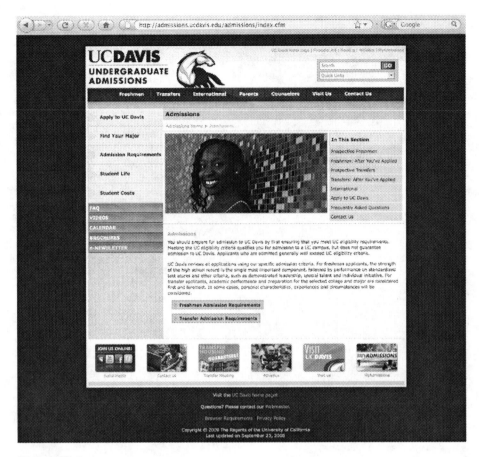

Figure 7.4

sites, and ".org" for nonprofit organizations. These can sometimes help in determining the legitimacy of some sites.

Search Engines

If you didn't already know the domain name of UC Davis, you could use one of many search engines on the Internet to find it. A search engine is like a directory for the Web. Some useful search engines are as follows:

Search Engine Name	URL
Google	http://www.google.com
Yahoo!	http://www.yahoo.com
AltaVista	http://www.altavista.com
WebCrawler	http://www.webcrawler.com
Go.com	http://www.go.com
Excite	http://www.excite.com

To reach a search engine, type a search engine address from the preceding list into your browser. When you visit one of these search engines, you will see a search box. Type in the keywords for a topic or person you want to research, and the search engine will list all the Internet sites it has indexed for that topic. Make certain your keywords aren't too broad or you will get thousands of useless list-ings. Narrow your keywords down to specific rather than broad areas.

Try different search engines. Some have better listings than others.

PRACTICE A-1: Reading on the World Wide Web

Directions: Place a *T* in the blank next to each of the following statements that is true.

_____ **1.** The Internet has become a major source for obtaining information on practically every subject.

_____ **2.** Reading on the Internet requires a different approach from the way we read printed text.

_____ **3.** A link is another term for the home page of a Web site.

_____ **4.** A Web site's address is known as a URL.

_____ **5.** A search engine can take you directly to the information you want on the Internet.

PRACTICE A-2: Understanding Web Sites

Directions: Answer the following questions in the spaces provided using the figures indicated.

Using Figure 7.1:

1. You are interested in finding out more about the students who attend UC Davis. What link would you click? _____

2. If you did not see a link for the information you wanted, what aids are provided to help your search? _____

3. How would you find the university's calendar of events? _____

_____

Using Figure 7.2:

4. How would you find information on financial aid? _____

_____

5. Is it possible to do off-campus coursework at the university? How do you know?

_____

Using Figure 7.3:

6. If you didn't find what you were looking for on this page, what link might you click on to find what you want? _____

_____

7. Where would you find information on the athletic programs at UC Davis?

_____

_____

Using Figure 7.4:

8. What would you click on if you wanted more information on transferring from another school to UC Davis? _____

_____

9. What would you click on if you wanted to know the dates of the Spring break?

_____

10. Where would you go to find information on when, where, and how to file an application for enrollment? _____

_____

PRACTICE A-3: The E-Mail and Blog Evolution

The Internet has brought with it another feature: e-mail. It, too, presents us with another way of reading. E-mail is often abbreviated, sometimes using symbols for words, such as the following:

:-) used as a smile
;-) used as a smile with a wink
:-(used to express sadness
8-) used as a smile from a person with glasses

These symbols and others are known as *emoticons* or icons that express emotion. As the use of the Internet expands, so must our ability to read "Internet talk."

While e-mail has many personal and business advantages, disadvantages also exist. For instance, unscrupulous marketers flood e-mail inboxes with annoying *spam*, unwanted messages ranging from stupid to sick. As e-mail providers work to find filters to separate spam from legitimate messages, spammers work just as hard at finding new ways around the filters.

Be a careful reader of e-mail. Don't fall victim to some of the scams. Many people have fallen for cleverly worded and promising spam messages, from "Congratulations! You've just won the lottery," to "Our product guarantees you a happier sex life." If there is no way to find out the e-mail's legitimacy, delete it.

Current figures estimate that millions of blogs are on the Web. *Blogs* are Web texts written by one or more people and frequently updated, sometimes daily. Blogs might be called an online journal of someone's thinking on a particular subject. Often they invite others to join in the conversation. Students use them as a way to share writing or questions about a topic.

As a reader, remember that any information you obtain from blogs may or not be valid. Ask yourself, who is writing the blog? What are their credentials? Is what they are saying logical?

Blogs can be fun reading. Just be aware of the information source before accepting the content as valid.

Optional Exercise

Directions: Type in *blogs* in any search engine, such as Google or Yahoo, and explore some of the blog sites listed.

B.   Practices Using the Internet

The following practices require that you have access to a computer. If you do not have a personal computer, your school will have computer services available in the library or learning center that you can use.

PRACTICE **B-1**: Using Search Engines

Directions: Find the following Web sites by using one of the search engines mentioned on page 310 and write in the URL.

1. *The Washington Post* _____

2. The Biography Channel _____

3. OneLook Dictionary Search _____

4. Women in Sports _____

5. Infoplease almanacs _____

6. The Rock and Roll Hall of Fame and Museum, Cleveland

   _____

7. Museum of Modern Art, New York _____

8. The Internet Public Library _____

PRACTICE **B-2**: On Your Own: An Internet Training Guide

Directions: As a way to learn more about using the Internet, work through the Virtual Training Suite offered on Intute and written by lecturers and librarians from universities in England. While the site is geared toward British students, it can be a useful tool in learning how to use the Internet to help you with coursework, literature searching, teaching, and research. The site can be found at http://www.intute.ac.uk.

PRACTICE **B-3**: Visiting Sites on the Internet

Directions: Practice reading from the following Web sites to see how different Web pages are designed. Notice the various uses of color, sounds, text sizes, and fonts. Ask these three questions of the Web sites you visit:

1. Who or what organization created the Web site?

2. Is the information trustworthy?

3. What purpose does the Web site serve?
Web sites:

http://www.ed.gov
http://www.peacecorps.gov
http://promo.net/pg/history.html
http://www.bartleby.com/references
http://www.nytimes.com

http://www.house.gov
http://www.doaj.org
http://www.onion.com
http://www.innerbody.com

After you have found and evaluated some of the Web sites, pick one. Then, on another sheet of paper, write a summary of your experience of reading the Web site and turn it in to your instructor.

C. Reading about the World Wide Web

PRACTICE C-1: Computer Use for Research and Information

Directions: As you read the following essay, apply what you learned in Chapter Two about reading for main ideas, supporting details, and identifying the author's thesis.

INTERNET RESEARCH AND INTERNET PLAGIARISM

from 123HelpMe.com

1   As wonderful as it is, the Internet is not the be-all and end-all of your research. A college-level term paper that uses only the Internet for information will probably not cover its subject adequately, and thus will not receive a high grade. There are several reasons for this. For one, the Internet tends to cover subjects more superficially than the printed literature, without the depth and context provided by a book. Most Internet sources also lack explicit citations to other sources for reference; such citation is an important part of articles found in professional journals and is one of the ways in which scholarly accountability is maintained.

2   Another important reason that the Internet should not be the primary information source for a term paper is the considerable variation in the quality of information available on the Internet. This variation is due to the Internet's lack of a standard for information quality. Printed, or "hardcopy," literature has a built-in safeguard to promote high quality information—peer-review. Peer-review means that the editor of the article or book has sent the manuscript to authorities in the subject matter (people like your professors). These reviewers evaluate the manuscript and reach a general consensus that the work meets the required standards. Reviewers cannot advise an editor to reject a manuscript simply because they might disagree with it. They can advise to reject it if there are flaws in the way in which the subject was investigated, if there are major internal inconsistencies, if the manuscript does not adequately deal with important counter arguments, or if the existing literature is not adequately referenced. Reviewers commonly offer suggestions to the writer for improving the manuscript before publication, and peer-reviewed publications are usually professionally edited as well. For example, this article has been peer-reviewed.

3   Another criticism of the Internet as a source of information for term papers is its ephemeral nature. The printed literature provides a permanent accessible record

123HelpMe.com, "Internet Research and Internet Plagiarism," 24 August 2009, http://www.123HelpMe. com/view.asp?id=22370.

stored in libraries. This is the knowledge base that scholars strive to improve and build upon, analogous to the foundation upon which a building is constructed. Information on the Internet, however, has no permanency, and is more like the shifting sands of a beach. What might be on a webpage today can easily be changed tomorrow. Information used to support an argument might not be there when someone tries to verify it later. In some cases, portions of the Internet are "archived" in order to preserve them for historical purposes; even so, this record probably has nothing like the permanence of published "hard-copy."

4   A final criticism of the Internet as a research tool concerns the sheer volume of randomly distributed material to be found there, and the difficulty of wading through it to locate specific information. This is like trying to find a needle in a haystack. Search engines help to solve this problem, but they have limitations. Search engines cannot, for example, help you choose an appropriate keyword for a search—a crucial skill when doing Internet research. Considerable thought must go into picking words or phrases that are fairly unique to your subject, or you will find that a search brings up lots of "bad hits," or inappropriate references.

5   Possible ways for quality control: check the web page where it resides: who put this information up? See below.

OPPORTUNITIES PROVIDED BY THE INTERNET

6   Despite its shortcomings, the Internet provides many research opportunities; as a starting point for finding an interesting subject, the Internet is unparalleled. It is analogous to an electronic encyclopedia with millions of entries and nearly as many authors. Since a few key words can locate many sources, you can readily determine the availability of Internet source materials for that topic. An Internet search can also alert you to controversial issues and differing points of view, which frequently make for good term paper topics.

7   For some types of information, the Internet is also unrivaled in its currency. In the area of climate research, government agencies and universities post some kinds of data to the Internet as it is collected. No printed reference can hope to achieve this degree of currency. However, this may not be all that useful for many term paper topics.

ASSESSING INTERNET SOURCES

8   It is important when using the Internet to evaluate your source. Several key traits should be used for evaluation purposes including currency, originality, accuracy, authority, purpose and objectivity (Kubly, 1997). These are discussed below. If you are skeptical about any of these traits after scrutinizing a source, the source should probably be discarded. As the old saying goes "if in doubt, leave it out."

9   Originality—Check the site for four essential elements: author's name, author's affiliation(s) or organization, page title, and page date. If one of these elements is missing you should probably assume that the author is not presenting original information, but rather is simply using information from another source. Most scholars want and deserve credit where credit is due. If you are still uncertain about the source of the information, check the document for citations and a reference list. Although not foolproof, the presence of references in an Internet source hints that the author understands and appreciates the need for verification of online information. This not only suggests a source with above average intellectual integrity, it also provides the opportunity to research the topic using the source's references. As a last resort, you might e-mail the page's author and ask about the source of the information.

10   Accuracy—Does the text contain any obvious grammatical, spelling, or punctuation errors? Do any statements or assertions in the document contradict other sources you have read? An individual or organization that does not concern itself with these types of errors cannot be trusted to provide reliable information.

11   Authority—Check the author's credentials if supplied. Does the author appear to be an authority on the subject. You might check a bibliographic database such as GeoRef to see if the author has published on the subject in peer-reviewed journals.

12   Purpose and objectivity—What is the intended purpose of the document; to inform, explain, or persuade? If informative or explanatory, are any significant conclusions drawn? If persuasive, does the author appear to have a bias? Does the author appear to provide only one side of a controversial issue? Does the author's affiliation lead you to question their objectivity? What is the intended audience for the document—the general public or the author's peers? In either case, are data supplied, and does the author indicate their source(s)? Is the methodology discussed so that the study can be replicated?

13   Ultimately, assessment of Internet sources requires critical thinking on the part of the reader. You must evaluate the quality of sources with respect to these criteria and decide for yourself whether or not to use a document.

WARNING AGAINST PLAGIARISM

14   One of the conveniences of the new Internet technologies is the cutting and pasting of text from one place to another. As a result, a sentence or paragraph from a webpage can be easily inserted into a term paper. This is wrong! The text of the term paper must be your own, and in your own words. To lift even a sentence—word for word or paraphrased—from another source constitutes plagiarism. Plagiarism is an intellectual dishonesty that in the scholarly world is the same as lying, cheating and stealing.

15   Some students believe that sentences or paragraphs can be lifted entirely provided that the source is cited. This is not correct. In the science world, sources for ideas or information are cited, but word for word text is hardly ever used except for historical purposes. Even if the source is cited, it is improper to paraphrase a sentence while retaining the original structure, because that implies the words are your own.

16   If you find a particularly elegant or useful phrase in the literature, it can be included in the term paper provided the phrase is within quotation marks and its source is cited. Larger textual passages should be indented, but this is very unusual in science articles (it is more common in the humanities and social sciences), and is generally discouraged in scientific writing.

17   Plagiarism can be avoided by reading the source material and taking notes and NEVER copying word for word. This must also apply to the Internet. Never cut and paste from a source into your term paper. As an added disincentive to cut and paste from the Internet, remember that, should your professor suspect that a phrase is not your own, the Internet could be easily searched for that phrase. Plagiarism from the Internet is very easy to catch!

Now answer the following questions.

1. Which of the following best states the author's thesis?

    a. There are several reasons the Internet can be a useful tool for term paper research, especially with the computer's ability to cut and paste material into a document.

    b. The Internet provides many opportunities for reliable research information on almost any subject.

    c. The use of Internet information in term papers requires critical evaluation of the accuracy and authority of the source and should never be used verbatim.

    d. Plagiarism is an intellectual dishonesty that in the scholarly world is the same as lying, cheating and stealing.

2. T /F The author believes that plagiarism can be avoided by reading the source material and by taking notes and never copying word for word.

3. T /F To check the authenticity of an Internet site, evaluate its timeliness, originality, accuracy, authority, purpose and objectivity.

4. Reread paragraph 2. What is the main idea? _____

_____

_____

5. What advantage does print material (hardcopy) have over Internet information?

_____

Summary Review Practice

Directions: To keep in practice what you learned in Chapter Two, write a one-paragraph summary of the article "Internet Research and Internet Plagiarism" and turn it in to your instructor. Begin your paragraph with the words, "In the article "Internet Research and Internet Plagiarism" the author believes that . . ." and continue by supplying its thesis and what you think is the most important support.

PRACTICE **C-2**: Reading about Internet Literacy

Directions: The following selection is taken from the book *Literacy in the Cyberage: Composing Ourselves Online* by R. W. Burniske. The author feels there are three basic questions students should ask when they read any Web site. These three questions are referred to as a "rhetorical triangle of *ethos, logos,* and *pathos*":

    Ethos: Who or what organization created the Web document?
    Logos: Is the document's argument or position logical and coherent?
    Pathos: What emotional appeals are used (visual, sound, textual) to persuade the reader?

If you need to, feel free to return to these definitions for clarity as they appear in the selection.

CASE STUDY: THE STATE OF THE ONION

R. W. BURNISKE

1   Mr. Bellamy, the instructor of a rhetoric and composition seminar for undergraduates, had repeatedly admonished his charges to pay close attention to sources they selected from the Internet. All too often, he thought, students would browse the

Web looking for something "cool" to put into their essays without considering the source of the information they borrowed. To exacerbate matters, they often failed to provide proper documentation, revealing a scholarly approach that was as casual as it was careless. In the most celebrated instance, one student's citation for a Web site said nothing more than "Internet." Now, as his students prepared for their final essay of the semester, a proposal argument, Mr. Bellamy felt obliged to teach them a lesson in a most unusual manner.

2   He would pull an April Fools' Day prank.

3   If successful, it would teach his students the value of visual literacy and the dangers of virtual gullibility. More than anything, he wanted to teach them how to read a Web document with a more critical eye, examining information through the filters of ethos, logos, and pathos. By now, they knew enough about the rhetorical triangle to apply it to written words. They seemed quite capable of analyzing newspaper editorials and short essays that had served as the topic of class discussions. However, something happened when they turned to online sources featuring colorful graphics, animated icons, motion pictures, and sound. To practice what he preached as a composition teacher—"show, don't tell"—Mr. Bellamy wondered how he might demonstrate the consequences of weak visual and textual literacy skills. He wanted to present his students with a document that looked real, even sounded real, but came from an unreliable source or delivered misinformation.

4   So he went online and used a search engine to locate satirical Web sites. He didn't know where to begin, because he had never before looked for online, satirical publications. He was surprised to find so many but finally settled upon an article in *The Onion*, a weekly publication that specializes in satire (http://www.theonion. com). The article, "America Online to Build Three Million Home Pages for the Homeless," claimed that one of the largest Internet service providers in the United States had announced ambitious plans for a unique social service. Beneath its bold headline, the article featured America Online's (AOL) logo, a picture of Steve Case, the chief executive officer of AOL, and the image of a homeless man pushing a shopping cart full of belongings through snowy streets. Among other things, the article claimed that Mr. Case said "there is room enough for everyone in cyberspace," and that this new program was inspired by the belief that "no American should be without an address."

5   Mr. Bellamy liked this very much. It was just believable enough to fool gullible readers. The bold headlines, standard journalistic features, and details of the bogus social program established enough ethos to persuade some students that this was an authentic report; the photos of a smiling Steve Case and the man with his shopping cart would capture them through the emotional appeal of pathos; finally, the argument, though clearly flawed, was just persuasive enough to make less critical readers think it a sensible proposal. Would his students see right through this, or would they fall into this satirical web of deceit? Would the seductions of visual imagery overwhelm their ability to critique faulty logic ("Give a person a homepage, and you have given that person dignity")? Would they notice how this satire played with words, combining the ideas of a "home" and an "address" to create its humor? Mr. Bellamy honestly wasn't sure what would happen, but he decided to give this a try, typing up a brief prompt for an online discussion, one that would help "show" students what he had tried to "tell" them throughout the semester.

6   On April Fools' Day, Mr. Bellamy greeted his students as he would any other day, then announced that he wanted to hold a synchronous, online discussion to examine a "proposal argument" in preparation for the final essay assignment of the semester. The focus of the discussion would be a proposal he had discovered while reading an online article. He then divided the class of 21 students into three discussion groups, with students numbering off so that the members of the respective groups were not seated beside each other. Students were given five minutes to individually read and study the one-page article on the Internet. They were not allowed to discuss it with their classmates before joining their online groups, which would have approximately ten minutes for their synchronized discussion.

7   Much to his delight, the groups conducted an extremely animated debate over this proposal. In fact, it was one of the liveliest synchronous, online discussions Mr. Bellamy had ever witnessed. Despite a deliberate prompt, however, the students failed to consider all three points of the rhetorical triangle. To his amazement and alarm, he watched 21 of 22 students fall victim to the prank, engaging in a heated argument over this most foolish proposal. Not until Mr. Bellamy interrupted to ask a question about ethos did 1 student out of 22 pause to consider the source of the information.

STUDENT REFLECTIONS

8   What did the students learn from this exercise? Following the synchronous discussions and the revelation that this had been an April Fools' prank, Mr. Bellamy asked each student to read the transcript of the synchronous discussions, which he posted on the class Web site, and then type a brief reflection on what caused them to fall for this foolish prank. In the first of these, Jennifer B. offers one of the most common reactions, lamenting her failure to consider the source and pay attention to the ethos of the Web document.

> I fell for this April Fool's trick because I assumed it was from a legitimate source. Being in a classroom setting, I did not think that the exercise would be fake. I was concentrating more on the assignment than I was on the source. In reading the Interchange that took place after reading the article, I noticed only one person in the classroom said anything about The Onion as the source. Even after it was posted that the document was fake, no one responded. It was as if no one cared and that they were more concerned with the other aspects of the exercise. I fell into the same trap as the rest of the class. It has taught the class and myself to always begin with the legitimacy of the source.

9   Jennifer B.'s comments reveal a disturbing tendency, which one might describe as the "transferal of ethos" from one source to another. In this instance, Jennifer and her classmates transferred the teacher's ethos, and their expectations for the kind of article their teacher would choose, to the Web document they encountered. Based on informal surveys of students, this seems a common phenomenon. In the following reflection, Brent S. reinforces this notion. He explains his misreading as a consequence of blind faith in the professor and susceptibility to the pathos of the text and images he encountered, which resulted from a preoccupation with the article's appearance.

> Why did I fall for this article? Well, first of all, I guess I believed it because Mr. B. told us to read it. It was something he had found and gave to us. That gave it some credibility in my mind. I thought, "Well, Mr. B. gave it to us,

it's most likely not a joke." Why would he give us something to discuss if it weren't real? Now I know why he did it, but that is the main reason why I thought it was real. I also believed it because it looked real. It looked like any other article you would find in an on-line newspaper. It had pictures. It just looked authentic. This experience has hopefully taught me to be more critical of the things I read, especially when they are on the Internet.

10   There is also the matter of the message. Where the first two reactions stress ethos and pathos, Kara W.'s reflection touches the third point on the rhetorical triangle. She notes the way in which preoccupation with an item's logos—and the heated debates it inspires—can blunt one's attention to other points on the triangle.

> I bought into the article simply because I did not check out the source or author. In fact, it seems that the entire group focused on the logos of his argument, and a little on the pathos. But no one gave a single thought on his ethos. We all overlooked the fact that there was no author, no credentials, and no justification as to why this guy has any authority to write the article. Strange, seeing as how this class emphasizes all THREE parts of the rhetorical triangle, and we manage to totally ignore one. In the future, we must all be more wary of where the information is coming from.

11   Obviously, statements like these are cause for hope, suggesting that this student has learned a valuable lesson about the rhetorical analysis of Web sites. As this final reflection indicates, an exercise such as this helps students learn a good deal about visual literacy and their own skills. Kelly, the author of the following reflection, had already created her own Web pages and used the Internet extensively for research, yet she couldn't resist the seductions of this satirical presentation. Rather than attempt to explain or excuse her misreading of the document, she seizes this opportunity to look upon her own mistakes and learn from them. Much to her credit, she draws valuable lessons from the exercise, recognizing her own tendencies and realizing the actions she must take in order to prevent future misreadings.

> It is interesting to see the discussion others had about the subject. It seems I was not the only one who was duped into thinking AOL was actually going to implement this program. It just shows how people are incredibly vulnerable. It is a little bit scary to think that I can be tricked so easily. This was a harmless joke, but if I believe everything I read then I could be giving people false information and perhaps harming myself and others. In the future, I need to look at the source more carefully. If I would have just looked at the address I would have seen that this did not come from AOL. It is important to examine the address. Who is writing it? Why are they writing it? What audience are they writing to? And what message are they trying to portray? These are some of the questions I need to start asking myself instead of immediately divulging [sic] into the article.

SEEING IS BELIEVING (AND OTHER SATIRICAL LESSONS)

12   There are many lessons to be learned from this exercise, but perhaps one of the most important echoes John Berger's earlier observation: "The way we see things is affected by what we know or what we believe." These students, who in many ways are fairly typical undergraduates at a public university, fell for this prank because of

what their eyes told them they were seeing. Aesthetically, this item looked like something they might find in the online version of a newspaper or magazine. The bold font style, the color photos, and the AOL logo made them believe they were looking at an authentic document. However, the key to this exercise, and one that Mr. Bellamy understood intuitively, is the manner in which the item is presented. Had the teacher prefaced the exercise by saying, "I thought we'd have some fun on April Fools' Day by looking at some satirical Web sites," students would have brought that expectation—that "belief system"—to their reading of the document. However, since the teacher tied the exercise to the students' assignment—a proposal argument—they brought different expectations with them, expectations that influenced what they saw and how they interpreted it. This speaks volumes about the importance of teaching visual literacy skills. Although educators may not think in these terms yet, the exponential growth of the World Wide Web and Internet connectivity in schools compels them to find ways to teach visual literacy. Exercises like Mr. Bellamy's may help students resist the seductions of fancy graphics and overcome the visual cues that excite the passion of pathos and overwhelm judgment of the author's credibility and logos.

Comprehension Check

Directions: Answer the following questions without looking back. Try to answer using complete sentences.

1. What is the author's thesis or main idea? _____

   _____

   _____

2. Why did Mr. Bellamy, the instructor, conduct his April Fools' Day prank on his students? _____

   _____

3. What Web site did Mr. Bellamy use in his experimental prank?

   _____

4. What features did the Web site have that made Mr. Bellamy think it would be useful in his teaching? _____

5. What did the Web site claim that AOL was going to do? _____

   _____

6. How much time were students given to read and study the Web page? _____

7. How many of the twenty-two students in his class fell victim to the prank?

   _____

8. John Berger is quoted as saying, "The way we see things is affected by what we know or what we believe." Explain what this has to do with reading on the Internet.

   _____

   _____

9. Circle any of the following that are lessons for reading on the Internet that students learned from Mr. Bellamy's assignment.

   a. Begin by checking the legitimacy of the Web source.

b. Don't believe what's on a Web site just because it looks "real."

c. Don't be taken in by the visuals on a page; examine them.

d. Don't believe everything you read, even if it's assigned by an instructor.

10. Do you think you would have been fooled by Mr. Bellamy's prank? Why or why not? _____

Vocabulary Check

Directions: Define the following underlined words from the selection.

1. He had repeatedly <u>admonished</u> his charges to pay close attention to sources they selected from the Internet. _____

2. To <u>exacerbate</u> matters, they often failed to provide proper documentation. _____

3. One student's <u>citation</u> for a Web site said nothing more than "Internet." _____

4. It would teach his students the value of visual literacy and the dangers of <u>gullibility.</u> _____

5. He went online and used a search engine to locate <u>satirical</u> Web sites. _____

6. There is room enough for everyone in <u>cyberspace.</u> _____

7. Would the <u>seductions</u> of visual imagery overwhelm their ability to critique faulty logic? _____

8. He wanted to hold a <u>synchronous</u>, online discussion to examine a "proposal argument." _____

9. She offers one of the most common reactions, <u>lamenting</u> her failure to consider the source. _____

10. <u>Aesthetically,</u> this item looked like something they might find in the online version of a newspaper or magazine. _____

Record the results of the comprehension and vocabulary checks on the Student Record Chart in the Appendix. Each correct answer is worth 10 points, for a total of 100 points possible for comprehension and 100 points for vocabulary.

Remember to make vocabulary cards for any words that gave you trouble.

Summary Review Practice

Directions: To keep in practice what you learned in Chapter Two, write a one-paragraph summary of the article "Case Study: The State of the Onion" and turn it in to your instructor. Identify the author and article title and summarize what Bellamy's students learned.

PRACTICE C-3: Vocabulary Review

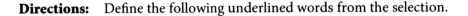

Directions: The following words are from reading exercises you have read in this chapter. Write each word in the appropriate blank. Any words you discover you don't know, add to your vocabulary.

scrutinizing	admonished	gullibility	infinite	permanency
lamenting	exacerbate	cyberspace	citation	ephemeral

1. One criticism of the Internet as a source of information for term papers is its _____ nature.

2. He wanted to teach his students the value of visual literacy and the dangers of _____.

3. Information on the Internet has no _____ and is more like the shifting sands of a beach.

4. Using the Internet, students can tap into an _____ variety of endless subjects.

5. If you are skeptical about the accuracy of a site's information after _____ the source, the source should be discarded.

6. The student offered one of the most common reactions, _____ her failure to consider the source.

7. The instructor repeatedly _____ his students to check the validity of their sources.

8. There is room enough for everyone in _____.

9. To _____ matters, students often failed to provide proper documentation.

10. One student's _____ for a Web site said nothing more than "Internet."

D.   Putting It All Together

Practice D-1: Timed Reading

Directions: The following selection can be used as a Timed Reading if so assigned. You may want to review the comments about timing your reading on pages 103–106 before you begin. Check your reading rate score from the last timed reading you did and try to read at least 50 wpm faster.

The article appeared in the *New York Times* in 1997. As you read for the author's thesis and main ideas, determine if the information is dated or if it still has value for today's Internet usage.

Begin Timing: _____

HOW STUDENTS GET LOST IN CYBERSPACE

STEVEN R. KNOWLTON

1   When Adam Pasick, a political science major at the University of Wisconsin at Madison, started working on his senior honors thesis this fall, he began where the nation's more than 14 million college students increasingly do: not at the campus library, but at his computer terminal.

2   As he roamed the World Wide Web, he found journal articles, abstracts, indexes, and other pieces of useful information. But it wasn't until he sought help from his professor, Charles H. Franklin, that he found the mother lode.

3   Dr. Franklin steered Mr. Pasick to thousands of pages of raw data of a long-term study of political attitudes, information crucial to Mr. Pasick's inquiry into how family structure affects political thinking.

4   The Web site containing all this data is no secret to political scientists, Dr. Franklin said, but can be hard for students to find.

5   "It is barely possible that if you did a Web search, you would show it up," he said. "Whether the average undergraduate could is another question." It would be even harder for the uninitiated to find their way around the site, he said. "One of the things you're missing on the Web is a reference librarian."

6   It is just such difficulties that worry many educators. They are concerned that the Internet makes readily available so much information, much of it unreliable, that students think research is far easier than it really is. As a result, educators say, students are producing superficial research papers, full of data—some of it suspect—and little thought. Many of the best sources on the Web are hard to find with conventional search engines or make their information available only at a steep price, which is usually borne by universities that pay annual fees for access to the data.

7   Mr. Pasick, 21, of Ann Arbor, Mich., whose conversation is filled with computer and Web search terms, admits that he would never have found the site, much less the data, on his own.

8   "All the search engines are so imprecise," Mr. Pasick said. "Whenever I have tried to find something precise that I was reasonably sure is out there, I have had trouble."

9   Dr. David B. Rothenberg, a philosophy professor at the New Jersey Institute of Technology, in Newark, said his students' papers had declined in quality since they began using the Web for research.

10   "There are these strange references that don't quite connect," he said. "There's not much sense of intelligence. We're indexing, but we're not thinking about things."

11   One way to improve the quality of students' research is to insist that students be more thorough, said Elliot King, a professor of mass communication at Loyola College of Maryland and author of "The Online Student," a textbook for on-line searching.

12   "Because information is so accessible, students stop far too quickly," he said. If a research paper should have 15 sources, he said, the professor should insist students find, say, 50 sources and use the best 15. When Dr. King assigns research papers in his own classes, he insists that students submit all the sources they did not use, along with those they finally selected.

13   The jumble in Web-based student papers mirrors the information jumble that is found on line, said Gerald M. Santoro, the lead research programmer at the Pennsylvania State University's Center for Academic Computing in State College, PA.

14   The Internet, he said, is commonly thought of as a library, although a poorly catalogued one, given the limitations of the search engines available. But he prefers another analogy.

15   "In fact, it is like a bookstore," Dr. Santoro said, explaining that Web sites exist because someone wants them there, not because any independent judge has determined them worthy of inclusion.

16   Dr. William Miller, dean of libraries at Florida Atlantic University in Boca Raton, and the immediate past president of the Association of College and Research Libraries, cautioned that free Web sites were often constructed "because somebody has an ax to grind or a company wants to crow about its own products." And he said that the creators of many sites neglect to keep them up to date, so much information on the Web may be obsolete.

17   "For the average person looking for what is the cheapest flight to Chicago this weekend, or what is the weather like in Brazil, the Web is good," Dr. Miller said. But much of its material, he added, is simply not useful to scholars.

18   Yet despite the Web's limitations, educators like Dr. King still see it as a way to "blast your way out of the limitations of your own library."

19   Some of the most valuable information comes from home pages set up by the government and universities. One example, said Dr. King, was research conducted by a student trying to find information on cuts in financing for the Corporation of Public Broadcasting. The relevant books in the college's library were few and outdated, he said, but, with his help, the student found full texts of Congressional hearings about public broadcasting's budget.

20   "Her essay no longer consisted of relying on books or magazines," he said, "but in getting raw data on which the books and magazines are based."

21   On the Web, students can also find electronic versions of the most popular academic journals, the mainstay of research for faculty and advanced students. Most university libraries now have electronic subscriptions to a few hundred journals. Dr. Miller warned, however, that while that may be a tenth of the journals in the library of a small liberal arts college, it is a tiny fraction of the journals subscribed to by a large research university, which may order more than 100,000. The trend is clearly toward electronic versions of academic journals, he added, but most are still not on line and the ones that are tend to be expensive. On-line subscriptions, for instance, can often run into thousands of dollars a year.

22   The time will surely come, Dr. Miller said, when most academic journals are on line, "but you'll need either a credit card number or a password" from an institution that has bought an electronic subscription. "And if you don't have one or the other, you won't get in," he said.

23   When Mr. Pasick turned to Dr. Franklin for help, the professor's expertise was only one of the necessary ingredients for success. The other was the University of Wisconsin's access to the Web site, as one of 450 research institutions that pay up to $10,000 a year for the privilege. (The site is operated by the Interuniversity Consortium for Political and Social Research, at http://www.icpsr.umich.edu.)

24   Even at an institution with the resources to take full advantage of cyberspace, there are some forms of assistance that the Web will never provide, some educators say.

25   Dr. Santoro describes academic research as a three-step process: finding the relevant information, assessing the quality of that information, and then using that information "either to try to conclude something, to uncover something, to prove something or to argue something." At its best, he explained, the Internet, like a library, provides only data.

26   In the research process, he said, "the Internet is only useful for that first part, and also a little bit for the second. It is not useful at all in the third."

Finish Timing: Record time here_____and use the Timed Reading Conversion Chart in the Appendix to figure your rate:_____wpm.

Comprehension Check

Directions: Answer the following questions without looking back. Try to answer using complete sentences.

1. What is the author's thesis or main idea? _____

    _____

2. Why do some students think that research using the Internet is easier than it is?

    _____

3. Why are many of the best sources on the Web hard to find or to obtain?

    _____

4. What does one professor suggest doing that would improve the quality of a student's research on the Web? _____

    _____

5. One person quoted in the article believes that the Internet should not be thought of as a library but as a bookstore. What does he mean? _____

    _____

    _____

6. Why, according to one source, are many free Web sites not reliable? _____

    _____

7. Who creates some of the most valuable home pages? _____

    _____

8. What is the mainstay of research on the Web for faculty and advanced students?

    _____

9. Dr. Santoro describes academic research as a three-step process. What are the three steps?

    1. _____

    2. _____

    3. _____

10. Why do you think the information in this article is or is not relevant today?

    _____

Vocabulary Check

Directions: Define the following underlined words from the selection.

1. . . . not at the campus library, but at his computer <u>terminal.</u>

    _____

2. As he roamed the World Wide Web, he found journal articles, <u>abstracts</u>, indexes, and other pieces of useful information. _____

3. Dr. Franklin steered Mr. Pasick to . . . information <u>crucial</u> to Mr. Pasick's inquiry.

_____

4. It would be even harder for the <u>uninitiated</u> to find their way around the site.

_____

5. Many of the best sources on the Web are hard to find with <u>conventional</u> search engines. _____

6. All the search engines are so <u>imprecise</u>.

_____

7. Because information is so <u>accessible</u>, students stop far too quickly.

_____

8. Web sites were often constructed because somebody has an <u>ax to grind</u>

_____

9. . . . or a company wants to <u>crow</u> about its own products.

_____

10. Creators of many sites neglect to keep them up to date, so much information on the Web may be <u>obsolete</u>.

_____

Record your rate and the results of the comprehension and vocabulary checks on the Student Record Chart in the Appendix. Each correct answer is worth 10 points for a total of 100 points possible for comprehension and 100 points for vocabulary.

PRACTICE **D-2:** Timed Reading

Directions: The following selection can be used as a Timed Reading if so assigned. You may want to review the comments about timing your reading on pages 000–000 before you begin. Check your reading rate score from the last timed reading you did and try to read at least 50 wpm faster.

Begin Timing: _____

YAHOO IN CHINA

WILLIAM H. SHAW AND VINCENT BARRY

1.   Shi Tao is a thirty-seven-year-old Chinese journalist and democracy advocate. Arrested for leaking state secrets in 2005, he was sentenced to ten years in prison. His crime? Mr. Shi had disclosed that the Communist Party's propaganda department had ordered tight controls for handling the anniversary of the infamous June 4, 1989, crackdown on demonstrators in Beijing's Tiananmen Square. A sad story, for sure, but it's an all too familiar one, given China's notoriously poor record on human rights. What makes Mr. Shi's case stand out, however, is the fact that he was arrested and

convicted only because the American company Yahoo revealed his identity to Chinese authorities.[78]

2.   You see, Mr. Shi had posted his information anonymously on a Chinese-language website called Democracy Forum, which is based in New York. Chinese journalists say that Shi's information, which revealed only routine instructions on how officials were to dampen possible protests, was already widely circulated. Still, the Chinese government's elite State Security Bureau wanted to put its hands on the culprit behind the anonymous posting. And for that it needed Yahoo's help in tracking down the Internet address from which huoyanl989@yahoo.com.cn had accessed his e-mail. This turned out to be a computer in Mr. Shi's workplace, Contemporary Business News in Changsha, China.

3.   A few months after Shi's conviction, the watchdog group Reporters Without Borders revealed the story of Yahoo's involvement and embroiled the company in a squall of controversy. After initially declining to comment on the allegation, Yahoo eventually admitted that it had helped Chinese authorities catch Mr. Shi and that it had supplied information on other customers as well. But the company claimed that it had no choice, that the information, was provided as part of a "legal process," and that the company is obliged to obey the laws of any country in which it operates. Yahoo cofounder, Jerry Yang, said: "I do not like the outcome of what happens with these things . . . but we have to comply with the law. That's what you need to do in business."

4.   Some critics immediately spied a technical flaw in that argument: The information on Mr. Shi was provided by Yahoo's subsidiary, in Hong Kong, which has an independent judiciary and a legal process separate from that of mainland China. Hong Kong legislation does not spell out what e-mail service providers must do when presented with a court order by mainland authorities. Commentators pointed out, however, that even if Yahoo was legally obliged to reveal the information, there was a deeper question of principle involved. As the *Financial Times* put it in an editorial: "As a general principle, companies choosing to operate in a country should be prepared to obey its laws. When those laws are so reprehensible that conforming to them would be unethical, they should be ready to withdraw from that market." Congressional representative Christopher H. Smith, a New Jersey Republican and chair of a House subcommittee on human rights, was even blunter: "This is about accommodating a dictatorship. It's outrageous to be complicit in cracking down on dissenters." And in an open letter to Jerry Yang, the Chinese dissident Liu Xiabo, who has himself suffered censorship, imprisonment, and other indignities, wrote: "I must tell you that my indignation at and contempt for you and your company are not a bit less than my indignation and contempt for the Communist regime. . . . Profit makes you dull in morality. Did it ever occur to you that it is a shame for you to be considered a traitor to your customer Shi Tao?"

5.   Whether profit is dulling their morality is an issue that must be confronted not just by Yahoo but also by other Internet-related, companies doing business in China. Microsoft, for example, recently shut down the MSN Spaces website of a popular Beijing blogger whose postings had run afoul of censors. Google has agreed to apply the Chinese censors' blacklist to its new Chinese search engine. And a congressional investigative committee has accused Google, Yahoo, and Cisco of helping to maintain in China "the most sophisticated Internet control system in the world." In their defense, the companies ask what good it would do for them to pull out of the Chinese market. They contend that if they resist the Chinese government and their operations are closed down or if they choose to leave the country for moral reasons, they would only deny to ordinary Chinese whatever fresh air the Internet, even filtered and censored, can provide in a closed society. It's more important for them to stay there,

From William H. Shaw and Vincent Barry, *Moral Issues in Business*, 11th Edition, Wadsworth, 2010, pp. 248–249.

play ball with the government, and do what they can to push for Internet freedom. As Yahoo chairman Terry S. Semel puts it: "Part of our role in any form of media is to get whatever we can into those countries and to show and to enable people, slowly, to see the Western way and what our culture is like, and to learn." But critics wonder what these companies, when they are complicit in political repression, are teaching the Chinese about American values.

6.   Some tech companies are turning to the U.S. government for help. Bill Gates, for example, thinks that legislation making it illegal for American companies to assist in the violation of human rights overseas would help. A carefully crafted American anti-repression law would give Yahoo an answer the next time Chinese officials demand evidence against cyber-dissidents. We want to obey your laws, Yahoo officials could say, but our hands are tied; we can't break American law. The assumption is that China would have no choice but to accept this because it does not want to forgo the advantages of having U.S. tech companies operating there.

7.   Still, this doesn't answer the underlying moral questions. At a November 2007 congressional hearing, however, a number of lawmakers made their own moral views perfectly clear. They lambasted Yahoo, describing the company as "spineless and irresponsible" and "moral pygmies." In response, Jerry Yang apologized to the mother of Shi Tao, who attended the hearing. Still, Yahoo has its defenders. Robert Reich, for instance, argues that "Yahoo is not a moral entity" and "its executives have only one responsibility . . . to make money for their shareholders and, along the way, satisfy their consumers." And in this case, he thinks, the key "consumer" is the Chinese governments.

Finish Timing: Record time here ——————— and use the Timed Reading Conversion Chart in the Appendix to figure your rate: ——————— wpm.

Comprehension Check

Directions: Answer the following questions without looking back.

1. How did the Chinese government discover that Shi Tao, a journalist, had anonymously posted state secret information on a Chinese Web site? _____

   _____

2. The information Mr. Shi posted was

   a. highly sensitive information on how to deal with protests.

   b. about a crackdown on Tiananmen Square in 1989.

   c. information about China's elite State Security Bureau.

   d. already circulated routine instructions on how officials were to dampen possible protests.

3. T/F   Yahoo admitted that it had helped Chinese authorities catch Mr. Shi but refused to supply information on other Yahoo customers.

4. What excuse did Jerry Yang, cofounder of Yahoo, offer as a reason for revealing Mr. Shi's identity? _____

   _____

5. What flaws did some critics find in Yahoo's decision to inform on Mr. Shi?

    a. Yahoo's subsidiary is in Hong Kong and has a different legal process separate from mainland China.

    b. When a country's laws are so reprehensible that conforming to them would be unethical, a company should withdraw from that country's market.

    c. Doing so is accommodating a dictatorship.

    d. All of the above.

    e. None of the above.

6. Which of the following companies are also complying with the Chinese government's request for some censorship and control of the Internet?

    a. Microsoft

    b. Google

    c. Cisco

    d. All of the above

    e. None of the above.

7. Why do some companies believe it is better to cooperate with the Chinese Government's requests? _____

_____

8. T/F Some tech companies want the U.S. government to pass a law making it illegal for American companies to assist in the violation of human rights overseas.

9. T/F Jerry Yang apologized to the mother of Mr. Shi.

10. T/F Defenders of Yahoo claim that Yahoo is not a moral entity and that its only obligation and responsibility as a company is to its shareholders.

Vocabulary Check

Directions: Define the following underlined words from the selection.

1. . . . a Chinese journalist and democracy <u>advocate</u>. . .

_____

2. . . .<u>embroiled</u> the company in a squall of controversy. . .

_____

3. . . . .embroiled the company in a <u>squall</u> of controversy. . .

_____

4. . . .declined to comment on the <u>allegation</u>. . .

_____

5. . . .Yahoo's <u>subsidiary</u> in Hong Kong. . .

_____

6. . . .to be <u>complicit</u> in cracking down on dissenters. . .

_____

7. . . .the laws are so <u>reprehensible</u>. . .

_____

8. . . .evidence against <u>cyber-dissidents</u>. . .

_____

9. . . .they do not want to <u>forgo</u> the advantages

_____

10. . . .not a moral <u>entity</u>. . .

_____

Record your rate and the results of the comprehension and vocabulary checks on the Student Record Chart in the Appendix. Each correct answer is worth 10 points for a total of 100 points possible for comprehension and 100 points for vocabulary.

Before you go on to the next chapter, make certain you understand any mistakes or problems you may have encountered in this chapter. It is important that you learn from mistakes, so don't despair when you make them. Accept mistakes as normal. Making mistakes is often the best way to discover what you do and don't know.

Remember to make vocabulary cards for any words that gave you trouble.

Questions for Group Discussion

1. As a group, discuss the moral issues raised in "Yahoo in China." Was the company a "traitor" to its customer, as Liu Xiabo believes? Was Yahoo right or wrong to assist the Chinese authorities? What would you have done if you were in charge of Yahoo?

2. Discuss what each of you has learned from reading this chapter. Each person should state something he or she didn't know about the Internet before reading this chapter. Who in your group has had the most experience on the Web and is willing to help those with less experience?

3. Referring back to "Case Study: The State of the Onion" (pp. 318–321), discuss the three fundamental questions referred to as _ethos_, _logos_, and _pathos_. How helpful will knowing these fundamental questions be as you read more Web sites?

4. Discuss how useful the Internet is or will be to each of you as students.

5. As a group, see how many of you can use the following words in a sentence. Make certain you learn the ones you still may not be able to use or recognize by writing the definition in the blank space.

a. admonish _____

b. exacerbate _____

c. cyberspace _____

d. synchronous _____

e. lament _____

f. abstracts _____

g. imprecise _____

h. terminal _____

i. obsolete _____

j. aesthetic _____

On Your Own

Pick ten new words you learned in this chapter, not necessarily those listed in question 5 for group discussion, and on a separate paper write a sentence for each word, using it correctly in context. Turn in the paper to your instructor

A Final Check

At the beginning of this unit, you looked at a diagram that illustrated the three facets of comprehension. Now you have completed the unit that is represented by the left leg of the triangle.

For the diagram below, fill in the blank lines in this section. Working with a partner or small group is acceptable if your instructor sets up groups.

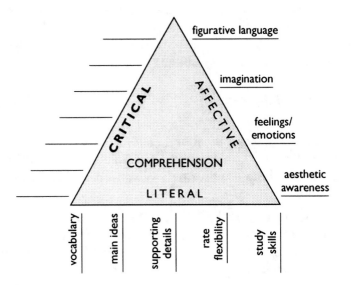

Hints: The first line has to do with information and judgments. The next four lines have to do with the author's worldview and how it influences our reading. The sixth line has to do with reading between the lines. The seventh line deals with what the reader does based on the information given.

When you have finished, check your answers with the triangle at the beginning of Unit Two.

Employers Are Monitoring Social Networking Sites

By LINDSAY EDELSTEIN

When John Ambrose, 24, interviews for jobs as a legal associate, he doesn't cite his hobbies as "anything that doesn't involve reading boring law books" or describe himself as a "party mongerer"—and he certainly doesn't have Hot Chip's "Playboy" playing in the background.

Until recently, these were among the details Ambrose, a third-year law student at Pace University, freely shared with tens of millions of MySpace users, and anyone else who landed on his personal Web profile. He figured he'd just as soon not share them with potential employers, though—which is why he wisely privatized his profile before starting his job search.

Not all job applicants are so proactive—and more are learning to regret it. While most job seekers have been schooled on how to present themselves in a cover letter or an interview, many overlook another important way employers get an impression of them: by trolling the Web for anything they can find.

Which means if you've got a page on a social networking site featuring photos of you mauling the stripper at your buddy's bachelor party, or if you write a blog that details your binge-drinking and bed-hopping exploits, odds are they're going to find it.

"The average job hunter doesn't realize that their potential employer is going to run their name in quotes through a search engine and keep digging until they find the dirt," says Todd Malicoat, an Internet consultant and the founder of the techie blog stuntdubl.com.

"Like it or not, your Google results are your new resume."

Four out of five companies perform background checks on some or all employees, according to a survey by the recruiting and staffing firm Spherion. And these days that means hitting the Web, whether it's checking networking sites such as MySpace or Friendster or just Googling your name to see what comes up.

Adam Zoia, founder of the headhunting firm Glocap Industries, says he relies extensively on the Internet.

"When companies do background checks, it's becoming increasingly common for them to Google people. If that's linked to YouTube or any other site on you, the prospective employer is going to see that."

Digging Up Dirt

Ask recruiters and HR professionals, and you'll get any number of stories about job applicants who've gotten snared in the Web (even if they're reluctant to attach their names to the stories, for fear of opening the door to lawsuits).

Zoia relates a story of an asset-management company that was seriously considering an applicant for a job as a healthcare analyst—until they ran an Internet search on him, and turned up an investment forum where he was freely sharing information about his current company's activities. Worried he'd dish about which stocks they were trading if he was hired, they decided to look elsewhere.

The human-resources manager for a major media conglomerate tells the story of a candidate whose page on MySpace got him into trouble when he applied for an entry-level sales job—not because of ill-advised Spring Break photos, but because it revealed his true ambition.

"It said his dream was to move to New York and become an actor, and that he was trying to get a full-time job to fund his trip—once he got settled here, he'd quit and pursue acting," she says. "Needless to say, the interviewer decided the guy wasn't right for the job."

The former creative director at a nonprofit near Union Square recalls deciding to do an Internet check on someone who was in the final stages of being hired for a job as a Web developer, after an exhaustive check of his resume and references.

"Using MySpace and to a lesser extent Facebook, we learned that he fancied himself quite the ladies' man. His suggestive screen name and provocative profile gave the whole office something to laugh about for hours." (They gave him the job anyway, but he didn't last long.)

Even after you're hired—sometimes well after it—online activities can become a problem. One of the stories that persuaded Ambrose to privatize his profile was from a friend who was reprimanded by a boss who saw his MySpace page, which made reference both to drug use and to the company he worked for, and listed the company's Web site.

"He felt that the guy shouldn't be listing his job alongside his other exploits—some of them being illegal," says Ambrose.

The head of HR for a large Manhattan firm recalls a previous job in which a site manager got far worse than a reprimand after administrators found his personal Web page on an erotic dating site, which featured photos of him in various nude poses. He was fired.

"It wasn't illegal, but the reason given was that as a manager he showed extremely poor judgment by making such a personal matter public, undermining his credibility and losing the confidence of the staff," says the HR exec.

In other cases it might be less clear exactly what the harm is. Almost everyone has tied one on at some point, so why should you be afraid to talk about it on your MySpace page?

The issue is less knowing that you passed out under the bar at Coyote Ugly than knowing that you're telling the world about it, says Zoia—adding that even if employers don't judge you the worse for it, they might be concerned about how it reflects on the company.

"Everyone, including the most successful people, did things in their youth—that's not the issue," he says. "An employer won't say, 'If I ever heard you got drunk, you won't get hired.' It's more that you did those things and you're advertising it."

Likewise, when an internship applicant's Facebook profile advertised his interest in "Smokin' blunts with the homies and bustin' caps in whitey," Brad Karsh, the president of the job-services firm JobBound, understood he was just trying to be funny—but "it raised doubts about his judgment and professionalism," he says.

As a result of the growth of cyber-sleuthing, college career counselors are increasingly warning students about the pitfalls of letting it all hang out on the Web.

False Security

Even when job hunters think ahead and take down private information from the Internet, they forget that a lot of online content is cached and remains accessible to others for a certain period of time after it's been deleted. "People may think that they've taken something down, but it may be seen by a person that digs a little bit," says Zoia.

Others might feel protected by the walls around a site such as Facebook, where profiles can be seen only by other members. But some employers seem to be finding ways around that. Tracy Mitrano, the director of Internet technology at Cornell University, says that when she recently spoke to a group of students about IT policy, one student told her she'd been asked by a corporate employer to look up a job applicant's Facebook profile.

"When I asked if any other students had been in similar situations, about five people raised their hands," she says.

As a result of the growth of cyber-sleuthing, college career counselors are increasingly warning students about the pitfalls of letting it all hang out on the Web.

"We've begun to talk about the MySpace and Facebook dangers," says Bob Casper, director of career services at SUNY [State University of New York] Oswego.

"Today's students have grown up in a wired world," he notes. "They may not be aware of the visibility they'll encounter by posting blogs and personal Web sites."

Many are wising up, though. In a recent survey, CollegeGrad.com found that 47 percent of college-grad job seekers who use social networking sites had changed or were planning to change the content of their pages.

Playing It Safe

Given the potential downside, are you better off avoiding networking sites and other Web activity entirely?

It depends whom you ask.

"We tell people point-blank, do not have a MySpace page or a Facebook page. Period. The end," says Zoia, whose high-paying clients include investment banks, venture capital funds and consultant firms. "Given that the stakes are high with these jobs, the level of scrutiny is high."

Top Internet recruiter Shally Steckerl takes less of a hard line, arguing that if you avoid coming across as a knucklehead, such pages can actually be helpful.

"It's OK, maybe even cool, to want to share your passion for movies, martial arts and Xbox 360—it shows that you're a three-dimensional person," he says.

Malicoat hopes that, as online background checks become more prevalent, companies will lower their expectations of online purity.

"A good employer will start to understand that if a marketing executive wants to have a few pictures online where they're out partying with friends that it might just be OK," he says. "I think the exposure to more of employees' personal lives will force employers to have a little bit more tolerance for extracurricular activities—or end up with bum employees with no personality."

ANALYZE THIS READING

1. Why should job hunters, as well as those currently employed, monitor their online behavior?
2. Describe common concerns of employers.
3. What advantages to having an online presence are discussed?
4. Explain how the many examples in this article function.

RESPOND TO THIS READING

1. Explain why you agree or disagree with Adam Zoia, founder of the headhunting firm Glocap Industries, who advises job seekers not to have a MySpace or Facebook page.
2. Because most employers these days will perform online background checks on job applicants, what, if any, changes will you make to your online presence when you enter the job market?
3. For many, online privacy and surveillance are now concerns. In the workplace and elsewhere, what issues do you have within this topic? On what single issue might you be motivated to argue?